Someone
to Be with ROXIE

The Life Story of
Grace Reed Liddell Cox
Missionary in China
1934-1944

MIRIAM G. MORAN

For Rush and Ruthie Hill

— the story of another young person who loved Yunnan —

Miriam G. Moran

ISBN: 978-1-4834-2910-6 (sc)
ISBN: 978-1-4834-2911-3 (hc)
ISBN: 978-1-4834-2909-0 (e)

Library of Congress Control Number: 2015905734

Because of the dynamic nature of the Internet, any web addresses or links contained in
this book may have changed since publication and may no longer be valid. The views
expressed in this work are solely those of the author and do not necessarily reflect the
views of the publisher, and the publisher hereby disclaims any responsibility for them.

Any people depicted in stock imagery provided by Thinkstock are models,
and such images are being used for illustrative purposes only.
Certain stock imagery © Thinkstock.

Lulu Publishing Services rev. date: 4/29/2015

For Grace Amanda
who has been to me the kind of daughter
I hope I would have been
to her grandmother

The approximate location of Chinese cities prominent
in Grace's story, using the spelling of her day.
(map outline by courtesy of http://d-maps.
com/m/asia/china/chine/chine18.gif)

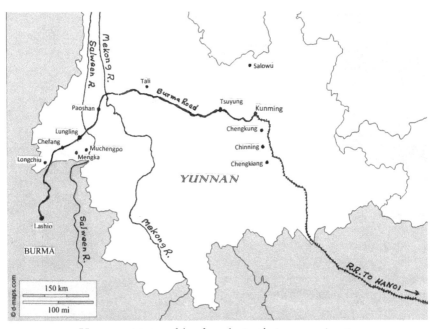

Yunnan cities and landmarks in their approximate
location, using the spelling of Grace's day.
(map outline by courtesy of http://d-maps.com/m/
asia/china/yunnan/yunnan05.gif)

CONTENTS

PART THREE: GOING HOME

FOREWORD

Grace Reed Liddell Cox was my mother. I wish I could remember her. She died of cancer when I was four years old, leaving me and my two younger brothers to learn about her only from others. Her sister, our Aunt Flora, told us stories from their childhood, and our father told us what he could, though even he had known her for just a scant five years. He carefully saved correspondence and mementoes, which I treasured, and I learned a few things from a photo album he had put together, but as I grew up, I wanted to know more. Who was she?

In 1982, the Overseas Missionary Fellowship (formerly China Inland Mission) published a new biography of J. O. Fraser, the British missionary who pioneered the work among the large Lisu tribe in western Yunnan province. Almost forty years earlier, Mrs. Howard Taylor, herself a China missionary, had written *Behind the Ranges*, but now J. O. Fraser's second daughter, Dorothy Eileen, was telling his remarkable story for the modern reader. Knowing he had been my mother's field superintendent, I read *Mountain Rain* eagerly, hoping I might find some mention of her. Instead, I found that she had apparently been forgotten. In the account of Mr. Fraser's death, the new biography stated simply that as he was dying, "He sent runners at once to get someone to be with Roxie" (Crossman 234).

I knew from Dad's album that the "someone" was my mother.

The author of *Mountain Rain* could not have known that—she was only five years old at the time. Neither could she have consulted her mother, who had died ten years before the book was published. A few of her parents' contemporaries were still living at the time she was doing her research, but apparently none of them had known, or did not recall, who it was her father had summoned.

Perhaps my mother's anonymity is an apt metaphor for her life. She was one of many single women who left home during the first half of the twentieth century to go to a country half a world away, devoid of personal comforts and conveniences. To them, that didn't matter. It didn't matter that they were risking a lifetime label of "spinster" because so few men were inclined to go. It didn't matter that they might not be "successful" or attain notoriety. Even personal safety did not matter. What mattered to them, as it did to the apostle Paul, was to "finish the race and complete the task the Lord Jesus has given me—the task of testifying to the gospel of God's grace" (Acts 20:24).

Some forty years after my mother's death, I received a box of letters which she had written, some dating back to high school. Her sister Flora had saved them, a few still in their envelopes. Some were for individual family members, some were "prayer letters" for the use of those who had promised to pray for her, some were letters *to* her, which she knew her family would enjoy seeing, but most were intended to be circulated among the family at large.

She wrote in longhand, rarely having to make corrections. The letters from China were written in ink on very thin paper, sometimes on both sides and in opposite directions to save postage, yet they were remarkably intact and legible. It has been my privilege to transcribe them, coordinate them with letters which my father had saved, and put together her life story as best I could.

Some of the geographical names my mother used have changed, along with the modernization of the Chinese language as a whole. Unless the name occurs in a direct quote, I have used the modern spellings, putting the former spelling in parentheses after the name's first appearance.

I learned things about my mother I had not known before—details about her wedding, for example. Her conversational style alone told me much. She wrote for the moment, sometimes not even bothering to date her letters. She abbreviated a lot, and was not bothered by an occasional misspelling or malapropism. I found her to be easy-going and uncomplicated, reserved but not timid, down-to-earth, fun-loving and witty, a gifted linguist, not inclined to spiritualize, yet possessed of a deep and abiding trust in her heavenly Father.

She was a foot soldier in the army of intrepid souls who were seeking to evangelize inland China. She wrote no books, left no journals, pioneered no new territory and held no high position, yet her life was hardly unremarkable. Her willing spirit and adaptability took her to widely disparate situations, from Yunnan in the southwest to Chefoo in the northeast, and back again. Returning from Chefoo she was chaperone for nineteen children as they traveled, first by steamer and then by train, to join their parents in Yunnan for the summer holiday. She was the amanuensis for Alfred Bosshardt as he dictated the account of his eighteen months as a prisoner of the Communist army, which was later published as *The Restraining Hand*. She was with J. O. Fraser when he died, and oversaw the erection of his tombstone. She filled in as local secretary in Kunming, managing the Mission office and keeping track of financial accounts, upwards of $10,000. Then, like many others, she was caught up in the political maelstrom of that decade (1934-1944), suffering terribly during her own escape from death along the Burma Road.

If she had lived to return to China for a second and third term of service, perhaps her name would have survived the fog of war and the political chaos of those years. But she died during furlough, leaving us to discover from her letters just who the "someone" was, who was called to be with Roxie Fraser.

ACKNOWLEDGMENTS

It will be obvious that without my mother's letters we would not have the wealth of information this book represents. I am indebted to my aunt, Flora Allen, for saving them, and to my cousins, Loretha Johnson and Jean Allen, who forwarded them to me after my aunt's death, along with her sketch of Liddell family history. I discovered that two of the letters (July 13, 1935 and April 14, 1936) were printed in *The Malvern Leader*, the newspaper for Mills County, Iowa, and I am grateful for the publisher's permission to use them.

It was my mother's letters that inspired my brother, John Cox, to visit Yunnan province in the summer of 2013. With Lieuwe Montsma as his very accommodating guide, he was able to trace our mother's route from Kunming to Baoshan, and witness what is left of the old Burma Road, along which she and our father fled from the invading Japanese army in 1942. I am indebted to him and to Lieuwe Montsma's website for valuable information (http://www.tinyadventurestours.com).

John also shared with me his expertise in editing and documenting, for which I am most grateful. Following the format of the Modern Language Association, outside sources are fully identified at the end of the book in an alphabetical list of Works Cited. In the text they are in parentheses, abbreviated, with relevant page numbers, and keyed to the listing in in the back. Any mistakes are entirely my own.

My brother, Philip Cox, enthusiastically supported me from the beginning, and used his careful eye in the initial proofreading.

My husband, Allen, a most patient sounding board, lent his steady hand with the maps. Our daughter, Grace Bailey, coaxed me along with practical advice and winsome good humor.

These are family members, but I also owe a debt of gratitude to Mair Walters, a friend who has blessed me more than she knows with her very real gift of encouragement (Romans 12:8).

Finally, I want to thank my father, Eric Cox. He too saved letters, diaries, and mementoes, carefully annotating each one. The photo album he made has been invaluable, not only for information, but for bringing to life the names and places in my mother's letters. The portrait on the cover of this book is from his album. It is of my mother in her early twenties, probably taken in 1930.

Also, it was from my father that I learned the foundational truth of God's gracious sovereignty, though he would not have expressed it that way. One of the first verses he taught me was Psalm 18:30:

> As for God, his way is perfect;
>   the word of the Lord is flawless.
> He is a shield for all who take refuge in him.

Many years later I became acquainted with a hymn which expounds that verse, the hymn which I have used to preface the three sections of this book. It was written centuries ago, yet the author, Samuel Rodigast, captured well the truths that sustain one in any century who understands that "As for God, his way is perfect." It is a hymn my parents probably did not know, but which aptly describes their experiences, and their response of faith.

Unless otherwise noted, Scripture passages are quoted from The Holy Bible New International Version, ©1978.

PART ONE

✠

WHY SHOULD
I NOT GO?

The harvest is plentiful but the workers are few.
Ask the Lord of the harvest, therefore, to send
out workers into his harvest field.

Matthew 9:37-38

Whate'er my God ordains is right: his holy will abideth;
I will be still whate'er he doth, and follow where he guideth.
He is my God; though dark my road, he holds me that I shall not fall:
Wherefore to him I leave it all.

Samuel Rodigast 1675

Chapter 1

Sister Number Four

It was time to go! With shells screaming overhead, they had no time to lose. Grace picked up the baby, Eric took her little case and their raincoats, and they ran. It was May 5, 1942, a crucial day in Chinese history, but all they knew was that the two big blasts they had heard were the bridge being blown up, and they thanked God fervently that they had gotten across.

By destroying the Huitong Bridge, the Chinese Nationalist Army had stopped the advance of the Imperial Japanese Army along the Burma Road. It left them with no way to get across the Nujiang (Salween) River, a formidable waterway flowing from the Tibetan Plateau to the Andaman Sea south of Burma. The river lay at the bottom of a gorge up to two miles deep in places, and the Japanese, now confined to the west side, were training their artillery on the soldiers and refugees trying to scramble up the east side.

Such was the predicament facing Eric and Grace Cox, missionaries with the China Inland Mission. Grace would later write a lengthy account of their ordeal, but how an all-American girl, born, raised, and educated in the heartland, would come to chronicle this episode of China's history is a story in itself.

* * * * * * * * * * * * * *

She was just a little girl, sitting in her family pew in the Evangelical Church in Oakland, Iowa. Her small stature, light hair, and very light blue eyes gave no clue that she was sister to the three taller girls with dark hair and brown eyes sitting with her as they listened to the father of a medical missionary in China appeal for help in that far-off land. "Not all can go," he acknowledged, "some because of poor health, some for other reasons; but all can pray and give." Her child's heart was moved, and her practical mind went to work. "I have no money to give," she reasoned, "but I have good health. Why should I not go?"

It is doubtful that in the banter on the way home anyone guessed that was the day Grace Liddell purposed to go to China. Neither could they have known the struggle that ensued in her young heart.

She was a happy child, growing up on a farm with seven siblings, secure in the love of good parents, blessed with an early education in the Bible and the ways of righteousness, but she was afraid. She didn't want to leave home, yet she knew that a big girl was supposed to be brave.

On another occasion, it was an evangelist who stirred her heart. His description of the foolish virgins who had come too late to the wedding banquet (Matthew 25) left a lasting impression. "I never knew you," they heard the bridegroom say, and the pathos of those outside the door moved her deeply.

She was born on December 1, 1906, on a rented farm just two miles west of the church where these speakers would later leave their imprint on her mind and heart. The farm was rented because, although her father had farmed successfully all his life, circumstances never permitted him to purchase a place of his own.

Her father was Peter Nelson Liddell, the oldest of seven sons and four daughters born in the United States to Thomas and Helen Liddell, who had emigrated from Rutherglen, near Glasgow, Scotland, shortly after their marriage. Thomas lived to be ninety years old, yet to the end he retained the distinctive Glasgow accent, making him almost incomprehensible to the younger generations. After working in the gold mines of South Dakota, he turned to smelting in the railroad yards in Omaha, Nebraska, before moving across the Missouri River to fertile southwest Iowa, where he purchased a farm.

As Thomas and Helen's oldest child, Peter knew farming well, yet he also knew something else: the brevity of life. He was just a boy when his uncle and aunt were gored to death by a mad cow. When he was nineteen, his mother died giving birth to twin girls, who also died. On his twenty-first birthday, with his father away on a visit to Scotland, he held his sixteen-year-old brother, Thomas, in his arms as he died of an infection.

Is this life all there is? What is the point? After losing his mother, infant sisters, and now his brother, perhaps it was questions such as these that drew Peter to the special meetings at the area's first church, Fairview Evangelical, located beside the cemetery where his family members were buried. His parents (Thomas and Helen Liddell) and his uncle and aunt (Andrew and Mary Liddell) were early adherents of the new church, and he attended with them, but it was when the Rev. G. L. Springer, its first pastor, held a revival that Peter's heart was stirred. What he heard gave him hope that this life is *not* all there is, that there is life after the grave, and that even this life can be meaningful for those united by faith with Jesus. He believed, and later, under the ministry of the Rev. D. C. Busenberg, he declared his intention to be a minister of the gospel he had embraced. This became his calling, although, by necessity, farming would remain his occupation.

Meanwhile, a young woman in the congregation had caught his eye. She was Lucy Anna Reed, whose family lived on a farm in the vicinity and had attended the church since its early days. At the time Peter met her, Lucy was a pianist at the church and taught a boys' Sunday school class, one member of which, James Davis, went on to become superintendent of men at Moody Bible Institute in Chicago. They made an impressive couple, she almost six feet tall and he taller still, and of solid build. Lucy could sing, and in time Peter found that his tenor voice blended well with her soprano. They were married on October 3, 1895, when Peter was twenty-five and Lucy was twenty.

It would be another three years before Peter could follow through on his call to the ministry. Meanwhile, he rented the Pierce farm, where he and Lucy welcomed their first child, Samuel Allen Reed, on July 22, 1897. They called him Samy, with one *m*. Little Samy was about a year old when Peter took his first charge as a lay minister in the Evangelical Church, as the denomination was then called. Over the next four years, he served churches in four different counties, including their own Pottawattamie County.

Since he lacked higher education, Peter decided to attend a school recently established by the Evangelical Church in Le Mars, a town about 140 miles north of Oakland. Lucy was in agreement, and to help support themselves, she opened their home to students who needed room and board, including James Davis, her former Sunday school student. Two daughters joined the family during this time: Flora Ellen, born on April 25, 1903, and Anita Marie, born on August 14, 1904.

After three years of study, Peter returned to farming. There is no indication that he resented this change of affairs. He was still a minister of the gospel, and he would continue to preach as he had opportunity, but he could not support a growing family with the resources of a country preacher.

He rented the Freeman farm, about a mile west of Oakland, where a fourth child joined the family: Lucy Janet, born on October 14, 1905. In addition to farming, Peter continued to serve as pulpit supply in the Evangelical Church congregations of the area. Fairview Evangelical Church, where he had come to faith, had declined in numbers to the point that it could no longer support a full-time minister. The historical record states, "Occasionally a minister would come and hold church services. One who came often was the Rev. Peter N. Liddell from Oakland, Iowa" ("Fairview").

From the Freeman farm the family moved again, and so it was that Peter's fifth child, Grace Reed, was born on the Judy farm. Little did Peter know that this child would go farther with the gospel than he ever imagined. Being the fourth of five girls in her family, she would be known as Sister Number Four to a people he had never heard of: the Lisu tribe in the province of Yunnan, China.

Because she was small, the family assumed she would be short like her Grandmother Reed. But she had large hands and feet, and, during a growth spurt in high school, she grew into them, becoming even taller than her sisters. Her hair also turned dark, but her eyes remained a stunning pale blue, prompting her mother to nickname her "Old White Eyes."

In search of more space, the family moved briefly to the Denton farm before settling at the Warnke place, a 120-acre farm with a creek, where they raised corn, oats, wheat, chickens, cows, and pigs.

Mr. Warnke, whom Flora described as a "dear old German man," would frequently walk the four miles from Oakland to observe the life and operation of the farm. Three more children joined the family there: Ralph George Smith on Christmas Day, 1908; Stella Merlie on February 13, 1910; and Virgil Niebel on January 8, 1913. Grace and Ralph were particularly close—both born in December, two years apart, and both with a propensity for mischief and fun.

The Liddell Family on the Warnke farm
Back: *Samy, Papa, Mama*
Front: *Ralph/Virgil, Merlie, Grace, Lucy, Flora, Anita*

This farm was the scene of Grace's earliest memories, and her home for the next eighteen years. Years later, when she was trying to win permission to do the arduous work of a tribal missionary in mountainous west China, she wrote:

> As for "roughing" it, what better background could one
> have than that of being one of eight on a 120-acre farm
> in the middle States. Rising at four o'clock, doing chores
> in biting below-zero weather, out into the field before
> daylight to pick corn, and helping throughout the year as

the season's work demanded. We as children were never coddled nor did we roll in the lap of luxury, but did have all we needed to give us good strong constitutions to endure the hardships of life.

Peter enjoyed his children—inviting contests of physical strength with Samy, buying the girls a new piano, and taking the three younger ones along to mend a fence, in spite of the temptations of a nearby bridge. "One time they were playing on that bridge, seeing how far they could hang from it, and [they] fell into the water head first," Flora recalled. "[But] Papa rescued them, [and] they went again next time."

As for Lucy, the farm could hardly have succeeded without her. In the summer, when it was time to thresh the oats and wheat, she would feed thirty-five to forty men, besides her own family, both noon and evening meals. It was she who got the horse and buggy out and took children to the doctor for broken bones—or the ingestion of kerosene. Yet with all of the cooking and washing and helping with chores, she found time to make rugs, do needlework, and teach her daughters to play the piano.

In the fall of 1917, Samy enlisted in the US Army. At twenty years of age, he was a year short of being eligible, but his father signed the papers for him and he left for boot camp in Gettysburg, PA, becoming one of his eleven-year-old sister's earliest correspondents. "Dear Sister Grace," he wrote, "I got your letter today and was mighty glad to get it. ... Don't you worry, I will send you a picture before long and you will get to see what I look like with my suit and gun." It was a machine gun. He was attached to the Sixty-First Infantry in France, taking part in the successful St. Mihiel Offensive, which was the first solo attack of the First Army, and in the large Argonne Meuse Offensive, which helped bring the war to an end.

The children rode a horse and buggy to their one-room country school where, in 1918, the seven younger Liddells comprised twenty-five percent of the student body. For one of her assignments, Grace chose to recite a poem which was an early indication both of her sense of humor, and her disdain for pretense. There were other options, but the thirty-two line poem, *The Dead Doll* by Margaret Vandegrift, was what she chose:

> You needn't be trying to comfort me—
>   I tell you my dolly is dead!
> There's no use in saying she isn't,
>   with a crack like that in her head…

The children also received faithful training in the Bible, and in what Peter and Lucy understood was holy living, i.e. no dances, movies, card parties, drinking, or other worldly amusements. Lucy could be stern and overbearing, but she also had a sense of humor which, with Peter's more easygoing nature, provided an amiable balance.[1]

Their home church was the United Evangelical Church in Oakland, where they attended not only Sunday services, but also prayer meeting and Christian Endeavor, which was a youth-oriented organization for Christian development and service. Although Grace had been touched by the need for the Christian gospel in China, it was at age twelve that she herself embraced it, when she "definitely accepted Christ as my Savior."

Four years of high school in Oakland were to follow. Since Oakland was four miles away by horse, she lived in town during the week with Mr. and Mrs. Mervin Gray and their two children, Laura Nell and Billy. Years later, in China, she received a letter from Laura Nell asking if she remembered telling Laura Nell about her desire to be a missionary in China.

Like her sisters before her, Grace took the Normal course, which meant that if she passed the state teacher's examination during her senior year, she would be certified to teach school. She graduated in May 1923 at the age of sixteen.

---

[1] Lucy's sense of humor could be harsh. Stan Allen, a grandnephew, recalls that when he was three years old, and Lucy was becoming elderly and infirm, "she would sometimes put her false teeth on the floor to scare any little kids that happened to be around."

Chapter 2

Serious Student with a Funny Bone

Although Grace had passed the state teacher's exam and was certified to teach school, her heart was set on college. The denominational school in Le Mars, Iowa, where her father had studied, had by this time become Western Union College, an accredited four-year college of liberal arts. Grace's four older siblings had all attended, though none had graduated, and she wanted to enroll.

The college was still owned and operated by the Evangelical Church, but promotional materials indicate that the school prided itself on being "unsectarian in character." Students were required to attend a daily morning devotional service in the chapel, and they were expected to attend services on Sunday in one of the city churches. The faculty came from a variety of denominations, the only requirement being that they be "men and women of Christian character as well as of sound scholarship."

Grace was accepted, but funds were tight. "Papa said if I could find a good place to work for my board that I had better take it," she wrote to her sister Flora. In exchange for a room and meals, she would help with the cleaning and cooking and other household chores, but the situations were not always congenial. After spending Christmas with her brother Samy and his wife, Jessie, it was hard to come back to the Dobberts.

> Mrs. Dobbert is so grouchy. I have cried every nite since I came back. One night I had to get up from the table. It is such a contrast. Everybody was jolly & in for a good time out there [at Samy's] & here all you hear is grunt for this & grunt for that. I sure will be glad when school is out. I don't know when I ever was so homesick.
>
> Yesterday while Mrs. Dobbert was gone I stuck her [cast iron] skillet in the stove & burned the gatherings of centuries off of the outside & half way down the inside, & then took ashes & sandpaper to it. Jessie told me how to do it. I don't know what Milady tho't. She had to blink her eyes because the reflection of the light was so bright when she opened the oven door. Ha! Ha!

During her senior year she was able to move to the dorm, thanks to help from Flora, who was by then teaching school. She wrote to Flora,

> It surely does seem good to be up here with the girls. I don't feel so much like an outsider anymore. … I sit at the head of a table this week. That means I must be first to take dessert, rise from table, & keep conversation going, etc. I guess I'll tell them to engage in silent conversation.

She was known for being smart and witty, with a good ear for language and music, but outside of the dorm she tended to be serious and quiet, bestowing her winsome smile sparingly. At the end of her sophomore year, the college registrar, who was also her biology professor, described her as "a young lady of excellent character and a good student…careful and conscientious in her work…of a quiet disposition and steady in her habits."

However, after a few weeks in the dorm, another side of Grace Liddell began to emerge. A classmate in high school had seen it. His indignant father told Samy it was "that blue-eyed sister of yours" who put the tack on Lawrence's seat and made him jump up and yell.

She enjoyed a good joke, typically slapping her thigh in her merriment. She was also a wonderful mimic, which served her well not only in making fun but in learning languages. One student wrote in her yearbook, "My ambition—to talk French like you."

As a math major she became known for her expertise in problem-solving, able to work not only her own trigonometry problems, but help others with theirs as well. On one occasion she was the only student who could solve a stubborn problem in calculus. "Western Union produces some math nuts as well as the U. of Chicago," commented one of her friends.

While she respected her parents' beliefs and standards of conduct, she was not necessarily bound by them. One woman with whom she boarded found it surprising that she was "so broad minded after being brought up so strictly." As a senior she attended movies on campus and even ventured to go with three other students to Sioux City, twenty-five miles away, to see the 1926 movie of *Ben Hur*.

Her roommate during her senior year was an underclassman named Cecelia. The two could not have been more disparate. Grace believed in working hard and being frugal, establishing habits that would build character and stand her in good stead as a teacher. Cecelia, on the other hand, was eager to be a sophisticate and make an impression in the world. Yet they became good friends and corresponded after Cecelia dropped out of college to seek her fortune in Los Angeles. In one of her early letters, Cecelia described a social gathering where she was determined to make a good impression, but had enjoyed a joke too thoroughly. "I forgot everything, let out a hearty laugh, and clapped my knee, just as you used to do," she wrote to Grace in friendly annoyance. "If you could have seen their faces!"

Grace had little appreciation for the luxuries and frivolities that enamored Cecelia, but when she ridiculed them, her friend chided her. "Sarcasm, you know, darling, is not very becoming in a school teacher." Grace's penchant for sarcasm was well-known. "It was from you that I first learned girls could attain perfection in the art of s-a-r-c-a-s-m," a young man wrote in her autograph book. But after college there is no more mention of it.

Grace took part in extra-curricular activities throughout her four years. She took voice lessons and sang in the glee club (first alto), as well as in the school's presentation of Handel's *Messiah* and the comic opera, *Mikado*, by Gilbert & Sullivan. She was a member of the Decameron Literary Society, and of the YWCA, whose object was "the saving of souls and the building of character." She also belonged to a gospel team that visited in the hospital and jail, and she faithfully attended midweek prayer meeting and both services on Sunday.

She graduated from Western Union College in June 1927, aged twenty years, with a BA in mathematics and a teacher's certificate for the State of Iowa.

Chapter 3

Reluctant School Teacher

While Grace was being as noisy (in the dorm), and funny, and smart, something else was going on beneath the surface. At some point before graduation, she attended a church service which proved to be crucial. "I listened to a message concerning the steps a Christian should take, one of which was consecration," she recalled. "That afternoon, I promised Him my life for full-time service." She was not one to publicize her dealings with God, and perhaps not many knew, but from that point on her early compassion for China was coupled with a deep devotion and loyalty to Jesus Christ. Her life was his, and she wanted to spend it in service to him in China, though the prospect was daunting. She had college loans to pay off, for one thing. Yet, until something clearly blocked her way, she was determined to follow through on her commitment

In order to start discharging her debts, she applied for a teaching position, and for two years (1927-1929) she taught seventh and eighth grades in Hastings, Iowa. This meant leaving the Oakland area, but it put her within reach of her extended family in Emerson. Her Aunt Flora, her mother's younger sister, who was to be like a second mother to her for the remainder of her life, had married Frank Kochersperger and settled on a farm near Emerson, about six miles from Hastings. Their two daughters, Wanda and Jean, were ten years younger than Grace and she loved them like sisters. Another close family member was her older sister, Flora, who was teaching at a rural school in the area. Sometimes, in order to have a touch with family, Grace walked the six miles from Hastings to Emerson for the week-end.

After two years in Hastings, she acquired a teaching certificate for Nebraska, "with specialization in French and Mathematics," and moved to O'Neill, where she taught at the high school and lived with Samy and Jessie. Meanwhile, her sister Flora had become engaged to be married to Sherman Allen, the widowed father of one of Flora's students. They were married in Maxwell, Iowa, 160 miles northeast of Emerson, at the home of a former pastor of Fairview Church, the Rev. D. C. Busenberg. As Grace and her parents traveled to the wedding, little did they know what a refuge this unassuming couple would become, providing a welcoming home not only for Grace, but for other family members as the need arose.

Just two months after Flora's wedding, the family was shocked by news of another kind. Peter Liddell, always healthy and strong, seemed to be failing, and on October 22, 1930, he died of an infection, followed by a stroke, at sixty years of age. All eight children were present at the funeral, and at the interment in Fairview Cemetery.

A bereaved Grace returned to O'Neill with Samy and Jessie to continue teaching at the high school. She was well regarded and had excellent references ("the rumor persists that there is no better all-round teacher in O'Neill"), but at the end of the second year (1931) she submitted her resignation. "I wasn't called to be a teacher," she explained. "I promised my life to the Lord…& taught only to meet debts accrued while going to school. I remember one time exalting so over a day's vacation that Samy, fed up, finally observed, 'Well, if I hated my job like you hate yours, I'd find another one.'"

And so, in faithfulness to her call, she began looking for a way to get to the mission field. She started with the Women's Missionary Society of the Evangelical Church, but after six months of protracted hopes, she received word that funds were insufficient to send her. "Teach for one more year," they advised, "and then try again." But she would not be put off. Judging from her later reflections, it seems she was also re-examining her faith. Was it intellectually defensible? What about the miracles? Is the Bible really inspired? All of it?

She contacted the School of Education at Northwestern University of Evanston, Illinois, thinking she might do well to take some graduate courses in Religious Education. Once again, however, funds were a problem. Enrollment was contingent on having part-time service to offset the tuition, but a letter from the school informed her that openings for part-time service had all been filled. "Teach for another year," they advised her, "and then try again."

She could have done that. She had one more year left on her Nebraska certificate, but before giving up, she contacted the family's long-time friend, James W. Davis, the boy who had been in her mother's Sunday school class and was now the superintendent of men at Moody Bible Institute. More recently, he had officiated at her father's funeral. Contacting him turned out to be pivotal.

Chapter 4

The Counsel and Care
of God at Moody

James Davis knew, as Grace could not, what was the theological tenor of the mainline seminaries, including the Religious Education program at Northwestern University. "Scholastically it would qualify," he assured her in a personal letter dated July 31, 1931, but he feared that the tendency towards neo-orthodoxy, the "cold" atmosphere, and the minimal Bible training would be a "great disappointment." He wrote to her as if to a daughter ("and I almost feel you are"), urging her to consider Moody Bible Institute. "You will get everything of value that would be offered in Northwestern, and from four to six times as much Bible training at the same time," he reasoned. Furthermore, she would be involved in hands-on ministry assignments, and be immersed in "the wonderful fellowship and atmosphere of this place." As for finances, she would need to come with sufficient funds for the first semester ($150), but after that, the school's Bureau of Employment would help her find part-time work.

In less than two months Grace was enrolled for the fall semester. She reflected on this change of direction in her testimony as a new member of the China Inland Mission, in the December 1934 issue of the Mission's monthly magazine, *China's Millions*:

When the choice of schools for training was to be made, His hand again intervened, turning my eyes away from a very modernistic school to the Moody Bible Institute. At this time Satan was making subtle attacks [on my faith], and God used as a means to clear the mists, men of scholarship who know and love Him, and who fearlessly and faithfully proclaim His Word. For them, I shall never cease thanking Him.

A year later (October 6, 1935) she explained it more fully in a letter to her cousin, Wanda.

I praise God for privileging me to attend the Moody Bible Institute and to sit under instructors with intellects to vie with any the world can produce, and yet who courageously and zealously proclaimed the "whole counsel of God." They were men who knew and loved Him. Before that I had tolerantly listened to those who tenaciously held to the full inspiration of the Word, but in the back of my mind sort of classified those same people as "unlearned and ignorant." But when I went to Moody, that mental reserve was annihilated. I praise Him that although I was so blind they had to take hold of my eyelids (so to speak) and lift them up before I could see, yet sight has been given me, and I have a Gospel of Life to proclaim now, and not an ethical code or measuring stick. … Often the works of these men who preach an ethical gospel are cleverly penned, and it isn't so much what they say as what they do not say and refuse to say.

Economically speaking, Grace could not have returned to school at a less opportune time. The stock market had crashed and the country was in the throes of the Great Depression. But she got together the $150 which she needed for the first term, made the 500-mile trip to Chicago, and enrolled at Moody Bible Institute in September 1931.

The school was founded in 1886 by evangelist D. L. Moody, not as an academic institution but as a training school for Christian workers. It had grown out of his compassion for people left destitute by the great Chicago fire in 1871, and it occupies today the same location in the heart of Chicago that it had when Moody founded it. Moody Church, which had its beginnings as a Sunday school in a Chicago saloon, is located about a mile north of the Institute.

While Grace was at Moody, she sat under the preaching and teaching of at least two evangelical greats of those days: Dr. James M. Gray, an ordained minister in the Reformed Episcopal Church, was president of the Institute, and Dr. Harry A. Ironside, self-educated preacher and writer, was pastor of Moody Church.

She clearly enjoyed her classes with Dr. Gray, though in her very first year he disillusioned her about some of her erstwhile favorites. It was the experience she had alluded to in her letter to her cousin Wanda: "...I was so blind they had to take hold of my eyelids...and lift them up before I could see...." She enjoyed listening to radio preachers such as S. Parkes Cadman, Daniel Poling, and Stanley Jones, but Dr. Gray cautioned against their subtle departures from Scripture, especially with respect to the deity of Christ. Sadder but wiser, Grace took note. "Guess they are all too modernistic, like Fosdick," she concluded.

At Moody she also came under the influence of Keswick teaching, sometimes known as the Higher Life, and the Victorious Life. A variation of the Wesleyan teaching on holiness which she had known from childhood, it took its name from the small town of Keswick in the Lake District of England, where, since 1875, an annual convention has been held to encourage Christian piety.

It was not surprising to find the Keswick influence at Moody since the school's first three presidents (D. L. Moody, R. A. Torrey, and James M. Gray) had all been impacted by it in some way (DeYoung). In fact, Moody may have created the need for it. His evangelistic campaigns in England (1873-75) left converts longing for personal holiness. They wanted victory over temptation and besetting sins, and the Keswick Convention, founded in 1875, provided speakers to address that need (Sawyer).

While the Keswick teaching was wonderfully helpful to many, others found it impossible and even dangerous, as J. I. Packer explains in *Keep in Step with the Spirit*. "The unreality of its passivity program and its announced expectations, plus its insistence that any failure to find complete victory is entirely your fault, makes it very destructive" (Packer 157). Grace's realism and sense of humor were a safeguard against seriously adverse consequences, but her letters do reflect Keswick teaching from time to time. For example:

- She explains her own conversion using the Keswick terminology of two stages—accepting Jesus as her savior at the age of twelve, and consecrating her life to him while at college.
- She writes of a convert who "is a believer, but a carnal Christian"—a distinction traceable to Keswick teaching.
- She laments her spiritual failures and vows that "henceforth the conflict is His, and His the victory," a stance reflective of the passivity in Keswick teaching on holiness.
- And she sometimes chides herself for sadness and fear as though they were signs of spiritual weakness, incompatible with "victory."

But as Packer goes on to observe, "When Christians ask God to make them more like Jesus, through the Spirit's power, He will do it, never mind what shortcomings appear in their theology. He is a most gracious and generous God" (Packer 163-164). Grace may have been lacking in theological precision, but a senior missionary would later recall that, like her Master, she was "so spiritual, & yet so understanding & human."

Moody Bible Institute offered three courses of training: missionary, general, and Christian education. Grace chose the missionary course with academic subjects such as church history, Christian evidences (apologetics), missions, and doctrine; and practical subjects such as home nursing, Bible story telling, public speaking, and homiletics. And, as James Davis had expected, she quickly discovered the "wonderful fellowship and atmosphere of this place."

The practical Christian work assignments he had mentioned included a girls' class at the Olivet Institute. Founded in 1888 by the Rev. Norman B. Barr, a Presbyterian minister, the Institute was a religious/social outreach on Chicago's Near North Side, in a slum area known as "Little Hell." Grace went armed with tracts to distribute along the way, and assured her family, "As yet no one has been surly or catty whom I approached." She also taught a class at a church in Chinatown on the South Side, and was there at the time of a murder. With characteristic candor she described it in a letter home.

> Last Sunday afternoon…a Chinaman was shot five times & killed, right in the street just about 2 blocks from the church. The body was still lying there after S.S., but there was such a mob crowded around the place that we couldn't see it (the body). The police wagon was backed up there & several policemen were milling around keeping the populace away. Virginia & I wanted to go up & see it, but Miss Lutz, an older lady who sponsors the girls, was afraid. She finally consented to let us slip up if we didn't go too close, while she kept the children. However, we were unable to see anything. She made us go clear around the block to evade the mob, & didn't leave us to do her visitation work until she saw we were safely on the [street] car & started home. She feared a town war & that more shots might follow.

Given her love of music, it is not surprising that Grace joined the General Chorus, or that she enjoyed singing under the direction of its amiable conductor, T. J. Bittikofer.

> He wanted us to sing [the word *prepared*] with three syllables—pre-par-ed. Well, it wasn't done. So he stopped & said, "Say 'par-ed.'" We did, & he said, "Pare him again." Well, by the time he was thru with us we sang it prepar<u>ed</u>.

In a later year, she was asked to join the student quartet, a precursor of the Moody Chorale, which still sings at the Founder's Week conference in February. Since 1901, the conference has been an annual event in honor of the birthday of D. L. Moody on February 5, 1837.

While she thrived in the atmosphere, and welcomed the challenges of her program at Moody, she was also being tested as a Christian. How would she hold up under the stress of unfair treatment? misunderstanding? foiled plans? difficult financial straits? Would she take offense? Her heavenly Father wanted her to know that she could trust him.

The school required that during their first term students live at the school, where the rate for room and board was nine dollars per month. Grace had this covered in the $150 she brought with her, but after the first term, students were obliged to find work or secure a live-in position. Staff members were assigned to help, but the job which they had hoped would go to Grace never did materialize, and she faced an unwelcome alternative: drop out of day school, find a live-in position, and take evening classes. But evening classes were not necessarily the same as day classes, meaning she could lose credits and perhaps postpone graduation.

Had she done right to come? Had she been presumptuous? "I am glad that I am not worrying about it," she wrote home. "I haven't lost a minute's sleep. I am deeply interested & concerned but don't worry a bit over it."

Meanwhile Mrs. James Davis invited her to stay with them until she found a job. The Liddell family friend had married and there were now three children: Mary, Merrill, and Russell. Grace had stayed with them before, and went frequently to their home to help Mrs. Davis with the housework, in return for what she thought was a lavish wage—sixty cents per hour, so this seemed to be an ideal provision. But Mrs. Davis was nervous and high strung and felt she must issue a condition: that Grace not visit and joke with the two boys. Grace was stunned. Joshing with younger brothers was second nature to her. At home she did it all the time with Ralph and Virgil. But Mrs. Davis felt it was immature.

Cautiously Grace asked if there were any other way in which she got on her nerves. "No," Mrs. Davis assured her, and complimented her on other aspects of her character. "Then, to speak in plain terms,"

Grace offered, "I simply talk too much." And much to her chagrin, Mrs. Davis agreed. Grace was used to being called reserved, and quiet, but not talkative. "I didn't <u>think</u> I was charged with that generally," she wrote home, "but I just gulped it down quick before I tasted the bitter."

In the end, Mr. Davis intervened. He advised that Grace not stay with them, and Mrs. Davis commended her for taking the news so nicely. "Thanks for my poker face!" she told her mother, relieved that she had appeared impassive, even though she felt otherwise.

The staff and the student body knew of her plight, and were genuinely sympathetic and concerned—praying with her, and giving her a reassuring pat on the arm. She even found an anonymous gift in her mailbox: five dimes wrapped in a little piece of paper with "Col. 4:2" written on it. (*Devote yourselves to prayer, being watchful and thankful.*)

As it turned out, she did drop out of day school. She secured a live-in position and enrolled in evening school for one term.

The family she lived with was Mr. and Mrs. Harding and their grown son, Raymond, and it was unlike any situation she had been in before. "Other women I've worked for have been more like a mother or sister to me," she wrote home, "but she is more like a slave driver. She hasn't any heart it seems."

The Great Depression gripping the country was no respecter of persons. Mr. Harding, in business for himself, was having difficulty making ends meet, and at least twice he and his wife turned to their student boarder to help them out. On one occasion, they needed money to buy heating oil, stock up on groceries, and redeem some items at a pawn shop. Knowing that Grace was saving money to move back on campus, they asked her for a loan. She obliged, though it left her temporarily without a penny.

It was a long semester. She grew so homesick that she even visited the Davises.

> She kissed me & seemed so glad to see me. Then Mary kissed me, & then Merrill & Russell came running to get theirs. Monkeys! I asked if they had their supper yet & Russell said, "Yes, we just want to top it off now" [i.e. have fun with Grace].

She did move back on campus for her final term. She took classes in both day school and evening school in order to make up for what she had missed, and she found work at the school library. But the wages were not hers for long. "I turn my library checks right back to the Institute so of course unless I make a little extra I have no 'pin' money."

She could ill afford another bill, but when she accidentally broke the thermometer she had been given to use in Home Nursing, she suddenly owed fifty cents. However, while she was doing some dusting for Mrs. Davis, a peddler came looking for old clothes to buy, and in exchange for three pairs of the boys' old shoes, he gave Mrs. Davis a quarter. Knowing the straits Grace was in, she promptly gave the quarter to Grace for her thermometer debt.

Later, when Mrs. Davis asked her to wash dishes after a lunch she was hosting for the faculty wives' Missionary Society, Grace had hope of another quarter. "It was really worse than threshers because of the type of dishes used," she wrote home, "...mostly thin glass-ware, sherbet dishes, Haviland, beautiful silver-ware, etc." Mrs. Davis trusted her to wait for her wages, and that night she dreamed it was a quarter. Since she was there for two hours and Mrs. Davis was "astounded" at the array of clean dishes, it is likely her dream was more than fulfilled.

The Institute itself was feeling the pinch. Grace wrote to her mother,

> I suppose that you know all the banks are closed in U.S. with the exception of S. Car., & maybe hers are now. [President] Dr. Gray said in chapel yesterday morning that we have enuf food in the house to last until Mon. eve, & enuf coal to last that long. By that time the banks are supposed to re-open. And he said that if they didn't that the Institute's credit is always good as they have always paid their bills. He added, "And in the mean time what are we going to do? We are going to <u>keep still</u>!! That's what we are going to do, & trust God."

At least one student in the audience knew exactly what he meant.

Chapter 5

Finding Her Niche in the CIM

During Grace's final year at Moody, the all-important question of future service came again to the fore. She enrolled in the Missionary Principles and Practices course, where students were introduced to various missionary societies. Not surprisingly, she was interested in the China Inland Mission (CIM), not only because it labored in China, but because its principles and practices clearly resonated with her. They had been hammered out in the crucible of personal experience by the founder, J. Hudson Taylor, and Grace saw their reasonableness.

Taylor had gone from England to China with a pressing burden for the millions in the interior who were dying without even hearing the gospel. Chinese along the coast were being reached, but no Protestant missionary had ventured into the inland provinces, and no mission society was ready to take that risk. Consequently, in 1865, Taylor founded the China Inland Mission, whose headquarters would be in Shanghai, not in far-off London, and whose goal would be to take the gospel into each of the interior provinces.

To meet that goal, he needed men and women who knew God and would risk their lives, if necessary, to work in inland China. Of necessity, such men and women would not be faint-hearted or ambivalent, but neither could they be headstrong. They would have to fit in with the overall strategy of the Mission. If a new worker believed that God was calling him to work in a particular province, Mission leaders would give his conviction due weight and consideration. But if there was a critical need for him in another province, the new worker would be asked prayerfully to reconsider, for the sake of the mission in China as a whole.

Grace was no stranger to hardship and sacrifice. Her heavenly Father had schooled her in the matter of trusting him for her needs, and that was how this mission operated. New recruits were to look to God for their needs, not to the Mission. The Mission could guarantee nothing but an equitable distribution of funds which had been received. Hudson Taylor had proven that "God's work done in God's way will have God's supplies," so it was Mission policy not to solicit funds, or borrow. They would "move man, through God, by prayer alone," and this remained the practice of the CIM for more than 100 years.

Furthermore, in the matter of remittances, all missionaries would be treated equally, regardless of position. Adjustments would be made for location (cost of living) and family size, but apart from that, the funds received in a given month would be divided equally. The general director himself would not receive a remittance any different from the newest recruit.

Finally, this mission was dedicated to evangelizing China, the very thing for which Grace had dedicated herself. She made application and was accepted, pending a successful course at candidate school that summer.

Even though she had lost ground by switching to evening school for one term, she graduated with her class on April 19, 1934, and returned to the bosom of her family in southwest Iowa, living with her sister and brother-in-law, Flora and Sherman Allen, on their farm in Emerson.

Two big events were to mark her summer. First, she made a trip back to Chicago: not to Moody Bible Institute, but to the World's Fair, as chaperone for her young cousins, Wanda and Jean Kochersperger. Second, she went by herself to Toronto, Canada, where the China Inland Mission had its candidate school for North America. There she would be observed and tested in various ways to determine her suitability for life as a missionary in China.

It never occurred to her that she might not pass the physical exam.

Chapter 6

Tested in Toronto

In Toronto, Grace was one of nine young people being screened for service in China at the CIM Canadian headquarters located at 150 St. George Street. Her roommate was Pearl Galloway, who had known Grace at Moody as "a rather formidable High school teacher." As her roommate, however, she saw her other side. "What a wonderful sense of humour! How often she cheered me up and made life a happier place -- and she was so gentle and loving," Pearl recalled.

During the weeks at candidate school, the new recruits would take orientation classes to further acquaint them with the CIM and with China. There would be elementary lessons in Chinese to test their aptitude for another language. They would be observed for their ability to follow instructions, work with other people, adapt to new customs, and handle the unexpected.

Grace successfully passed all the evaluations except the one she thought would be easy: the medical exam. In Chicago a doctor had declared her well and healthy, but in Toronto another doctor found that she had low blood pressure, anemia, and badly infected tonsils. An operation to remove the tonsils would cost her four days, and put her that far behind in her study of elementary Chinese.

What did it mean? If she couldn't pass the physical exam, she couldn't go to China at all—a prospect unthinkable to her. "Somehow I just know the Lord will enable me to pass the examination and be accepted," she told her family. "I have heard His call to China since childhood and & I believe it's China—tonsils or no tonsils."

It turned out to be "no tonsils," but the anemia lingered, making her acceptance still uncertain. What was she to think? Had she been mistaken? Would she get to China? Her letters indicate only that she faced such questions with equanimity, and with undiminished trust in her heavenly Father. "Maybe it will [be] my lot to stay at home," she wrote. "I want His will, knowing His grace is sufficient." It was no glib acquiescence. If she had to go back, she would need nothing less than the grace of God to make the necessary explanations and adjustments back home.

Meanwhile, she made the practical decision to focus on raising her hemoglobin level. One doctor advised her to go to the country for a week—an attractive measure for those who could afford it. Instead, she sat in the sun to do her reading, took long walks, sunbathed on the beach, and played tennis. "If [it] doesn't come up it won't be my fault," she declared.

It did come up, and she did pass the physical examination. She was cleared to go to China as a new worker. But the next question was, When? The country was still reeling from the Great Depression, and it might not be until the next year (1935) that she could go. While she waited, she again made her home with the Allens in Emerson, Iowa.

Chapter 7

"Come with Me to China"

The light turned green sooner than Grace expected, and she scrambled to make it. On October 18, 1934, she learned she would be sailing the very next week. She had just eight days to prepare her outfit, pack her trunks, say good-bye to her scattered family, make the train trip to Seattle, Washington, and proceed north to Vancouver, BC, where she would board the ship. It was such an abrupt turn of events that she wondered if she could comply, but she knew her heavenly Father hadn't brought her this far only to forsake her. "With him all things are possible," she reminded herself.

Her sister Flora dropped everything to help. To find items that could not be purchased locally, they took a day to go the nearest city of any size, which was Omaha, Nebraska, fifty miles away. Their return trip gave Grace a foretaste of travel in China. The last stretch was eight miles of muddy road—three of them on foot because the car became mired in mud, and a tire blew out just as evening began to fall. They took shelter in the Champion Hill church building until someone could come with a team of mules, but even mules were not equal to the task. The car would not budge. Instead, the two sisters rode home in a lumber wagon. This experience might have been enough to discourage anyone less resolute, but a beautiful rainbow appeared as dawn broke, and Grace took heart.

Another surprise came on the day that she was to leave, a "final touch," as she called it. At noon she learned that her evening train had been rescheduled for two o'clock that afternoon, leaving her just two more hours! Hurriedly she tied up loose ends, bade farewell to her loved ones, and was on the train with her luggage when it pulled out of the station. Family members waiting on the platform watched as the train moved off into the distance, taking her away for seven years (which lengthened into ten) from all that was familiar and dear.

She was alone. Or was she? As she settled into her seat, she remembered an anonymous quote: "Our Lord does not say, 'Go for me to China'; but, 'Come with me to China.'" Her heavenly Father was with her as the train took her farther and farther west. She saw his handiwork in the big skies and beautiful mountain scenery of the West, and a hymn of praise came easily to mind:

> Before the hills in order stood,
> Or earth received her frame;
> From everlasting thou art God,
> To endless years the same.

Two passengers took particular interest in her. One was an older woman who had graduated from Biola (Bible Institute of Los Angeles). "This lady bought my supper at Billings (onions on liver) and gave me a dollar bill to be applied on the subscription to some secular magazine that I might keep up on current events." Another was a woman whose curiosity was piqued. "Now just what is your purpose in going out?" she inquired. "Is it to educate the Chinese?" Grace quietly affirmed her priorities. "I told her my main objective was to tell them the gospel story," she explained. Education could come later.

When the train arrived in Seattle, she was met by Mr. Charles Judd, the CIM secretary in Vancouver, BC, who was holding a copy of *China's Millions* to identify himself. Three other young women arrived that same day: Pearl Galloway (who had been Grace's roommate at Candidate School), Pearl Strot (from Moody), and Ruth Temple (from Northwestern Bible Institute in Minneapolis). The three stayed together at the YWCA, where Mr. Judd had booked a room for them on the fifth floor (at seventy-five cents per person), thinking it would give them a good view of Puget Sound. But after sitting upright all the way from Iowa, it was the bed that loomed large in Grace's view.

While in Seattle they ate with chopsticks at a Chinese restaurant, obtained visas at the Chinese and Japanese consulates, and visited a new little church where people were informed and encouraging. "They are spiritually awake and are whole hearted for missions," Grace wrote. "They had something to say besides 'Good luck.'"

While she was on the West Coast, Grace hoped she might rendezvous with her younger brother, Ralph, who was now with the Navy, aboard the USS *Utah* in Bremerton, Washington. When they could not arrange a meeting, Dr. Glover, CIM Home Director for North America, asked Mr. Judd to keep an eye on her. She hadn't seen Ralph in four years, not since their father's funeral in 1930, and now she would be adding seven more years. Would she be melancholy? Irritable? Certainly she was disappointed, but Mr. Judd could report that he saw no tendency toward despondency or peevishness, neither of which would bode well for the mission field.

From Seattle she traveled north to Vancouver, BC, where she stayed in Mr. Judd's home until it was time to board the Japanese ship, the MS *Heian Maru*, bound for Yokohama, Kobe, and eventually Shanghai. She sailed, as expected, on October 26, 1934. A "box of beautiful flowers" was waiting for her in her cabin, wired by her Aunt Flora. And for the voyage she had seven companions of like mind and purpose. In addition to the three single women who had been with her in Seattle, two couples were going out under the Brethren Church: Mr. and Mrs. Cuff, who had been in China for thirty-six years, and Mr. and Mrs. Baehr, who were new workers.

The voyage would take twelve days, introducing Grace to such new experiences as room service, seasickness, crossing the International Dateline, and a birthday feast in honor of the Emperor of Japan.

Grace with Pearl Galloway (left) and "our little stewardess,
Kamiyama" on the M. S. Heian Maru

About five days into their journey a violent storm came up. "The waves went over the top deck & smashed unmercifully against our portholes," Grace wrote. "Looking out the port hole one could see valleys as long as several houses & then whee! we would slide into one & roll over the top of the crest...." The rolling and pitching of the ship made it vibrate until she wondered how it could not help but snap in two.

A storm at sea was something she had always wanted to witness, but except for a few brief minutes she was confined to her bed, where an analysis of the construction of her room led her to worship.

> Lying here in bed [seasick], I count approximately
> 300 inch head bolts in the ceiling of this one room &
> note 3 steel rails the size & shape of those of a railroad
> reaching the length of the ceiling, each of them having

at the exterior end a steel triangular brace with about a 12" hypotenuse.

But I just know there is more than human prowess that keeps the old ship from collapsing. I take my hat off to man whose brain devised such a wonderful construction as the ship which can successfully buffet the angry waves of the deep; but I bow in reverence before the maker of man.

On the morning of the twelfth day, passengers could spot Mt. Fujiyama, and by noon the ship was docking at Yokohama. The three days in port gave Grace and her friends the opportunity to visit Tokyo, where they found "rickshaws and Packards, occidental and oriental dress of both men and women, leather shoes, wooden shoes, and no shoes at all."

They glimpsed from a distance the grounds of the imperial palace, and took a drive to the mountains, admiring the terraced hillsides and visiting several shrines, including "the big Buddah at Kamakura." Then there was the poignant sight of "hundreds of school children with rosy cheeks and intelligent smiling faces, dressed in modest uniforms of dark blue, standing in rank [but] bowing to idols."

The next stop was Kobe, where they visited "the 'Kiku,' or chrysanthemum show," an impressive display in honor of what has been Japan's national flower since 910. A train then took them to Nagasaki, where they rejoined their ship.

Finally, on November 17, three weeks after sailing from Vancouver, they heard a fog horn from the light boat coming to escort them, signaling that they were within fifty miles of the harbor at Shanghai, China. Excitement ran high, but because of dense fog passengers could see nothing. Eventually they spotted the boat, and the sun came out as they navigated their way to the harbor through a variety of fishing junks and freighters.

Having just spent a week among the colorfully-dressed Japanese, they were startled at the "drab blues, grays and blacks" of the Chinese. Even the harbor seemed cluttered and dowdy. The junks hoisted sails that were "gray, ragged and patched." Several passenger boats were so laden with passengers that Grace could only compare them to "a coopful of chickens on a hot day." On the Huangpu (Whangpoo) River, sampans housed "thousands of Chinese coolies." Interestingly enough, she saw her own name in large capitals atop a tall building along the shore, but she was not beguiled. *Liddell Bros.* was a long-established English trading firm with no ties to her family in Iowa.

As the ship reached its dock, Mr. Slade of the China Inland Mission was on hand to meet the four young women and take charge of their baggage. Coolies scrambled to help, vying for customers and bargaining for a wage. When a coolie whom Grace had engaged withdrew, she engaged another, only to have the first one come back and argue furiously that she was his fare. "They sounded quite vicious but were really quite harmless," she wrote reassuringly, and in the end, the first one prevailed. She watched in wonder as he came up out of steerage carrying on his back a case of hers marked 209 pounds. It contained a bookcase with her books, and at home had required at least two men to carry it.

The next step was to get through customs, and pay a tax on any furniture they were bringing in. With grateful amazement, they watched as officials opened only a token trunk or two and checked the rest through, including the one containing Grace's bookcase.

Chapter 8

Mission Headquarters

The nerve center of the China Inland Mission was at 1531 Sinza Road in Shanghai. In Toronto, Grace had become familiar with the Canadian office, but the headquarters in Shanghai were the administrative offices for the entire Mission. There was also a Mission home, staffed to care for missionaries, guests, and new workers such as the four whom Mr. Slade was escorting from customs.

At the Mission home, they were welcomed by the venerable Mr. D. E. Hoste, who had been general director of the CIM since Hudson Taylor appointed him in 1902. In the following year, 1935, he would be succeeded by Mr. George Gibb, putting Grace and her friends among the last Mr. Hoste and his wife would receive.

Everything was strange: the city, the Chinese language all around them, the quaint customs, and the English tenor of the Mission home in which they were guests, yet they found they were not strangers. They had been prayed for by name as each one became known to the Mission family, and upheld in prayer as they made the long voyage across the Pacific.

In their rooms each young woman found a bouquet of flowers and a verse with a personal note of welcome from Mr. and Mrs. Hoste. Grace took to heart the verse they had chosen for her: Isaiah 26:3 (KJV), "Thou wilt keep him in perfect peace whose mind is stayed on Thee." She would need a mind at peace to work effectively in the face of a strange and challenging culture, the constant meeting of new people, and even physical danger.

That very evening, at the weekly prayer meeting, she learned anew that inland China was not a safe place. A civil war between the Chinese Nationalists and the Chinese Communists had been going on for seven years, and bandits, often interchangeable with Communist soldiers, were a constant menace, especially to foreigners. Foreigners could be captured and held for ransom. Or killed.

Alfred Bosshardt and Arnolis Hayman, two missionaries who had been captured six weeks earlier in Guizhou (Kweichow) province, were in fact being threatened with death at that very time. They had been walking home from a conference with their wives, two children, and a single missionary, Grace Emblen, when they were seized by Communist soldiers and held for $700,000 ransom—$100,000 per captive. Eventually the wives and children were released, but Miss Emblen and the two men were forced to join the Red Army (Chinese Communist Party) on its Long March, which was actually a prolonged and harrowing retreat from the White Army (Chinese Nationalist Party) through some of China's most difficult terrain. Miss Emblen was abandoned when she fell from exhaustion, but the two men were forced to trek more than 2,000 miles with the retreating army—an experience which Grace would help to chronicle in days to come (Bosshardt 5, 13).

The prayer meeting that evening was thoughtful and well-organized, and Grace warmed to its sincerity and depth. The two captives were a focal point, but not to the exclusion of other outposts, where, in spite of political unrest, rough living conditions, financial straits, intransigent officials, and illness, missionaries seemed to be gaining a foothold for the gospel. "It was a privilege to hear workers from the field tell of His blessing on their work and to pray with them for the needs of the various stations," she wrote.

A brief stay in Shanghai acquainted the newcomers with its modernity—"wide paved streets, street cars, traffic 'cops,' electric lights, telephones," and a bus which was bigger and more grand than any Grace had seen in the US or in Canada. They spoke over a Christian radio station and visited the Bethel School, where Christian nationals such as Dr. Andrew Gih were being trained to evangelize their own people. Grace would later work with two Bethel graduates in remote Yunnan.

Leaving Shanghai, the four new workers, escorted by Mrs. Mathews, a senior missionary, boarded a train for the CIM language school in Yangzhou (Yangchow), 150 miles north. The train took them as far as Zhenjiang (Chinkiang), where they visited a spot hallowed to the China Inland Mission: the cemetery where Hudson and Maria Taylor are buried, along with two of their children, and many other CIM workers who had laid down their lives in China.

The next day the women, escorted by Mr. Best for this leg of the journey, boarded a motor launch to travel the remaining fourteen miles via the Yangzi (Yangtze) River. At Yangzhou they would spend six months in language school (November 1934 – May 1935) before learning what part of inland China would be their particular field.

Chapter 9

Language School

If Shanghai was modern, Yangzhou was ancient and primitive. Transportation was by foot or rickshaw. The streets were alleys, some so narrow the new visitors could touch the walls on either side without extending their arms.

Grace and her friends joined about twenty-five other young women at the language school, also known as the training home. (A similar school for men and married couples was in the neighboring province of Anhui [Anhwei].) They studied not only the language, but Chinese customs and manners, the geography of China, the highlights of CIM history, the Mission's principles and practice, "and instructions for probationers." They learned how to get along with co-workers from other countries besides their own: England, Canada, Sweden, Germany, Switzerland, New Zealand, Australia, and the United States. "All speak English, but American is understood," was Grace's wry observation.

The "mother" of the home was Mrs. Rowe from England, with three single missionaries serving as teachers: Miss Williamson, Miss Griffeth, and Miss Wilson. At least three Chinese men came in daily to teach writing and pronunciation, and a number of Chinese servants were on hand to help with cooking and maintenance of the property. Some were Christian, but not all. "My private teacher is a Buddhist, my writing teacher a Confucianist, & my conversation teacher is a Christian—Mr. Poh (Baw)," Grace explained.

The language study was "fascinating…but we make progress only on our knees." The days were structured to help. "No studying is allowed after 5:15 in the afternoon or before 9 in the morning." And recreation was mandatory: "We have an hour of strenuous exercise at noon, playing basketball, walking and running. I choose to run a mile at least—seven times around the garden." At other times they also played baseball and ping pong.

Grace and her friends found five others who had been with them in Toronto, and together they became known as the Toronto Nine. Four of them formed a quartette, with Grace as second alto.

Language School Quartette
L-R: Grace Weir, Pearl Strot, Pearl Galloway, Grace Liddell
Early 1935

The language classes themselves provided comic relief, although they had to learn not to laugh. When Mr. Poh commented that one of the American girls, "the tall girl with a long face," had her words correct but spoke too fast to get the tones right, Grace knew he had been talking about her. That afternoon when he called on her to use "I heard" in a sentence, she responded, "I heard that Mr. Poh said my tones are bad &

that my face is long." He good-naturedly admitted it, but in an effort to save face, stated he meant that *she* was long and her face was *big*.

Miss Griffeth then explained to them all that in Chinese etiquette it is unacceptable to cause anyone to lose face, and it is unseemly to laugh, even over humorous mistakes with the language. "When you laugh, you lower yourselves greatly in the estimation of the Chinese. You will never in all the world be able to lead them to Christ," she declared.

Grace hadn't been at language school more than two weeks when terrible news came from the neighboring province of Anhui. Two CIM missionaries in their first term of service, John and Betty Stam, had been beheaded at the hands of Communist soldiers, leaving their three-month old daughter alone for more than twenty-four hours before a Christian Chinese pastor found her and took her to safety.

For Grace and the others at the training home the news came as a sober reminder of the gravity of their calling. "Several of us knew John at the Moody Bible Institute and some…also knew Betty," she wrote in somber reflection. She asked friends at home, "Will you pray for me that I may be able to grasp the language readily and be enabled to tell forth His love to those who have never heard?"

Meanwhile, there was no time like the present to begin. Even though they were novices, the young missionaries went out among the Chinese in Yangzhou. They could at least help their Chinese servant distribute tracts.

They watched as the servant gave one to the Islamic imam, earnestly explaining the gospel to him. As they left the Confucianist temple, a teenaged boy ran after them, asking for a tract, and they saw firsthand how cruel heathen worship could be. "On his head were pairs of spots where candles had been burned in worship ceremonies, and the hair doesn't grow. The spots were a little smaller than a dime and about ¾ of an inch apart." Another young man "shied and sprang down the bank and almost whimpered as he looked at me with terror written all over his face," Grace wrote. Too late she realized it was her dark glasses that had frightened him.

She had taken to wearing colored lenses because of a social custom she was finding hard to embrace. She had been brought up to look people in the eye. "It is in the eye that I find the personality—they are the windows of the soul, so to speak." But here it was considered immoral to look a Chinese man in the eye. Dark glasses allowed her to look where she pleased, but it never occurred to her that they might also be taken as evidence that white people are, indeed, "foreign devils."

Grace wrote to her family of two other local customs, one noisy, and one colorful. The new workers could hardly miss the total lunar eclipse which took place while they were there, given the raucous accompaniment on the ground. Believing a dog was swallowing the moon, the citizens of Yangzhou shot firecrackers and beat tin pans and drums long into the night, until the dog gave it up. A more serene and enjoyable custom was Yangzhou's colorful lantern festival.

> Last night we could see them from our window, [people] drawing the big ones along on wheels & carrying the smaller ones by hand. They all had candles inside & really were very pretty. The largest ones were about the size of a bushel basket. I don't know when they made all of them or where they kept them all. Some were made of paper & some of some kind of thick shiny stuff. The fine network in some of them was most intricate.

It was a delight to Grace to find a warm, spiritual camaraderie among her new friends at language school. "We have been having a blessed time in fellowship with the Lord," she wrote. "Many of our spare periods & every evening until 10:00 & after have been spent in prayer. I never knew time to pass so quickly." They prayed for the Holy Spirit to equip and anoint them for their work ahead, and they prayed spontaneously, often more than once.

As for herself, Grace was sensing a disconnect in her life, and the only way she knew to deal with it was with the passivity of Keswick theology. "I want to walk in His strength alone," she wrote. "Walking in my own strength [while] serving Him with my mind has kept me in bondage, but by His grace henceforth the conflict is His, and His the victory."

With eight countries represented at the language school, there were bound to be differences of opinion about world affairs. It was December

1934 and the trouble brewing in Germany was a concern to Grace. The Nazis had a majority in parliament and Hitler was now president as well as chancellor, but the new workers from the Liebenzeller Mission, a German Lutheran associate mission of the CIM, seemed unfazed by his growing influence and control.

> Sister Else has been trying to enlighten me concerning Hitler. They think he is "the it," and say he protects the Christians, & that had it not been for him the communists would have driven all the Christians out of Germany.

The young German missionaries believed Hitler would be an ally of the church. ["He] wants to get rid of all sects & have the one true church," Sister Else explained. But as an American, Grace could only be skeptical. "Why doesn't he, as a gov't. official, keep his finger off the church?" she asked her family in her weekly letter of April 13, 1935. "If he is helping the church I can only believe it is as a means to an end."

When the next issue of *Moody Monthly* arrived with a disturbing article about Hitler, Grace shared it with her new friends, but to no avail. "[They] laughed at it & said the people in other countries didn't understand."

"Then why all the smoke?" Grace reasoned to her family. "Where there is so much smoke, there must be a little fire."

Events would soon vindicate her suspicions, but for the time being it was a moot point. She and the German sisters shared a loyalty deeper than their own nationalities. Their first loyalty was to Jesus Christ, and they were in China to help extend his kingdom. Later she would write home of the "great work" she saw the sisters doing in Yunnan, work "which requires grace from our Lord to carry on."

By April, Grace and Pearl Strot had progressed in their study to the point that they were ready to take their exams at the end of the month, a month short of the usual six months.

The oral exam lasted about fifteen minutes and consisted of two parts. First came reading aloud—a real challenge, as Grace noted: "One girl from England was so nervous that she broke down & cried right in the middle of her reading." Second, each student was expected to answer ten simple questions asked by a Chinese speaker other than her personal teacher.

The written exam consisted of three parts, administered over two days. Unlike most students, Grace took the option of writing it in Chinese character rather than Roman script. Afterwards, in the privacy of her room, she took out the big joke book her cousin Jean had given her, and she and Pearl "had some mental relaxation."

The Chinese language course consisted of six sections. Students completed the first section at language school, but the remaining five would be administered from Shanghai as independent studies. Missionaries would enlist the help of a local language teacher and, when they felt they were ready, would request the exam, take it, and send it back to be graded.

About the same time as the language school exams were being administered, the general director, Mr. George Gibb, visited the training home to designate the new workers to their respective fields of service. He did this in consultation with each individual missionary, taking into account her own leading and inclinations, and in consultation with those who had observed her during language school. But in the end, the decision was his. As general director, it was he who knew what kind of workers were needed, and where. Realizing the critical importance of this decision, Grace asked those at home to pray with her that her designation be according to God's will, and that she be acquiescent in it. There is no mention of anyone being disappointed.

> I wish you could visualize the Home at the time when Mr. Gibb came to make the designations. The air was full of excitement and anticipation. On the wall in the hall hung a map of China. As each girl came from her interview with Mr. Gibb, and her appointment was known, a small flag with her name on it was placed in the proper place on the map. By the time the group… were all designated the map was well covered with flags. The four of us who came across the Pacific together are in four different provinces.

As escorts were available, and as peace from communistic invasions warranted it, groups left the Home to go to their respective provinces. We never knew when a telegram would come from Shanghai telling us to leave as soon as possible. One day a telegram came about 11 o'clock for a party of nine to leave. In two hours' time five of the nine had packed, eaten their dinner and were off. The other four left the next morning. As each group left we formed two columns for them to march through and sang [a triumphant] chorus composed by Mrs. Rowe.

Grace's station was to be the city of Chengkiang, some 2,000 miles away in the western province of Yunnan, and her letters indicate she was most content with this designation. It was to become her "beloved Yunnan." But there was a caveat relating to her experience as a teacher in the USA.

Mr. Gibb "made me" promise to be willing to go to Chefoo [the CIM boarding school] to teach anytime the call should come…. Several of the girls have the same thing hanging over their heads. I may never be asked to go & again I may…. It would be nice to <u>know</u> in a way, but it is better to trust & abide.

Meanwhile, a small flag with her name on it was placed on Chengkiang, Yunnan, and another, with the name of Helen (Clare) Lassen from Seattle, WA, was placed beside it.

But when would they go? Their departure date had been canceled once, due to Communist army activity in Yunnan, and there was no knowing when it would be safe for them to make the journey. At the same time, the other girls continued to depart, making it "lonesomer & lonesomer as each group goes," Grace admitted.

Her dear friend from Toronto days, Pearl Gallagher, had gone to Anhui, the province where the Stams had been stationed. Pearl's roommate had moved to the room vacated by *her* best friend ("for sentiment's sake"), leaving Grace alone and exhausted from the strain of studying for the exam. She was also deeply concerned about her sister, Flora, whose first baby had been stillborn and who was now expecting another. Grace's earnest belief that a "victorious" Christian is not overwhelmed forbade any show of weakness, but she was emotionally spent. "Am sorry to say it was hard," she wrote. "Was shamed before them all because my old eyes just naturally wouldn't behave. It hurt too, to think that I was thus failing Him."

On May 9, news from home eased her mind and lifted her spirits. She might have had the news earlier, had a letter from Grace's mother gotten through, but even five weeks after the fact, it was still a tonic: Sherman Merrill Allen had arrived safely on April 3, 1935, and mother and baby were doing well. They called him Merrill, and as Grace received letters describing his development and baby ways, she undertook to make a "Merrill book," a scrapbook of pictures and excerpts from his mother's letters with which to surprise Flora when she returned home.

That night, sensing Grace's need for companionship, "Pearl Strot came in & slept on the extra bed in my room...."

But the next day Pearl, too, left for her appointed station.

Chapter 10

Westward to Yunnan

As it turned out, Grace and Clare were among the last to leave the training home. After Pearl Strot left, it was another three weeks before they and two others were cleared to travel. They began their 2,000 mile journey on June 3, 1935, arriving at Kunming, the capital city of Yunnan, about a month later.

A three-day stopover at Mission headquarters in Shanghai gave them opportunity to do some shopping, but more memorable to Grace was the privilege of being asked to walk with Mr. Hoste, the recently retired general director. That was how he preferred to pray: aloud, while walking with a companion, and Grace treasured the experience. "One who has walked so long with the Lord has more than worldly wisdom to pass on," she discovered.

From Shanghai the four new missionaries and their companions, Mr. and Mrs. Browning, traveled by passenger ship to Haiphong in French Indochina, with stops at Swatow, Canton, and Hong Kong. "We couldn't have asked for a more delightful journey than the one from Shanghai to Hong Kong," Grace wrote. "Canton was interesting to us because it is the port to which all the early missionaries came."

At Hong Kong she was fascinated to see Chinese sailboats in the path of their oncoming vessel, with merchants waiting to climb aboard "by an ingenious hook & rope method" to hawk their wares among the passengers. A launch took the young women from the ship to the city, where they were hospitably welcomed by Mr. and Mrs. Ritzie at the Basel Mission, a Swiss organization working in southern China. During their brief visit they were happy to be tourists, enjoying as many experiences as they could in the historic port, including a ride on the funicular railway to the top of Victoria Peak.

But a less pleasant voyage awaited them as they boarded Butterfield & Swire's ship for Haiphong. Rough seas sickened almost everyone, prompting Grace to resort to a bit of sarcasm. "…the…economy in the dining room must have pleased the captain greatly," she quipped in a letter home. The cabins were no refuge, being suffocatingly hot, but the crew was kind, offering apples and fresh orange juice whenever they wished. And the second mate let Grace briefly take the wheel—a feat which would have intrigued her future husband, who was himself a ship's officer at that time.

They had been cautioned that Haiphong might levy an exorbitant duty on goods, even goods in transit, "and we had prayed much about it." However, after several hours of opening boxes and examining the contents, "one official's heart began to change & he took pity on us. He had [the baggage men] go see the chief. The chief wrote a note to the effect that our goods could be passed…& so although we had to open all but my bookcase, not one thing was taxed. Praise the Lord!!!"

In the city of Haiphong they met some Annamese, a Mongolian people who, as part of the French colonial empire, had learned to speak French as well as Chinese. Grace first encountered the effects of betel nut among them. In general, she found them "better looking than the Chinese as long as they keep their mouths shut. They chew some kind of nut which makes their lips very red & their teeth as black as charcoal. When they smile it looks as tho they have no teeth at all."

They stayed in a French hotel which boasted a bidet in each room, but none of the young women knew what to make of it. "As there was no stool, we just supposed that was what this was supposed to be, yet tho't it very strange that there was no toilet paper. However we used it, all of us, only to learn later upon inquiry that there was a stool around the corner in a separate room & paper, too. Did we laugh?!!! But we still don't know what that thing is."

The next leg of the journey was a three-day train trip northwest to Kunming, along a railway opened by French engineers in 1910. Rice fields abounded as long as the terrain was level, and Grace knew her farming family would be interested.

> The rice was in practically every stage from the planting to the tall green. I suppose each little patch was about the equivalent of a square rod. It is remarkable how they have one plot flooded and another dry, sometimes the two adjacent. The partitions were about a foot high & made of mud. One would naturally think it would seep thro' from one to the other, but it doesn't seem to.

By the end of the first day their hard-working steam engines had pulled them through Hanoi and on up to the Yunnan border, a journey from sea level to a height of more than 5,000 feet in about 240 miles.

Yunnan means "south of the clouds" and indeed, the higher they climbed, the closer were the clouds, but the origin of the name is more prosaic. Just north of Yunnan is the province of Sichuan (Szechwan) where the summers, by comparison, are very cloudy, thus putting Yunnan "south of the clouds" (Montsma, "Yunnan").

The young missionaries were on the train three days, but because of frequent mudslides the train did not travel at night. Passengers were obliged to get off and find an inn for themselves.

> We could have put up at French inns but they are so very expensive that we chose the Chinese instead. They told us these inns were the exception in cleanliness, accommodation etc. But we had boards to sleep on instead of springs. There were mosquito nets but with holes torn in them. Our visitors consisted of mosquitoes, fleas & rats. (In the average Chinese inn the varieties are more in number.) Our Chinese meals were served in our rooms, & yes, we ate with chopsticks.

The second day took them into Yunnan, where the train followed river beds through amazingly steep gorges, with sides rising perpendicular to the tracks. "We could see where in several places there had been landslides & the slide had been banked or walled with stone, & sometimes a tunnel dug through the slide." They went around switchbacks and through a chain of 200 tunnels, "some so long that the smoke [from the steam engines] caused one to cough." They had their first glimpse of Yunnan's lush vegetation—palm trees, banana trees, pomelo and pomegranates.

The third day brought them to a plateau, another impressive sight in their new province. It was "a basin or plain surrounded by mountains on every side & the plain itself a checkerboard of small rice fields & other vegetation" with "little villages nestled close to the sides of the mountain."

By five o'clock that afternoon they arrived at Kunming, the provincial capital, where a welcoming party of five missionaries was waiting to help carry their baggage. But there was none.

When crossing into Yunnan, they had stopped for baggage inspection and duty fees, but because there was not time for inspection, they had been instructed to leave their baggage behind. It would be on the next day's train, the official assured them, and the officers at Kunming would do the inspecting.

Knowing what an ill-fated arrangement that could be, "we prayed much about it." When they went to the station the next morning, they were relieved to find that the luggage had arrived as promised. Furthermore, "[we] didn't have to pay one cent, except Barbara who had to pay on some medical supplies." The officials weren't even interested in their trunks. Kathleen did have a canvas carryall with about two yards of leather straps around it, which the inspectors just cut off as if they were rope. "Nothing can be done," Grace explained. "We just have to take the spoiling of our goods cheerfully." (Little did she know how much more of that spoiling was in store for her.)

As the China Inland Mission moved inland, it was important to establish a home base for missionaries in each province. A property large enough for an administrative office and a guest home would be acquired, and normally a couple would be designated to serve as local secretary, and as host and hostess, usually on a short-term basis. When Grace and the other new workers arrived at the Kunming Mission home, Mr. and Mrs. Arthur Allen were in charge. The young women had a week to recover and adjust, and then for Grace and Clare, it was time to travel the final twenty-five miles south to Chengkiang, their appointed station.

PART TWO

✠

ON A CHECKERBOARD IN CHINA

"My time in China has been more or less a game of checkers…."
(Letter to General Director Gibb, December 1938)

Whate'er my God ordains is right: he never will deceive me;
He leads me by the proper path; I know he will not leave me.
I take, content, what he hath sent; his hand can turn my griefs away,
And patiently I wait his day.

Whate'er my God ordains is right: though now this cup, in drinking,
May bitter seem to my faint heart, I take it, all unshrinking.
My God is true; each morn anew sweet comfort yet shall fill my heart,
And pain and sorrow shall depart.

Samuel Rodigast 1675

Chapter 11

Baptism by Fire in Chengkiang

Although Grace was asked to relocate several times in China, no situation was as perplexing as the first. The problem was not the location, with yet another dialect, strange customs, and unfamiliar food. That she expected, and accepted. It was her senior missionary, renowned for her zeal as a missionary, but impossible to live with. "Lord, is it I?" she would wonder as tension mounted and the atmosphere chilled.

When she and Clare arrived in Chengkiang on July 4, 1935, they were the latest in a succession of missionaries who had come to this city, distinguished for being "the only walled city on the plain." A church had been established and Chinese evangelists were actively engaged. In addition to working on their second section of Chinese language study, Grace and Clare would be helping with teaching and evangelism under the supervision of their senior missionary, Miss Grace Hoover. Like Grace and Clare, Miss Hoover was from the United States. In fact, when she was on furlough, she briefly met Grace Liddell at Moody Bible Institute.

Traveling first by train, then rickshaw and huakan, it had taken Grace and Clare a full day to travel the twenty-five miles south to Chengkiang, accompanied by Mr. Robert Porteous, acting superintendent of Yunnan. The huakan was new to Grace—a rope seat suspended from two bamboo poles carried on the shoulders of coolies. It could be embarrassing.

51

The coolies were greatly disconcerted because of our size, & we could hardly blame them. Clare & I are about the same size [nearly six feet] & Mr. Porteous is a tall man. ... When we came to a very small mountain (very great & steep hill), we got out & walked, also walked down the other side. It is customary to do that, although they carry their own people up hill & down. ... Mr. Porteous told us we weren't to walk anymore until after lunch. But soon we came to quite a little rise, & I surely did feel like a scamp having those little men laboriously pack me up there, so I told them please I wanted to walk. I didn't know whether they understood my dialect or not, but [they] got it the first time, & stopped immediately. I walked up that knoll & down, & then waited on a little bridge for them to catch up. Instead of being grateful, they made as if to go on, indicating another very slight rise in the distance, but I took hold of the pole & told them I wanted to ride now, so they stopped & let me on.

As they approached the city Grace's huakan was in the lead. A man standing on a knoll called out, "Peace be unto you, missionary," but the dialect was so different from what she had learned in language school she was at a loss to know how to reply, "so I just smiled and went on." Then she met a group of children and adults who had walked a mile out from the city with the same greeting, "Peace be unto you, missionary," and again she smiled and went on, while the group remained to welcome Clare and Mr. Porteous. Then, much to her chagrin, "the coolies carried me right down thro' the streets with all eyes fastened upon me. Yes, I did feel like two cents. I thought they never would come to the compound."

The compound was a two-story house and garden rented by the CIM, with Miss Hoover in charge. It was a large house, affording a room apiece to Miss Hoover, Grace, Clare, and each of three Chinese female employees, including the new workers' language teacher. The house also accommodated the Chinese pastor/evangelist and his family, and the landlord.

We had a nice supper of mashed potatoes, fried chicken, gravy, fresh tomatoes & several other good things. After supper the Christians had a little reception for us where they served us sweets & apples & tea. Different ones gave little messages of greeting & Mr. Porteous gave the response.

Mr. Porteous returned to Kunming the next day, leaving Grace and Clare to settle in, with Miss Hoover as their mentor. Grace wrote home admiringly of her senior missionary. "We are privileged to have a senior worker with such a good command of the language and who has the work at heart." They wore Chinese clothing—a wadded gown with trousers underneath—but the Chinese mistook them for men "because of our size & big feet." By contrast, Miss Hoover was small, with small feet, and Grace could see that the Chinese liked that in her. "What hope have I?" she asked whimsically.

Actually, she had more hope than she realized. Arthur Allen had observed her not only during the few days she was in Kunming, but he was in a position to hear reports from Chengkiang. After learning of her untimely death he wrote, "I remember when Grace first came. The Chinese really liked her, [which] isn't always the case by any means. She had a way of reaching the hearts of the people in Chengkiang. I'm talking about what the Chinese told me."

At Chengkiang
L-R: Grace Hoover, Clare Lassen, Grace Liddell, Bible-woman

The dialect in Chengkiang was not only different, but formidable. "The first day I came upstairs from class feeling almost sick at my stomach, it was such a strain," Grace reported. Chinese is a tonal language, but the expertise she had gained at language school seemed useless to her now. "We have to change all of our tones but one..." Their days as new workers would be divided between more lessons with the language teacher and visiting among the people to try out the new dialect.

Other things were sadly familiar with what they had seen in Yangchow. Idolatry was on full display, and they saw vividly the hopelessness of people without knowledge of the true God.

One night last week, all the idolaters were worshiping their ancestors, by burning paper money, paper shoes, & clothes for them to use in the spirit world. Each person's belongings were sealed in a neat paper package and burned in order. Some piles would more than fill a bushel basket. As each packet was thrown on the fire, a dipper-ful of soup with bits of food in it was thrown on the ground for the departed spirits, but dogs came up & ate the bits. At the same time one stood with a glass of wine & poured a bit over his little finger & onto the ground, offering up wine to the spirits. As one looked up & down the street it seemed there was a fire in nearly every doorway.

We walked around the block. On one street several women were wailing in a most blood-curdling manner. We peeked in at one house where it was going on... [A] big black coffin sat just inside the door. Candles were burning & food sat at the foot of it, where the mother knelt and wailed. ...

One day this week we were walking around the town a bit & stopped in at a temple to look around. Grace [Hoover] sat down on the door-step beside an old woman & tried to make plain to her darkened mind, the way of salvation. ... It was chilling to see that old woman actually laugh as Grace told her of Christ's vicarious atonement, His dying on the cross and shedding His blood for our sins. She said that in all her experience she had never had anyone laugh at the plan of salvation. ...

Besides the ongoing challenge of language study, each woman took a turn at cooking for a week, which included baking the bread and going to market. When it was Grace's week to cook, she reduced her study to "3 or 4 hours a day."

There were also villages to visit, with a Chinese Bible-woman to do the teaching. They made these visits on foot, going sometimes as far as five miles each way.

And there was the monthly visit to the leper colony, a six-mile trip which they took on horseback. Grace had grown up around horses, but the pack saddle she was obliged to use was punishing. It was "a wooden structure with two cross pieces about eight inches apart and standing about three inches above the horse's back," which no amount of padding could disguise or make comfortable. She considered riding bareback, until they removed the saddle and she saw the open sores on the animal's back. So, being young and physically fit, she joined the Bible-woman on her own two feet, "and enjoyed every bit of it."

The leper colony was pleasantly situated beside a lake, but was itself a place of pathetic hopelessness. It consisted of a group of about sixty men, women and children, cut off from their families and isolated from society, waiting for the inexorable progress of their disease to take its toll. Treatment, but not a cure, was available in Kunming, but who could get there? About all they could hope for was that someone who had been to Kunming would return and share some new tip for coping. The missionaries had no cure, but by visiting once a month they could show the compassion of Jesus, and bring the message of hope and life which could be theirs in him, regardless of their physical condition.

Life in Chengkiang did have its lighter side. Grace enjoyed watching Mr. Tseng, the primary evangelist, in action.

> Saturday evening after…a short message, he was suggesting topics of prayer for the various ones present. He said, "Mr. K'o, you pray for your daughter that she won't be so ornery. Mr. Teng, you want to sell medicines, but you sit at your booth half asleep and can't sell anything. You ask the Lord to help you in your work." …And so he went the rounds, hitting each nail on the head. They knew it was true, but they only laughed, because he does it in such a way they can't be offended.
>
> When we go out to the villages, he sells Gospels. You should see him. After his message, he starts to sell them for a copper or so each.[2] He simply puts the book into their hands & says, "Here, this is yours, give me the money for it," & they nearly always do it.
>
> He is certainly longwinded. The last two Sundays he has talked for one full hour. The men like to hear

---

[2] The copper was the basic unit of Chinese currency, gradually replaced by the yuan in the late nineteenth century, but apparently still in use in 1935. "History of Chinese Currency" (wikipedia.org).

him, but the old women get tired & get up & go out. You should see the children sit and listen to him. Little youngsters, 12 years old & down, sit & listen as tho they are enraptured. His own children are all there.

The evangelist, Mr. Tseng, preaching in Chengkiang on market day

Grace enjoyed the evangelist's children, often writing home of the little three-year-old boy, En-kuang. Using her family's endearments, she refers to him as "a little captain," "a little mischief," "this little tad," and "little scoot" as she describes his impish behavior.

> Tonight the little three year old, En-kuang, occupied my lap most of the time during service, and part of the time entertained himself pulling the hair on my arm. When I came home, he wouldn't let go my hand. I tried to tell him "goodnight" but he wouldn't have it. So I told him to kiss us goodnight & then go. He kissed Grace & me, & I started upstairs with my lamp, but here he came. So I told him goodnight again & that I'd see him again tomorrow, so he took his hat off and bowed. Come to find out, he was after a cinnamon roll [which

I had made the day before]. He led Grace [Hoover] to the kitchen and pointed up to the breadbox.

It was the care of a baby girl that began to strain Grace's relationship with her senior missionary, Grace Hoover. The infant's family lived in back of the Mission compound, and since the mother was a Christian, it was quite natural that one day her older sister should bring the baby over for the missionaries to see. "She was wrapped in old blue denim rags—quite clean considering—[but] was broken out badly with the heat," Grace explained, so Miss Hoover gave her a bath, and Grace and Clare helped put together a hasty layette.

> You should have seen us scurrying around to make clothes for the lassie. Clare cut a little dress out of an old blue voile of hers. I folded a dishtowel, cut a hole in it for a neck & made a slip. Another dishtowel made the binder; a table napkin the "nappie," a Turkish towel the inner blanket, & a fourth of Grace [Hoover]'s red wool blanket made the outer wrap. Clare furnished powder, I supplied olive oil, Grace found some castile soap. When she became hungry the sister took her home. …
>
> They never make clothes for [babies] until they are about a year old & [there is] reasonable assurance that they are going to live. Until that time they are dressed in old rags. They think it quite a novelty to see the baby so clean & in white. They don't dress babies in white as it is symbolical of death.

Before long it became apparent that Miss Hoover wanted the infant to be *their* baby. The parents were willing to give her up, and Miss Hoover did eventually take her as her own, but meanwhile Grace and Clare were expected to take part in caring for her and making her clothes. "We asked [Miss Hoover] if we couldn't buy material, but she says it is difficult to find anything soft enough." So they appropriated their own towels and blankets, just as Miss Hoover was doing.

And what of language study? Miss Hoover had passed all six of her exams, but Grace and Clare juggled their ongoing study with the demands of the baby, each one taking her for a week.

> This last week was my week to take care of the baby. The mother usually brings her about breakfast time. After breakfast I'd bathe her, feed her & toddle her on my knees until she was asleep. One day I held her on my lap practically the whole day long....

A measure of relief came when Grace and Clare took a "day off." It was market day, and they packed their lunch and sewing and walked out four miles to Fuxian Lake, "our beautiful lake," as Grace called it. Only a girl from the farm would take note of the way pigs went to market. "They tie their feet together & carry them on a pole. Sometimes they are put in baskets & a basket hangs on either side of a horse's back, pigs squealing as pigs can." After wading in the lake, they shared their lunch with some curious teenagers, reluctantly starting home when it began to rain.

That evening Grace entertained Clare by reading *Knee-Deep in June*, a poem by James Whitcomb Riley. It described the relief of that day so well, and Grace reproduced the dialect so convincingly, that "Clare laughed till the tears rolled down her cheeks. Our kitchen girl came in and thought it great fun to see Clare laugh so hard." It was August 1935 in Yunnan, but it might just as well have been June 1920 on the Warnke place. "It sounded like Ralph might have written it."

> Tell you what I like the best --
> 'Long about knee-deep in June,
> 'Bout the time strawberries melts
> On the vine, -- some afternoon
> Like to jes' git out and rest,
> And not work at nothin' else! ....

"Oh! It did just seem good to get out all by ourselves," was Grace's telling comment.

On another day, they visited a village about three miles away with Mr. Tseng, the evangelist, and two Chinese Christian men who went along to help. "We had a lot of fun," Grace wrote, and described it for her family.

> It was market day in the village and there were hundreds of people there. The men put up posters and preached in four different parts of the village. One old lady followed us from place to place and said she loved to listen. It's strange how the old women seem less obdurate and more ready to forsake idolatry and accept Christ as their Saviour than the young women....
>
> Then they took us to a tea shop (now don't visualize a cozy little nook like the tea shops at home). This place was crowded with men, & there wasn't a single table empty. So Mr. Tseng asked some to move so that we could all sit together. They graciously did so. Oh, the tea tasted <u>so</u> good. It was quite warm, & we had walked a bit, & with hats on. There were smaller bowls from which to drink. As the large bowls (about the size of a teacup at home) became empty, the waiter would come along and fill them up with boiling water. We kept him busy for awhile.
>
> Mr. Tseng went out on the street and bought us some cake. [It] is about the time when they offer cakes up to their ancestors (but the people eat them themselves). Well we had some of that kind. It was quite good—very sweet. Clare didn't care for hers, so warily dropped a greater part of it on the ground & asked me to oblige by kicking it under the table, so I did. No one saw. ...
>
> Then we had the walk home. We had some pretty nice chats with [Mr. Tseng and the helpers]. Can understand them a little better, but imagine they feel like showing us their heel dust just plenty of times.

In spite of these periods of relief and a sense that she was gaining in the language, Grace's letters from Chengkiang began to betray some concern. They were more introspective. She seemed to be in some kind of spiritual trouble. Specifically, she wanted friends to pray that she would daily "die to self," that she be "victorious," that she let the Lord "perfect that which concerneth me," no matter how much it might hurt. In short, life with their senior missionary was becoming increasingly difficult, though Grace wrote of it only with great reluctance, and then only to her beloved Aunt Flora, her mother's sister.

> Grace is certainly zealous for winning souls, and takes advantage of every opportunity to preach Christ, and is not easily daunted. But her temperament is such that it makes an excellent weapon for accomplishing that humility which I desire. She doesn't hesitate to set me down good & hard, justly or otherwise, and sometimes quite cutting....
>
> Sometimes I just long for a good old hearty laugh and wonder if I'll forget how, by the time I go home. When Jean's letter came telling about the "old biddies" in the rain, & your letter about Doris in the cemetery, I was thoroughly enjoying them, but heard a "Sh!" So when I finished Jean's I let her read it, & I think she didn't even smile. You know, I think sometimes a good laugh is as good as a tonic. …

Still, such was her self-discipline that she kept her thoughts to herself. "I never breathe a word about Grace to Clare," she told her Aunt Flora, "but am sure she sees it and feels it, too."

How easy and natural it would have been to compare notes and criticize. Or, given Grace's facility for mimicry and sarcasm, how much fun they might have had at Miss Hoover's expense. But their situation was far too serious. They were new workers, still unfamiliar with the dialect around them, dependent on their senior missionary for everything in terms of becoming established as missionaries. They could ill afford to be incompatible. For one thing, the Chinese believers looked to the missionaries to live in harmony and peace with each other. But more importantly, their commitment to the Love that "always protects" was too deep to permit open complaint or argument. Miss Hoover's good name would not suffer at their hands.

When Clare went to Kunming for several days, leaving Grace alone with Miss Hoover, "I prayed definitely about the stay of the two Graces together," Grace told her Aunt Flora. There would be no buffer, no English-speaking friend with whom to take a walk. No one but her heavenly Father.

For awhile the situation seemed to improve. Instead of finding fault, Miss Hoover was congenial and helpful. She even offered Grace a piece of candy she had received from home. "The candy wasn't so good, but oh I praise the Lord for what prompted her to do it," Grace wrote.

Another break came when Clare returned, and Miss Hoover left the two new missionaries in charge of the compound for a few days, while she visited other villages with Mr. Tseng and the Bible-woman. When she returned, she asked Grace if she would like to take the same kind of trip, and Grace readily agreed. She was away about a week, traveling on horseback with Mr. Tseng and the Bible-woman to villages some thirty miles distant. It gave her complete dialect immersion, since she spoke and heard no English all that time. They crossed two mountain ranges, stayed overnight in an Islamic inn, and Grace spent a day in bed with stomach flu before they returned home, but they had been a happy trio.

Sadly, once those two trips were over, things returned to the status quo. Miss Hoover's reformation was short-lived. The old tension was back, and Grace found it hard to sleep. She asked for prayer that she be able to go the second mile as gladly "when acrimony characterizes the speech of another as when loving-kindness is the characteristic." To make matters more difficult, Clare was being reassigned to another station, leaving Grace on her own with Miss Hoover.

At the same time, she was improving in the language to the point that she could teach Scripture verses to the women and lead Sunday morning devotions. The latter was "quite a nervous strain" because the audience was mostly men. (Women were not inclined to attend because they could not read.)

There is our evangelist, with his pencil and paper jotting down notes; there is Mr. Suen, retired on a postmaster's pension; there is Mr. Yang, … whose pronunciation is somewhat different from ours (and I wonder how much of what I say he can understand); there is Mr. Teng (*Dong*) who sells medicines, and Mr. Ko, who has a little general merchandise shop. Besides these regular attendants, there are those of our own household, and the evangelist's wife and older children.

In spite of all of the perplexity and strain, Grace could still laugh at herself. She wrote home of a day when she and Miss Hoover had gone with the Bible-woman and the language teacher to gather pine needles on a nearby mountain.

The Bible-woman & I lost the teacher and Miss Hoover, and while trying to find them, [we] ran across an old woman sitting on the ground. I asked her if she had seen our two friends, and she answered "No." Elated, I turned to the Bible-woman and said, "Marvellous, she understood." Only to have the old woman come back at me with, "What do you think your cows would be doing away up here?"

Chapter 12

J. O. Fraser –
A Friend in Need

A week before Christmas 1935, Mr. J. O. Fraser paid a visit to the work in Chengkiang. He knew Miss Hoover, but as field superintendent for Yunnan he wished to meet the new worker now stationed with her. Grace had heard of him. He had come from England in 1908 and had pioneered much of the work in western Yunnan, particularly among the Lisu tribe. In order to translate the New Testament into Lisu, he first had to reduce their language to writing; in doing so, he had devised what came to be known as the Fraser alphabet.[3] The great distances between stations, coupled with primitive means of travel, made it difficult for a field superintendent to visit often, but now he was in Chengkiang and Grace was glad to meet him.

"I like him very much," she wrote. "He gave me some most helpful advice both in the language...and in the spiritual walk."

It was the kind of encouragement and support she had been missing, but his visit was all too short. "A small group of us escorted him to the city gate, but when we came back I walked a little ahead of the rest until my eyes decided to behave."

There was to be a field conference in the middle of January, just three weeks hence, and that became a bright spot on her horizon. The

---

[3] In 1992, the Chinese government declared the Fraser alphabet to be the official script for the Lisu language.

field conference brought together all the missionaries from a particular area for reports, advice, mutual encouragement, and prayer. Mr. Fraser would be there, and she would see Clare again.

Meanwhile, she joined the local Christians in their celebration of the birth of Jesus. They had been singing carols since the end of November, but in order to keep the chapel decorations new for Christmas day, they waited until December 23 to put them up. There were no garlands and poinsettias and candles, but new pictures, posters, paper chains, and mottos framed with evergreen twigs. They went caroling, and the children recited Scripture passages, and they had a wonderful feast for both the morning and afternoon meals.

> The men prepared [the feast] with Mrs. Tseng's help. They worked nearly all day long the day before Christmas, & two of the men slept on the seats in the chapel the night before Xmas, so as to be here on hand in the early morning, and also because they worked until nearly midnight the night before. ... Each [guest] paid $3.00 for the two meals—not quite 3¢ apiece in U.S. currency."

It was a proper Chinese feast, with Chinese customs and etiquette. Rice came first, with one guest filling the bowl for each of the others at their table for eight, including Grace. Next, the person beside her stood up, reached with his own chopsticks to take meat and vegetables from the serving bowls in the center of the table, and placed them in her bowl. It was the neighborly thing to do, and it obviated the need to pass anything.

But how to convince them when she was full? She knew to place her bowl on the table and stand up, urging the others to continue eating, but before she could stand, someone would put more rice in her bowl, and courtesy required that she finish it. There were two possible solutions. One was to place her hand over her bowl, "because sometimes they slip around and drop it in over one's shoulder." Another was to hold the bowl in her lap, but even that was no guarantee against someone crawling under the table with a dipper of rice.

The missionaries had decorated a tree in their courtyard with paper flowers, candles and streamers, and there were gifts for the household members and the children, but underneath all the festivities, Grace's private anguish persisted. She was so troubled she could not write home, and the record is silent from Christmas 1935 until February 1936. The situation had become unbearable.

She had been cautioned by older missionaries never to go over the head of a senior worker. It could create disunity and rifts, for one thing, and it would most certainly put Grace herself under closer scrutiny. She was still a new worker, after all, and Miss Hoover was a seasoned missionary.

At the field conference in mid-January, however, she took the risk of approaching her field superintendent, despite the word of caution. "Sometimes we can rely upon the counsel & advice of man," she explained to her sister Flora, "and sometimes He leads directly contrariwise." With relief, she found Mr. Fraser totally sympathetic.

Since she was going to Kunming for her second section language exam in February, Mr. Fraser told her to be prepared to stay awhile, and he asked Miss Hoover to accompany her. Miss Hoover stayed just two days, but it was long enough for Mr. Fraser to determine that Grace Liddell needed to stay "several months." This was news to Miss Hoover, and she was not pleased. The evangelist, Mr. Tseng, had already moved to another station, and now she was losing her junior missionary. She informed Mr. Fraser that she would not stay in Chengkiang alone, but she did return for almost a year, continuing to care for the baby. Shortly after her return, the cook and both teachers also left.

Grace wrote to her at least twice, but received no response, not even to her request that she send her "the base to the waterless cooker Mama gave me & the enamel chamber of mine which she had been using for the baby." A chamber pot could be replaced, but a replacement for the cooker base would have to come from home. Miss Hoover did write a note to Clare, but "it wasn't a very nice one."

"I do feel sorry for her," Grace concluded, "can't help it, but I actually believe had I stayed there I couldn't have stood it. Sleep comes much better now...."

She had also done some heart searching. She had been at Chengkiang only seven months. What had gone wrong? In a letter to her sister Flora (March 1936) she suggested that part of the trouble had been her own "self-will." But what *do* you do when your senior tells you to use a procedure that you know is clearly not the best way to do a thing? She prayed for the grace to do it the inferior way, if necessary, for the Lord's sake. "If I am driving in a nail, & someone suggests doing it differently, I want the grace to do it differently, although I know my way is right, just to crucify this self, & particularly self-will." Her prayer for humility was being answered, however rough the means.

Meanwhile, Miss Hoover was causing the other Yunnan missionaries grave concern. She had decided to take the baby home with her to the USA. The parents were agreeable. It was an opportunity for them to make a little money, which Miss Hoover was willing to give; but when they raised their demand, she absconded with the baby and headed north to Kunming.

In the end, she did not go home to the States. She got as far as the Mission home in Shanghai, where General Director Gibb asked her to stay and help at headquarters. When Mission leaders later requested that she return to Gansu (Kansu), the province where she had previously worked for eight years, she agreed to go. (No mention is made of what became of the baby.)

But what would Grace Liddell do?

"I suspect this has been about as disappointing a shock to you as it has been to me," she wrote to her "dear Floras." She didn't expect them to understand "until you have been out here and gone through it…. We are in the enemy's stronghold here," she told them, "and he exerts every effort to defeat our Lord." She spoke of "nervous strain" and "tired nerves," of "defeat where once there was unconscious victory." It all caused her "to realize more & more my utter weakness, & dependence upon Him," and she recalled the promise that welcomed her when she arrived at the Mission home in Shanghai, "Thou wilt keep him in perfect peace whose mind is stayed on Thee."

When Grace had first visited Kunming, on her way to Chengkiang, Mr. and Mrs. Arthur Allen were in charge of the Mission home. Now, seven months later, it was under the care of Mr. and Mrs. Fred Hatton, and a number of other guests were also in residence: five evacuees from the neighboring province of Guizhou; a young couple who had come to the capital for dentistry; and the senior missionary in Kunming, Mr. J. David Harrison, and his wife, Kathryn.

It was the Harrisons with whom Mr. Fraser wanted Grace to live during this extended stay in Kunming. They were Moody alumni, having been students about ten years before Grace enrolled. They married in Shanghai in 1927, and now had three children: Jimmy, at the CIM boarding school in Chefoo, and Marjorie and Carl, still at home. They would be moving into a place of their own just around the corner from the Mission home, and Mr. Fraser asked Grace to move with them, along with three other single ladies: Mildred Wright, Doris Trefren, and Irene Barberini, also known as "Barbara." The Harrisons would be Grace's senior missionaries, and, as Mr. Fraser expected, it was a good match. "They are a real blessing & help to me," she wrote, "and I pray I may be to them."

Since Grace had completed both the written and oral parts of her second section exam, she settled down to study for the third section. In Chengkiang her teacher had been an inexperienced girl of nineteen, but here she was pleased to have the same teacher as Mr. Harrison, who, although he had completed all six sections and spoke fluent Chinese, continued to study with a language teacher.

But what else would she do? Mr. Fraser had said she should stay in Kunming for "several months," but she had no clue what the future held after that. "Pray with me His will be done," she asked her "dear Floras."

Little did she know the wonderful assignment for which her heavenly Father was positioning her.

Chapter 13

Eyewitness

At the Kunming Mission home, prayer was fervent for the protection and release of Arnolis Hayman and Alfred Bosshardt, the missionaries captured two months earlier by the Communists in Guizhou province, and still being held in captivity. Neither man was young. Mr. Hayman, who had come to China from New Zealand in 1913, was forty-four years old at the time he was seized. Mr. Bosshardt, a Swiss citizen born in England, was thirty-seven. When ransom demands were not met, the men were forced to continue with the Sixth Army on its grueling Long March. At one point, they braved an escape, only to be turned in by local farmers and recaptured three days later. The punishment was predictable. They were bound and sentenced to death. But a higher authority was in command, and in God's providence, the Communists' sentence was never carried out.

The CIM was assisted in its effort to secure the missionaries' release by Mr. Hermann Becker, a member of the Liebenzeller Mission, an associate mission with the CIM. (Grace had met Sister Else and others of their new workers at language school.) Because Mr. Becker had once saved the life of the nephew of *Ho Long*, the Communist general of the Sixth Army (Bosshardt 275), he was in a position to negotiate with them. On November 18, 1935, he succeeded in securing Mr. Hayman's release, and none too soon. After almost fourteen months of captivity, he was sick, emaciated, and weak. However, after a period of recuperation and rest at home, he returned to China for ten more years of active missionary service.

Mr. Bosshardt should have been released at the same time. Mr. Becker had sent the required money, and Mr. Bosshardt had seen evidence that the officials had received it. But they denied it, insisting there was enough for only one, and Mr. Bosshardt was led back to his quarters.

Meanwhile, the Communist army was advancing in Yunnan. The Mission home in Kunming had already welcomed missionaries fleeing from Guizhou, but as the situation worsened, missionaries also came from the north of Yunnan and then from outstations around Kunming. Because the city was well garrisoned they could be relatively safe—not only from invasion, but from brigands outside the city walls.

As Easter 1936 approached, the missionaries in Kunming, including Grace, gathered each evening of Easter Week at the Mission home to pray for Mr. Bosshardt, for the Chinese Christians left in the evacuated stations, and for their own protection and spiritual well-being.

> On Wednesday evening hearts seemed peculiarly drawn out in fervent supplication on behalf of Mr. Bosshardt. As Mr. Hatton was pleading for him, suddenly his prayer changed from supplication to praise for answered prayer for Mr. Bosshardt. One evening Mrs. Porteous prayed that we might have the joy of seeing him walk right into our compound.
>
> On Friday there was a day of prayer, at the close of which we partook of the Lord's Supper, it being Good Friday. Our hearts were stirred because we were conscious that our Lord was meeting with us.

By the close of Good Friday, the Communists were rumored to be approaching the city. Grace returned to the Harrisons' home, along with the others living with them, while men from the Mission home went to find out what they could. When no word came, "we went peacefully to sleep," but not for long. "[We] were roused from a sound sleep by a terrific pounding at the front gate." Cautiously the women answered the door, fearing it might be a Communist soldier, but it was Mr. Hatton from the Mission home. Word was that the army was just five miles away, and he urged them to get to the train station immediately, where a train was waiting to take people south if necessary.

Ironically, the city had been left unprotected. The soldiers who were usually on guard had been deployed to outlying cities and villages, where pilots flying overhead had spotted Communist activity. Since no activity had been detected around Kunming, it was assumed the city would be safe.

> We hurriedly dressed, taking with us scarcely more than a toothbrush and Bible. Mrs. Harrison had been ill with the flu and had been up [from bed] just one day. Bathrobes and blankets were wrapped around Marjorie, age four, and Carl, age two, and we began the half hour's tramp to the station.
>
> The streets were pretty well cleared but a few rickshaws were available for some of the mothers. Soldiers at intervals would stop us and inquire as to who we were and where we were going. As we reached the station excitement filled the air and more people trooped in—Germans, French and the English speaking nationalities, business men as well as missionaries. A special train was waiting and we were invited to sit in the cars for a rest as they waited for more news.
>
> Meanwhile we were praying for and greatly concerned about two [Chinese] mothers in the hospital, one with a one-day-old baby and the other with a two-day-old baby. The hospital is outside the city wall. After some time, here came the mothers on stretchers, carried by the missionaries, as other help was not available. We kept waiting, with an occasional word of encouragement from the American consul. A general was making a complete round of the city to see that everything was all right.

In spite of the tension and the late hour, Grace was able to take note of the whimsical scene in the waiting room:

> …a nicely dressed young lady asleep on top of one of the tables. On the floor under a table, with a basket for a pillow, lay a gentleman of large stature soundly sleeping. The chairs were all occupied by nodding forms. In one big easy chair lay the English consul fast sleep. Just outside sat two Chinese on some boxes. They sat with their backs together, heads touching. Each was a back rest for the other and both were asleep.

In the end, they were spared. The alarm had been caused by a group of soldiers coming dangerously near the city as they cut across the country. Then, for some inexplicable reason, they turned away. At the same time, government troops were being called back to the city, and enough had arrived through the night that by five-thirty in the morning the consuls gave permission for people to return home.

It wasn't until they were on their way that they could laugh at the sight they presented, and no doubt it was with an amused smile on her face that Grace recorded the comical details. One lady had forgotten her glasses but remembered to put on a string of pearls. Another wondered if her husband had remembered his teeth. Others had tumbled out of bed into whatever clothing was closest at hand. A little girl trudged along with her dress over her nightie.

Yet, though they arrived safely at home, there was no assurance that the danger was over. Saturday passed without incident, and Easter Sunday was normal, but "Monday morning as we were eating breakfast a Chinese boy came in to tell Mr. Harrison that there were two Chinese gentlemen to see him," and that changed everything.

The men had come from Mr. Becker to say they now had money to negotiate the release of Mr. Bosshardt. Mr. Harrison promptly escorted them to the appropriate authority, only to learn that Mr. Bosshardt was already free and would be in the city that afternoon.

"Oh, the joy of it, the faithfulness of our God," Grace exulted. "Before the word came, some of us were studying and some were busy at other things. But immediately a holiday was declared and we said 'goodbye' to books for that day."

Since the Mission home was already full, it was decided that Mr. Bosshardt would stay at the Harrisons' home around the corner, and how eagerly Grace and the others made the preparations!

Mildred Wright was using the guest room, but she gladly moved to a camp cot in the attic. The guest room opened on to a veranda, which the women furnished with a day bed and a screen. Doris Trefren and Irene Barberini walked half a mile to purchase a bouquet of sweet peas for the room, while Grace placed her mother's Bible on the nightstand and a plate of chocolate candy on the dresser.

But what would he want for supper? Mrs. Harrison was at a loss to know. Would he be able to eat? Was he suffering from malnutrition?

Sensing the momentous nature of what would be happening that day, a small group of the household gathered for prayer. "Nothing was too small or insignificant to bring before Him," Grace observed, including Mrs. Harrison's quandary about supper. "Upon arising from her knees she knew it was to be chicken broth. So a chicken was bought and stewed to a tasty broth."

At three-thirty that afternoon, the men left to meet Mr. Bosshardt. They had planned to wait for him at the city gate, but in their anticipation they walked on until they met him—nearly five more miles. It was hard to believe it was he. He had walked 2,500 miles, a captive of the Sixth Army on their Long March for 560 days, about a year and a half. He was dressed in Chinese clothes, the same clothes he had been wearing for the last four months, it turned out, and his beard had grown long. But he still had a sweet tooth. He ate the chocolate bar they had brought so hungrily that they were concerned. Then, after one more bite he refrained, saying simply, "It's good."

Eagerly they heard his story. He had not escaped. He had been released, and it had nothing to do with Mr. Becker. What saved him was his citizenship: he had been born in England of Swiss immigrants but had retained his Swiss nationality. His captors explained that since they were now distinguishing among nationalities, and Switzerland was not imperialistic, they would let him go. They gave him Communist tracts, some money to engage a huakan, and instructions that he was not to leave until morning. He slipped the tracts into a book he was carrying, and his captors moved on during the night. It was Easter eve.

In wonder his mind went back sixteen months to Christmas eve in 1934. He and Mr. Hayman sat bound in a small room awaiting their sentence, with guards posted to make sure they did not communicate. When morning came and he realized it was Christmas Day, "our Lord sent a message to me in one word which made a world of difference—'Emmanuel—God with us.'" Since he was forbidden to speak this comforting Name aloud, he took some bits of straw and carefully spelled it out in English on their rough floor, and Mr. Hayman understood. "Knowing we should be imprisoned no longer than He would allow, we rejoiced in tribulation" (Bosshardt 51).

Now, as morning came, it was Easter Sunday, 1936, and he was a free man. Though his bonds were nothing compared to the bonds of death which had bound his Savior, they had been loosed. In his joy, he would gladly have walked to the nearest town, but found that his legs were "almost useless." He ended up accepting a ride on the back of a friendly tribesman as far as a farmhouse, and there he waited until a mountain chair and coolies could be found to take him the rest of the way (Bosshardt 211, 249, 259).

The town had recently been pillaged by the Communists, so when the Nationalist soldiers searched him and found Communist tracts tucked in his book, they were immediately suspicious. They took him first to one official and then another to be inspected and interrogated. Finally, when they were convinced he was innocent, they gave him a good meal. He hired a huakan, and a contingent of Nationalist soldiers accompanied him until he met the party coming to welcome him, five miles from the Kunming city gate. Earlier he had imagined himself arriving in Kunming, walking the short distance into the CIM compound, and surprising everybody. But given his condition, it was well that his friends had surprised him.

It was after dark when the missionaries back in Kunming received word that the welcoming party was returning. They were bringing Mr. Bosshardt by rickshaw, and they would be going straight to the Harrisons' home, not first to the Mission home, as those waiting had expected, and they would need a flashlight to light the alley.

When they finally arrived, Grace was touched by Mr. Bosshardt's humility and gracious demeanor.

>Weak though he was, he greeted us with a smile and shook hands....

>As he entered the house he was invited to enter the sitting room, but protested he was too dirty. A chair was placed in the hall for him and he reluctantly sat down, only to quickly rise when [someone else] offered to shake hands with him. The group spontaneously sang the doxology and he stood to sing with them. The joy was too great and tears flowed down the cheeks of several. A short prayer of praise was offered and then he proceeded upstairs to the bathroom where a hot bath awaited him.

>He had not washed his face for 24 days. Even with description you could not imagine the filth he was enduring. ... He told those who assisted him that in one day he killed 500 body lice and the next day over 500. His garments were wrapped in an oil sheet, saturated with kerosene and burned. Fortunately he had managed to escape head lice.

>...As he came from the bathroom he looked like a different person. Mr. Harrison had given him a shave and haircut. More friends who had not yet met him were waiting in the upper hall. Again there was the gracious smile and the reluctant acceptance of a seat.

>Little Jackie Graham, age four, went over to shake hands with him and Mr. Bosshardt asked him for a kiss, wherewith Jackie threw his arms around his neck and kissed him.

>The group could not refrain from singing again, this time "How good is the God we adore," and again Mr. Bosshardt stood and sang with the rest. "We'll praise Him for all that is past and trust Him for all that's to come." Another short prayer of praise was offered

in which he was committed unto the Lord. After thanking the group and expressing the fact that he was overwhelmed, he was taken to his bedroom. …

Can you imagine how a nice clean bed with white sheets would look to him after a year and a half of filth? He could only shake his head.

The first thing he noticed and expressed his appreciation of was the Bible. With a soul especially appreciative of beauty, the second thing he noticed was the bouquet of sweet peas and then the bananas of which he is particularly fond.

Had our Lord guided in all these small details? There is no question in the minds of those of us who prayed. Was the chicken broth appreciated? If you could have seen the bowl being refilled you would again have seen an answer to prayer.

Mr. Harrison asked him if he would like for him to read a passage of Scripture before retiring and he asked for the 124th Psalm, [which concludes]:

We have escaped like a bird out of the fowler's snare;
   the snare has been broken, and we have escaped.
      Our help is in the name of the Lord,
         the Maker of heaven and earth.

Mr. Bosshardt slept well, but when the doctor came to examine him in the morning, he learned how ill he was: in an advanced stage of beri-beri, suffering from pleurisy, bronchitis, a weak heart, and sprue (a disease of the small intestine). The British consul transported him to the hospital in his automobile, but after examining him, the doctor's prescription was for complete rest, quiet, and good nutrition, all of which could be supplied in his room at the Harrisons'.

Grace summed up the whole experience in a psalm of her own:

The children of the Lord cried unto Him night and day for a year and a half.

They cried unto Him seven nights in succession. On the fifth day they cried unto Him from morning until evening.

The Reds turned away from the city and went in the opposite direction and the prisoner was set free. Blessed be the name of the Lord.

Chapter 14

Sidelined in Kunming

As the excitement of that memorable Easter week-end in 1936 began to fade, Grace wondered again where she might next be designated. Would she be suitable? Compatible? Peace came only as she stayed her mind on God. "There is rest in knowing that He does know," she wrote later that month to her praying friends at home. She was eager to get back to work, even if it meant teaching at Chefoo, the CIM boarding school, which now seemed a real possibility. "Praise Him for making me willing," she wrote, "but I think I should always have the hope of coming back [to Yunnan]."

By July the question had been tabled, for a surprising reason: she was asked to stay in Kunming and work with Mr. Bosshardt on the story of his captivity and release. He was not strong enough to write, but he could describe his experiences, and as he recalled his eighteen months of captivity, Grace took his story down in long hand.

It wasn't what she had had in mind, but it was what she needed: working over a period of four months with congenial company. When Mr. Bosshardt's wife, Rose, came from Shanghai to join him, Grace found her equally personable. Their lives became "a real benediction."

The task was considerable, both for Mr. Bosshardt in his weakened condition, and for his assistant with her pen and paper, but they worked together harmoniously. "I am sure you were the Lord's gift," Mr. Bosshardt would later tell her. As for Grace, "This task was taken as from our Lord, and has been a great blessing." She estimated there were "around 60,000 words" in his narrative, and they wrote it again before committing the manuscript to be typed.

When Grace discovered that Mr. Bosshardt had a sense of humor, she ventured to offer him the loan of her prized possession, the joke book from her cousin Jean.

> ... I took it into his room one day, & while I was talking to him Mrs. Bosshardt picked up the book to look at it. She would smile occasionally & peek over the top of the book as tho she wanted to share [it], but as he was busy talking she kept silent.
>
> Just as I was leaving I said to him, "Mr. Bosshardt, I don't know whether you'd enjoy this or not." He took it saying, "Well my wife seemed to be enjoying it." ...
>
> In the daytime he rests on a little day bed on the veranda. After we came up from dinner yesterday we peeked out the window & there he lay soundly sleeping, and with the joke-book by his side.

The original plan was for Mr. Bosshardt's story to be one of three included in a single book. Mr. Hayman would submit his story, as would Mr. Becker, who had negotiated Mr. Hayman's release. But in the end this proved impractical. Only Mr. Bosshardt's story appeared, with an abbreviated form of Mr. Becker's account. It was published in November 1936 by Hodder & Stoughton, with Grace's title: *The Restraining Hand*. When she received her copy, Grace found that Mr. Bosshardt had inscribed it, "To the real author of this book."

Grace with Mr. and Mrs. Bosshardt (left) and Mr. and Mrs. Harrison
August 1936 in Kunming

During the time Grace worked with Mr. Bosshardt, her circle of acquaintances in Yunnan grew. She met other missionaries as they passed through the Kunming Mission home, including one family which would figure large in her life in days to come: John and Isobel Kuhn, with their little girl Kathryn. John and Isobel, both graduates of Moody, had come to China a few years ahead of Grace.

> My! I enjoyed the Kuhns so much. He is Mrs. Harrison's brother, but is much more subdued—very calm, quiet & gentle. She is very attractive in personality and both full of fun. Their lives were a real blessing to me—a savor of Christ.

She met another kindred spirit in the person of Mrs. Carson (Vercia) Cox, a Quaker missionary from the USA who would become a dear friend (but no relation to Grace's future husband). As Grace's work with

Mr. Bosshardt came to a close, "Auntie Vercia" asked Grace to keep her company for a few days.

> She is a lovely woman and I enjoy staying with her. She is over fifty years of age. … The last evening she played her guitar & we sang hymns, read a portion of Scripture & had a season of prayer together. She paints beautifully…and she is so full of fun, but at the same time deeply devoted to our Lord.

By the end of August, nearly four months after his release, Mr. Bosshardt was well enough to travel, and the doctors gave their permission. He and his wife made the long journey to Switzerland, where he continued to recuperate before returning to China four years later.

> We went with them to the train yesterday morning and not only the missionary community, but the Amer. & British consuls and others were there, too. … Margie [Marjorie Harrison—4 yrs old] rode home with me in a rickshaw & said, "When I get home I want to cry." But I didn't have to wait that long. The kiddies both learned to love Uncle & Auntie Bosshardt as they called them, & the love was mutual.

With her temporary assignment now completed, Grace was once again looking into an unknown future. She liked Kunming, and she especially liked the Harrisons. In fact, she thought she would like to stay.

> My stay here with Mr. and Mrs. Harrison has been very happy, and their lives, too, have been a real blessing. They have been like a brother and sister to me, and the little children, too, have grown into my heart….
> I should love to have this home [with Harrisons] as my headquarters, and go out from here with a Bible-woman for two or three months to some out-station,

then in again long enough to get my breath and then go to some other out-station. But it must all rest with our Lord, and we want to do according to His will and desire for us.

While she waited, she continued studying for the third section language exam, spoke at various meetings, sometimes in Chinese, and went with Mrs. Harrison to visit in the villages. She helped Miss Minnie Kent with a five-day Bible School in Chengkung, the station to which Helen (Clare) Lassen had been transferred. However, during the time Grace was helping Mr. Bosshardt, Helen had been transferred again, this time to Chefoo, where she wrote glowingly to Grace of her new situation, hoping that Grace would soon follow. "So confident is she that I will be coming later that she even told me what dress & shoe shops to patronize in Hong Kong & Shanghai. I do hope she is mistaken," Grace admitted.

When she returned to Kunming, a letter from Mr. Fraser indicated that he felt the same way. "I cannot help hoping, if it be the Lord's will, that we may not yet have to lose you for Chefoo," he wrote. And, sensing she felt awkward about having had to leave her first station, he reassured her, "I also have perfect satisfaction in your having been transferred from Chengkiang to the capital—I have never felt a moment's misgiving about it."

Chengkiang had been her baptism by fire, but it had not devoured her. She had earned the respect of her superintendent, and she had proved in new ways the faithful care of her heavenly Father. She was also wiser. When she came across a clipping by Samuel Chadwick, a Wesleyan Methodist preacher in England, in which he described the fruit of the Spirit in "newspaper English," she saved it. It was Galatians 5:22-23, where he rendered the grace of longsuffering as *a forbearing patience in provoking circumstances and with trying people.*

Chapter 15

Introduction to Tribes Land

Grace remained in Kunming two more months: taking care of necessary dentistry, pressing on with her language study, and helping with the wedding of her friend, Irene Barberini, to fellow-missionary, Albert Allen. She also received an invitation to visit tribes land. Mrs. Browning, a young missionary wife and mother, asked Grace to keep her company in Salowu, the CIM center for work among the tribes northeast of Kunming, while her husband itinerated in the area. Depending on the condition of roads and trails, it was a six-day journey from Kunming, and she would be there for about six weeks.

There were pros and cons. She wanted to prepare for her third language exam, and Mrs. Browning had told her that Salowu would be "a nice quiet place to study for final review and for writing." On the other hand, friends in Kunming warned her that "there will be little studying done with three babies under 18 mo. in the home." (Little Consie was seventeen months old, and the twins, Bill and May, were two months old.) But Grace reasoned that the children would make it "a challenge to study all the more." She would miss seeing Jimmy Harrison when he came home from Chefoo School for Christmas, "but if it means Mr. Browning will be able to go out & visit the stations I will be willing to sacrifice that pleasure." Besides,

... It will be a wonderful opportunity to see the tribal work, which is quite different from the Chinese. It is so much easier to pray for these places, too, when one has been there and actually seen them.

She packed her belongings into three forty-pound baskets and a bedding roll, all of which coolies would manage with carrying poles. On October 22, 1936, she set off with the new Mr. and Mrs. Allen for their station, Wuting, which was half way to Salowu. It was her first visit to northern Yunnan and she reveled in the beauty.

Crossing rivers and streams on stones or planks, climbing staircase precipices, which take one up, up, up until it is a venture even to look down, drinking in the beauty of the surrounding hills, [make] the journey... anything but a monotonous one. ...

It was Saturday morning when they arrived at Wuting. Since Grace would not be going on to Salowu until Monday, she and Barbara visited Sapushan, a neighboring Miao tribes station, on Sunday, arriving unexpectedly and during the church service. It was impressive.

What a sight to behold that big one room chapel with dirt floor, & with saw horses for seats, seating between 400 & 500 people. And can they sing!!! It was good to hear them. It is generally recognized that the tribes excel the Chinese in their appreciation of music, but this particular tribe is outstanding in that respect.

As the message was in Miao, [Barbara] & I understood only what few words were the same as Chinese. It was communion Sunday & ... around 150 partook of the Lord's supper—tea serving as wine, and a coarse corn bread for bread.

As planned, on Monday Grace set out for the rest of the journey to Salowu, a distance of another sixty miles. Albert Allen was to escort her for thirty miles to a station where Mr. Browning would be waiting to take her the remaining thirty miles. But a rendezvous in tribes land was not always successful. Good connections depended on good runners. A runner might start out with a message, only to be sidetracked, or waylaid, resulting in the message arriving late, or not at all. So they were not unduly surprised to reach the inn at the halfway station and find no sign of Mr. Browning. Perhaps he himself had been delayed.

> [Albert and I] had our supper, prepared by the boy who cared for our horses as usual, then put up our beds.
> Because the inn was so crowded, we strung up an oil sheet for a partition & Albert slept on one side & I on the other. ... I heard a bang as a bottle of canned milk hit the floor, & then Albert called & said it was rats after our lunch. But I let him crawl out and rescue it. I thought...it was time to get up, but it was only 10:30, so gladly I went to sleep again.

By five o'clock the next morning, Mr. Browning still had not come. How long should they wait? Albert had the thirty-mile return trip to make, which was at least a two-day journey on foot and horseback, and Grace was reluctant to have him wait on her account. She would be safe enough in the company of the coolies, she assured him. The horse boy was a young Christian whom she trusted, and eventually Albert consented. "[W]e both expected Mr. Browning any minute, so we had a word of prayer & parted."

Within five minutes, Grace and the horse boy did indeed meet Mr. Browning coming towards them on the trail. Not surprisingly, they learned that the message had not reached him in time. A rumor of robbers on the trail had detained the runners. After mutual greetings, they turned their horses toward Salowu and reached the Brownings' little home just at dusk, where "<u>such</u> a lovely supper awaited us." It was a harbinger of six pleasant weeks to follow.

The Brownings worked among the Nosu tribe, on a station that had been established in 1920. Grace did not know a word of the language, but she delighted to be in their worship service. There was a "family feeling," which she had not noticed among the Chinese. They smiled broadly and gave generously of their produce to help support their own Nosu pastor. Unlike the Chinese, who could be indifferent to the gospel, "our Lord seems to have peculiarly blessed [this] tribe in turning them unto Himself by the literal hundreds."

But there were other stations to be built up, and Grace had come to keep Mrs. Browning company while her husband set out to visit them. Despite the warning that she would get little studying done, she was ready for the third section exam by the time she returned to Kunming. Furthermore, she had made a friend of little Consie, though she had been "scared to death of me" at first. A bit of chocolate bar had helped.

> Consie is quite friendly now. Today…[s]he wouldn't quiet down for even her mother. So I went to her & held out my hands & said, "Consie, want chockie?" Smiling through her tears she reached out her hands to me & away we went.

Back in Kunming, Grace took the exam the week before Christmas. Later she received a letter from Mr. McPherson, assistant China director in Shanghai, congratulating her on passing it "with such an excellent grade." He also noted something else. "I see that you have fallen in love with the Tribes' people."

Actually, she was eligible to go to the tribes, now that she had completed her third section of Chinese. Furthermore, she had been advised by both Mr. Harrison and Mr. Fraser that she was "peculiarly" qualified for tribal work.

But what of her Chinese? She had struggled with this question some months earlier, though she had told no one about it. If she started learning a tribal language, she feared she would forfeit the good foundation she had gained in Chinese. On the other hand, if she were to go to Chefoo, she would lose much of her Chinese anyway.

As it turned out, her next assignment was not to the tribes, and not to Chefoo. It was to work alone in Chinning, a Chinese city situated about half way between Kunming and her first station, Chengkiang. It was Mission policy to send single women to work in pairs, or to assist a married couple, not to work alone. But Chinning was to be a temporary assignment, and Kunming was just a two-hour bus trip away, so the decision was made that she would go.

> At the beginning of the New Year [1937] I expect to go alone to an outstation, Chinning. As not even a Bible-woman will be there to help it will mean drawing on Him for my every help. I am looking forward to this service with joyful anticipation, the least of the joys not being closer and sweeter fellowship with our loving Lord.

Chapter 16

Shallow Stakes

As the only white person in the city of Chinning, Grace was a novelty. Town ruffians stood below her window and called out in a dialect she understood all too well, "Ole foreign billy goat." Missionaries who preceded her had left a handful of believers, but only one seemed glad that she had come. "Am sad to say that apart from one dear old soul, Mrs. Cheng (Chun), hypocrisy and coldness seem to characterize the believers," she wrote to her praying friends at home.

Grace at Chinning
On the left is a woman with bound feet who walked
thirty miles to attend Bible School.
On the right is "our faithful old Christian, Mrs. Cheng."

Her living quarters were two rooms above the chapel in a building rented by the Mission. Unpainted and sparsely furnished, they were adorned only by the dust and dirt descending freely through cracks in the tile roof. When Grace undertook to scrub the floors, the landlord cautioned her against it, lest the water rot the boards. And there were rats. Nevertheless she made it her home and settled in to a routine of Bible classes, reading classes, home visitation, and studying for the fourth section of her language exam. Still, a companion would have been nice.

> Heard a noise at one of the bedroom windows the other night, as though someone had a hold of it & gave it a violent shaking twice. A little later I heard the roof tiles rattle. I flashed my light toward the window, cleared my throat & went back to sleep—after praying that I be not allowed to lie foolishly awake in fear & dread.

By the time she left six months later, the ruffians had changed their tune. Using her Chinese name, they stood under her window and called out, "*Li chiao-si*[4] is a good person." On one particular Sunday she counted thirty-four children and young people in the chapel.

Her six months in Chinning were punctuated with evangelistic efforts elsewhere, including a ten-day Bible school in Chengkung, where she again helped Miss Minnie Kent. Perhaps it was at this time that Minnie witnessed Grace's exceptional ear for language, as she recalled it many years later. Exasperated with her horse because nothing she said or did would induce him to budge, Grace resorted to the command she had heard the horse drivers use. Though she had no idea what it meant, she repeated it perfectly, and it worked. However, unknown to her, J. O. Fraser was within earshot and he also heard it. Taking her aside, he gently advised her not to do it again: it was a string of colorful curse words, unseemly for use by a missionary!

Her time in Chinning was also interrupted by a stint as local secretary at the CIM office in Kunming. Mr. Hatton was recovering from typhus and had been advised to take a month off from his administrative duties.

---

[4] *Li* = Grace; *chiao-si* = teacher, or religious teacher

Since Grace was already at Kunming for the periodic field conference, she seemed a timely replacement, except that she had no experience.

> ...I went over and helped Mr. Hatton get out the monthly reports for our province, work out the trial balance, etc., then he left me to begin the new month. It was a <u>real</u> nervous strain at first, with orders to fill, books to keep, etc., and attending conference at the same time. ...
>
> The big trick is to get the cash to come out right each night. One night I was out $3.50 & Mr. Harrison came along & gave it to me out of his own pocket & told me to go home & forget about it. The next morning I found the mistake. Another evening I was out 50¢ & Albert Allen came along & gave it to me, but he, too, got it back the next morning. They have had a lot of fun about "making up the cash," & taking their turn at it. Tonight it came out just right the first time I added it up. There was over $11,000 to account for. It was a <u>big</u> relief....

One of the decisions to come out of the field conference was that Grace would leave Chinning and join Minnie Kent in Chengkung. Minnie was alone since Helen Lassen had gone to Chefoo, so the plan was for Grace and Winnie to live together and make a two-point parish of Chengkung and Chinning, fourteen miles apart.

Grace could see the wisdom of this decision, but she had reservations. She was making good progress on her fourth section of language study, thanks to the teacher whom Mrs. Cheng had secured for her, and there was Mrs. Cheng herself. Grace hated the thought of breaking the news to her. "She won't be able to understand why Chengkung can have two missionaries and Chinning can't have any."

And she was right. Mrs. Cheng could not understand. "[She] is begging & prays every day that our Lord will keep me here.... She brings me things now, too, to try to work on my feelings...." When a lack of good drinking water made Grace slightly ill, Mrs. Cheng saw it as "of the Lord to keep me here so I couldn't go away." But Mrs. Cheng was the only one. "Really believe the others don't care a whole lot."

So Grace prepared to move again. "How true it is that we cannot drive our stakes very deep," she reflected. "We just must be ready at beck and call to go when and where it is desired we should." At least in Chengkung she would no longer be alone, and instead of just one committed Christian, there was a thriving group of more than fifty believers, with a resident Chinese pastor and his family.

Then Minnie Kent changed her mind, and for a time Grace wondered if she would make the move after all. Minnie had asked permission to move to another province. "If Shanghai sanctions the move, then I <u>may</u> be allowed to stay in Chinning," Grace told her family. After all, if she was going to be alone, she might as well be alone in Chinning. In the end, Shanghai did sanction Minnie's move, but Grace was still asked to go to Chengkung.

Grace and Minnie were together for just one week before Minnie left (June 1937), but plans were underway for a new worker to join Grace. She was Miss Dorothy Burrows, a nurse, newly arrived from England. Kathryn Harrison had met her in Kunming, and knowing of Grace's unhappy experience in Chengkiang, she wrote to reassure her. "You two will just hit it off fine. She is like you in some ways. ... She's made of good missionary stuff—nothing soft about her. ... She is spiritually minded too."

But nurses were in great demand in Yunnan in the 1930s; doctors and hospitals were few and far between. Consequently, when Mrs. Harrison escorted Dorothy to Chengkung to meet Grace, it could not be to stay. Mrs. Arthur Allen in the south was afflicted with a urinary tract infection, and in the north Irene (Barberini) Allen was having difficulty with her first pregnancy. Dorothy was their only medical help. Given the long distances and protracted means of travel, no one knew when she might return.

Meanwhile, Grace enjoyed settling in to more congenial living quarters—"the house here is <u>so</u> much nicer than the one at Chinning"— and she found "a young Mrs. Cheng" in Li ta-ma, who helped her manage the two-point parish.

[We] went out to a village yesterday, hung our song sheets & posters up on a couple of nails poked in a mud wall, & sang & spoke to the gathered crowd. The Lord certainly gave grace & courage, & they seemed to understand. We each spoke about 15 min. … I picked out one old lady in the crowd & talked directly to her. Understand she is a kind of witch.

Tomorrow night will be prayer meeting at Chinning, then there will be three & maybe four services on Sunday there. Li ta-ma said she will give her testimony in the evening, so that will relieve me somewhat.

As June passed, Grace began looking for "interesting news" from her sister Flora. It came almost six weeks after the event, but was nonetheless satisfying: little Merrill had a baby sister, Loretha Grace, born healthy and well on June 10, 1937. "Am quite happy & proud to have two dear little namesakes," Grace responded. (The first was Donna Grace, her sister Merlie's second daughter, born on December 8, 1936, and on June 28, 1937, came a third: Grace Alice Umhofer, the daughter of friends from Moody.)

By mid-August Grace was still alone in Chengkung, enjoying her work but looking forward to having Mrs. Harrison and a Bible-woman come from Kunming to help with a five-day Bible school. When she heard that their bus had arrived, she ran to meet them, but immediately saw that something was wrong. Where was Kathryn's broad smile? Suddenly Grace knew news had come from Chefoo School.

We had no sooner entered the house than [Kathryn] put her arm around me & I could feel her hand trembling. She then opened her purse & gave me a letter. "Do I have to go?" I said.

The need at Chefoo was critical. With just two weeks before the new term was to start in late August, one of the teachers, Miss Philips, had been thrown from a rickshaw and was in the hospital with a concussion.

But why turn to Grace Liddell? Yunnan in the southwest was about as far as it could be from Chefoo in the northeast. Grace knew of teachers closer to the school whom the Mission directors might have chosen. And why now? Now that she was settled and gaining some traction in the work that she loved? It made no sense.

> My heart has been like lead, & the services like funerals. This work I dearly love. The school-room is like a cage to me, give me the wide open spaces—the wider the better. I love the country & the country people, & feel a definite misfit amongst the [formal, regulated staff at Chefoo.]

Then came a ray of hope. Thanks to the Japanese attack on Shanghai on August 13, 1937, it would not be safe for her to travel. Since telegraph wires had been cut, making it impossible for messages to get through from headquarters, Mr. Fraser made the unilateral decision that she should stay in Yunnan for the time being. Grace could see where it might even be permanent.

> Chefoo is quite safe [from fighting]. So if school opens at the end of this month & they carry on, & the Lord continues to block my way here, then they cannot but hunt for somebody else.

However, during the last week of August the situation cleared and a second telegram came, reaching her on a visit to Chinning. DIRECT TO CHEFOO. She gathered up her things, but the journey back to Chengkung only mirrored her dismay.

> I left...with a coolie about 3 o'clock in the afternoon. The horse was so tiny and had such a big sore on its back that I rode only about an hour and walked the rest of the way. We arrived home about ten minutes of eight in the dark, wading through mud, slipping and sliding in great fashion.

As we stumbled along a suggestion of Dr. Samuel Zwemer's [came to mind], "When you feel lonely look up at the stars." Glancing up I saw only one and stumbled on.

Just a few yards from our own door I tumbled over a steep five-foot bank into a stream of dirty water. After trying to climb up and sliding back a time or two, managed to get up as dirty as a pig. Li ta-ma was in bed, but got up and fried some eggs and heated bath water.

She had one day to pack, find a horse and coolie, and make the thirty-mile journey to Kunming.

Chapter 17

A Little Sad at Chefoo

Chefoo School was located in a seaside port north of Shanghai, now called Yentai (Chefoo). Hudson Taylor had discovered the port's restorative climate in 1879, having become extremely ill with dysentery. The fresh sea air and wholesome food were exactly what he needed, and during his seven-month recuperation, he began to envision a rest center for missionaries worn out and oppressed by the relentless heat of the interior. In time his vision grew to include a school for missionaries' children. If such a school had been available, he and his wife, Maria, would not have had to send their children back to England. Even homeschooling could not protect them from the heat, poor diet, and the stress of constantly moving from one location to another. In 1870, five-year old Samuel had died of an ulcerated stomach just weeks before he was to join others on a ship to England.

Consequently, Chefoo School was established in 1881 and grew to accommodate all thirteen grades in the British system. The school admitted not only CIM children, but also children of other missions, and children of diplomats and businessmen. Among the more notable students were Henry Luce, who went on to become editor of *Time* Magazine, and Thornton Wilder, American playwright and novelist.

By the time Grace joined the faculty in 1937, Chefoo included a Girls School, a Boys School, a Preparatory School for the primary grades (ages five through ten), some co-educational classes, a hospital, sanitarium, and business department. Since the majority of CIM missionaries were from Britain, Chefoo was run on the British system, but American influence was gradually being introduced. When she arrived, Grace was one of four Americans on the staff, two of whom were friends from former days—Pearl Galloway and Helen (Clare) Lassen.

Trusting, if not comprehending, Grace began the long journey to Chefoo. First came the train trip south from Kunming to Haiphong, but since part of the track was under water, "we had to pile out & step into canoes & be pushed [by coolies] across to where a second train was waiting to take us on." At Haiphong she boarded the coastal steamer *Taiyuan*, bound for Hong Kong. Normally, it would bypass Hong Kong and go up the coast to Shanghai, where Grace would transfer to a steamer going to Chefoo. But Shanghai was under Japanese control. The only option was to transfer ships at Hong Kong, making the voyage to Chefoo almost two weeks long.

Once aboard, Grace's hopes for a reprieve revived as she heard the captain announce that when they reached Hong Kong, ships might not be leaving for Chefoo.

> So I may get to go back "home" to Yunnan yet. It's rather like walking on thin ice, never knowing whether a step should be taken until after I've stepped. The whole thing is a mystery to me. ... But peace comes from knowing His hand is in it all. The way is dark, but He is leading....

However, when they reached Hong Kong she discovered that ships *were* leaving. The SS *Hupeh* would be sailing for Chefoo in three days. She also learned that she was to have a companion: little six-year old Kathryn Kuhn, daughter of John and Isobel Kuhn, whom she had met in Kunming just a year earlier. Kathryn would be enrolling at Chefoo and Grace would be her escort, but how Grace received this information was an adventure in itself.

A passenger on board the *Taiyuan* relayed to her the fragment of a message he had happened to hear over the radio in Haiphong: Grace was to report somewhere when she disembarked. She guessed, correctly, that it was the Phillips House, where CIM missionaries lodged when in Hong Kong. At the Phillips House, the hostess had a message for her to go to still another place, where she found two ladies from CIM headquarters in Shanghai, stranded following their vacation because of the fighting in the city. They had received a telegram from General Director Gibb asking them to intercept Grace and instruct her to wait in Hong Kong for the Kuhns, who were returning from furlough. She was then to escort little Kathryn to Chefoo. But would they arrive before the SS *Hupeh* was to sail?

The answer came within a matter of hours when a Japanese steamer pulled into port with the Kuhns on board, entirely unaware of the plans for Kathryn. With the Japanese still fighting in Shanghai, they had assumed it would be impossible for Kathryn to go to Chefoo until after the Christmas break, and were planning confidently to take her with them all the way to Yunnan. But a telegram was awaiting them in Hong Kong: SEND KATHRYN TO CHEFOO WITH GRACE LIDDELL. It was devastating news. "I was totally unprepared to give up my girlie so soon," Isobel confessed (Kuhn 65-66).

They had three days together, but inexorably the day of departure came. Grace wrote:

> The parting was extremely hard. [John & Isobel] went out to the big boat with us in the launch, [but after they returned to the wharf] it was up to me to comfort the poor little kid with tears running down my own cheeks. I sat her on the railing of the boat & gave her my hankie & she waved & sobbed, stopping between sobs long enough to have her picture taken with a smile.
>
> When we could no longer see them she asked to go to the cabin where the promised chocolates were. She soon composed herself & there was only an occasional tell-tale sob. She crawled up on a bench & peered out through the port-hole singing to herself, "No, never alo-o-ne...." She sometimes weeps a bit at nighttime, but is all right if I lie down beside her.

There is a Christian mother, Mrs. Longdon, on board taking her little boy, Ramsey, to Chefoo, too. Besides there are two little girls on board so she has had delightful days on board ship & has been very brave.

They were at Tsingtao, within one day of Chefoo, when the ship's crew decided to go on strike. Rumors of cholera at the next port had alarmed them, and they refused to go on.

They took their bedding and everything…but later enough of the table boys & cooks came back, so we could have supper. But it is impossible to pull out without the fire stokers & the sailors.

As it turned out, they were delayed just one day, which Grace used to study for her fourth section language exam.

By the time she arrived, school had been in session three weeks. "I haven't felt the least bit anxious or fearful," she wrote. "I've known only perfect peace—just a little sad because of leaving Yunnan."

There might have been reason to fear. The night before they arrived, a Japanese battleship focused a powerful searchlight on the SS *Hupeh* as it steamed by, and when Grace arrived she saw "considerable preparedness."

Trenches are dug. Huge piles of sandbags are dotting the water front along the beach the full length of the city. Flags are painted on U.S. & British buildings. A large G. Br. Flag…is roped to the ground on the hockey field…. Jap planes fly over almost every day— just scouting. A siren blows to warn that it is a Jap.

But the daily routine of school life continued undisturbed, and Grace did her best to fit in. She was assigned to the Girls School, but also had two classes of boys.

The teachers here are kindness & love itself & do everything but spoon feed me in helping me get started.

I don't know how they could be nicer. But everything is so very, very proper & I'm so easy-going that it is like being in a straight-jacket. Today I went to church wearing a tam, carrying my coat on my arm as it was too warm walking. The girls marched in all wearing light coats, prim little hats, & wearing or carrying gloves. I just naturally don't belong here, I belong in Yunnan.

Something else concerned her. She noticed that the British staff members were skimming the milk and taking the cream for their own use. A German missionary, Miss Erna Bachmann, was likewise troubled, and later recalled how she and Miss Liddell collaborated to make sure the children were given whole milk to drink.

The three children from Yunnan had a special place in her heart.

This afternoon I went down to the Prep. School & took little Catherine Fraser, Kathryn Kuhn & Jimmie Harrison to church with me. So they sat with me instead of the other children. I never see them unless I make a special effort.

One morning Pearl G. said a little girl wanted to see her "auntie." It was Kathryn. When they told her I had come I could hear her little feet just flying from the hall. She had been having an especially lonely time....

The schedule was different from anything Grace had been used to. Instead of having a full day off on Saturday, they had Wednesday and Saturday afternoons free. As she expected, science was one of the subjects she was asked to teach; others varied from map drawing to algebra. As an American, she found her British students amusing.

Can you blame me for smiling when in their science notebooks "soda" is spelled "sodar" and "beaker" is spelled "bekah"? Then of course I write Z on the board and call it "zee" and they answer "zed;" I say "nee-ther" and they answer "ni-ther."

Grace with some of her students on a picnic by the sea at Chefoo

When she was not in the classroom, she was studying for her own language exam, and writing reassuring notes to parents back in Yunnan. Normally, their children would be coming home for a month's vacation at Christmas, but with war clouds hovering, most of the students and staff would be staying at Chefoo for Christmas 1937, and Grace assured the parents of her special care and attention.

The faculty worked hard to make it a memorable time. They arranged games, set up a flood light on the playground for roller skating after dark, gave concerts and readings, went on hikes, and prepared elaborate stunts for Christmas Day.

Grace also used the vacation to take her fourth section Chinese exam, which she passed with ease. "Now that leaves two more exams if I want to take them, & I think I do," she told her family. "But no more have to be taken unless it is for tribes work."

Before she left Yunnan, Mr. Fraser had suggested that she might return in the spring. It was the prayer of her heart, and as time went by, she watched eagerly as circumstances unfolded to permit it. Additional staff members arrived, and within a few days the anticipated word came from Mr. Gibb: he "greatly appreciate[d] all that you have done for us at this time in Chefoo…." Later a telegram came appointing her "to escort the Yunnan party home in the spring." Grace would remain in Yunnan, and one of the children's mothers would escort the children back to Chefoo after the holiday.

As she wrote the news to her praying friends at home, she reflected on the past few months. Had her presence been of any particular blessing to Chefoo? She had answered a call and filled a need, but she had won no child to Christ. But perhaps her heavenly Father was more interested in what the experience would mean for her.

> I do not know…what blessing is the fruit of my coming here, but the blessing which has been my portion is that He has added unto me love. Christ in me has taught love for the children and for my fellow-workers in a way that I have never known before. And to have met so many of our Mission here, and seen the work done here has given a knowledge and acquaintance which will make for effectual prayer. He will have in me, I believe, a more consecrated and fruitful worker than before.

Her love for the children, especially those from Yunnan, was a lasting memory for Catherine Fraser. As an elderly saint in 2007, she recalled Grace's "warmth, her friendliness, her love and care for children… I was timid and shy," she admitted, "[and she] was always especially nice to me and I can remember how much that meant to me."

Catherine's best friend was Kathryn Kuhn, the same age as she, and in the same room, and equally fond of Miss Liddell. Grace wrote home:

> Often when I go in to see Pearl Galloway, the little girls are in their room just off the hall, playing with their dolls etc. Sometimes I slip up behind Kathryn Kuhn & cover her eyes but she always guesses who it is because my hand is so big. If she sees me before I get to her she lets out a series of "Oh! Oh! Oh!" and comes running with arms outspread.

She captivated the boys in her US geography classes by reading to them James White's account of the discovery of the Carlsbad Caverns in New Mexico. "They are usually naughty and noisy. But that morning they were so quiet that I had to fight to keep from smiling."

On March 12, 1938, she boarded a coastal steamer with nineteen children in tow. Thirteen would go as far as Hong Kong, three more to Haiphong, and the remaining three—Catherine Fraser, Ruth and Stephen Metcalf—would go on with her by train to Kunming, Yunnan. (Kathryn Kuhn would come later, as soon as travel conditions would permit her parents to make the journey out of the mountains to Kunming.) The nineteen children were a handful, with three older boys who delighted to tease the younger ones and make mischief even during prayers, but she managed it without incident.

The train ride north from Haiphong "was frightfully dirty & the children especially are like little pigs." As they neared Kunming, Grace organized a clean-up. "It was quite a game to watch the transformation as each came from the washroom." They hadn't seen their parents in over six months, and excitement was running high—except for Catherine Fraser. When word came that her parents would be delayed for a day, it was hard to be excited. "Naturally [she] was very disappointed but didn't cry. She [just] said rather meekly, 'I got all cleaned up for nothing.'"

She was asleep when Frasers did arrive the next evening. Impatient to see her, they woke her up, and as Grace watched, "I had to get out & use my hankie."

Chapter 18

Farther West

Once Grace was back in Kunming, the Christians in Chengkung hoped she would return to them, and old Mrs. Cheng in Chinning hoped she would return to her. "Is *Li chiao-si* coming back [to Yunnan]?" she had asked Mr. Harrison. When he assured her she was, she replied, "Thank God the Heavenly Father. I think of her a lot, pastor." But the decision was made that Grace should go to neither place.

Winifred Embery, a second-generation CIM missionary from Australia, was stationed in Baoshan (Paoshan), about 220 miles west of Kunming, but for health reasons she had most recently been in Shanghai. Her co-worker, Kathleen Davies, was marrying and moving elsewhere, and Winnie was returning to Baoshan alone. Grace wondered if they might be asked to work together. "It would be a pleasure and a delight to work with one who loves our Lord and the Chinese people as Winnie does and who serves Him so faithfully and unsparingly," she wrote home, "[but] I do not know whether those in authority have any thought of sending me West or not... [T]he matter has been committed wholly unto Him and He will lead as pleaseth Him."

Those in authority *had* thought of it, and within a month Grace was eagerly preparing to move farther west with Winnie. Not only was she going with a compatible partner, but this move would put her in close proximity to the work among the tribes in western Yunnan. Among her possessions were now two puppies, *Nip* and *Tuck*.

Harrisons dog had nine little black & white puppies. So I'm taking a couple of them tomorrow to Paoshan with us. Have a wire basket in which to carry them. Cut up my old tweed knickers to make blankets for them. They are over a month old now & steal the mother's food sometimes, so think they will quite stand the trip.

Most of the way west was too rugged for anything but a horse, but the Chinese and Burmese were busy hacking from the mountainous terrain a crude road that would eventually stretch 717 miles from Kunming to Lashio, Burma. This they accomplished, mostly by hand, in less than two years. Known as the Burma Road, its purpose was to facilitate the transport of military troops and supplies (Montsma, "Burma Road").

The Burma Road also facilitated the travel of missionaries. Grace and the group with her were the first missionaries to use the stretch from Kunming to Dali (Tali). Besides herself and the puppies, the group consisted of Winnie Embery, Miss Lydia Chiao (a Chinese Bible teacher from Baoshan), three married couples, and one child: Catherine Fraser's little sister, Dorothy Eileen. A truck or "bus" could take them as far as Dali, but beyond that the road was incomplete.

Travel on the Burma Road was seldom smooth.
Here passengers help the driver extricate the "bus" from a mud hole.

The CIM had a Mission home at Dali, where the three couples and little Dorothy stayed for a few days while Winnie, Miss Chiao, and Grace, with her puppies, traveled the remaining eight days by horseback. In her letters, Grace refers to their road as "the horse path," or "the old horse road," apparently not realizing she was on the famous southern Silk Road, which Marco Polo had traveled in the thirteenth century (Montsma, "Southern Silk Road"). Actually, it was much more a path than a road. About six feet wide, it consisted of large stone blocks, many of which were missing due to heavy rains, while those remaining had been rounded into boulders by the passing of the centuries. Rather than winding its way around a mountain, so as to keep level and make the ascent gradual, it went straight up and then down again, as Grace discovered.

> The road was real rough & rocky, making a very difficult footing for the horses. ...[W]hen the climb is steep each step means a strain & lunge for the horse to the next stone, sometimes a foot higher than the one before it.

But the beauty was breathtaking.

> For miles & miles all around us we could see mountain peaks & more mountain peaks all gaily bedecked with cumulus clouds, tiny & great, like tufts of cotton scattered at random. ... All along the way were white lilies, orchids, eidelweiss, ferns & many other like flora. The ferns were simply gorgeous. The large fronds standing quite erect, slightly cupped at the top, & the whole plant had the shape of a mammoth tulip or lily standing several feet high.

When they came to the Lancang (Mekong) River, the approach alone was formidable. Like the Nujiang River farther west, the Lancang is a major waterway through Southeast Asia. Originating in the Tibetan Plateau, it flows south through six countries before emptying into the South China Sea below Vietnam, and like the Nujiang, it has cut deep ravines through the mountains of Yunnan. Grace described the approach. "We climbed down [on horseback] for 3 ½ hours, which was very tiring as it required almost constant bracing of one's knees." On the next day they faced the ravine itself.

> Down we went, winding back & forth around the hair-pin curves—fifteen in all. At the bottom we crossed over on an old swinging bridge & one couldn't help but wonder how long the old rickety thing had been in use & how many more minutes it would still hang.

She was apparently describing the footbridge running parallel to the old Gongguo bridge (Montsma, "Bridges"). Once across, the climb up the other side was equally challenging. An inn at the top provided a night's rest before they pushed on to the Mission home at Baoshan. It was June 7, 1938, when they arrived, complete with the two puppies.

They found the Mission home alive with activity. Lisu tribesmen had come on an errand for the Kuhns, who lived farther up the canyon. They needed sugar and flour, and hoped the Mission home had some to spare. A steady stream of Chinese Christians came through to welcome Winnie back. A telegram arrived to say that the Frasers had left Dali and would be arriving soon. And, not to be overlooked, "an independent worker from the States, Miss Hunter, had cake & bread baked for us & so we soon had a cup of tea."

When the Frasers arrived three days later, Grace was especially glad she had brought the puppies. In Kunming, five-year-old Dorothy had little Carl Harrison to play with, but in Baoshan there was no one except Nip, now himself alone since Tuck had taken sick and died. "She finds the little pup good company," Grace wrote.

In an area where workers truly were few, it seemed extravagant to have four in Baoshan, so the decision was made that Grace and Winnie would move to Yuwang, a town just a day's journey south, where there was a group of believers with no missionary. Baoshan would still have Mr. and Mrs. Fraser and Miss Chiao to tend and expand the work there.

The Mission had acquired a house in Yuwang, and sometime in July 1938 Grace and Winnie moved there to begin work in what Mr.

Fraser described as a "large and needy district." Their home consisted of two small rooms on the second floor. Downstairs were two more small rooms, one of which was a little chapel which opened on to the public road. On market days they had a ready audience for their simple presentation of the gospel truth, while on other days they visited in homes, held classes and meetings, and Grace pressed on with the fifth section of Chinese.

The dialect in Yuwang was "atrocious" because the "the first and second tones are switched around." But with her aptitude for language, and diligent study, she gained enough proficiency to take the Sunday services when Winnie was visiting a town where there were, as yet, no Christians. Three had shown some interest in the gospel, and it was possible that Winnie and Grace would both go there for a couple of months later on.

However, before Winnie could return, Grace was urgently summoned back to Baoshan.

Chapter 19

Someone to Be with Roxie

Mr. James Fraser, beloved superintendent for West Yunnan, was dying. On September 21, 1938, he had gone to bed with a headache. His wife, Roxie, six months pregnant with their third child, had no inkling it was anything more than that, but within four days he was gone, a victim of malignant cerebral malaria at the age of fifty-two.

As the headache worsened, he sensed that it was serious and "sent runners at once to get someone to be with Roxie" (Crossman 234). If others knew, they had forgotten when it came time to write his biography that the person he summoned was Grace Liddell in Yuwang.

Hastily Grace made the necessary arrangements and arrived in Baoshan on September 24. Mr. Fraser was unconscious, with his fever climbing, and Baoshan had no medicine available that could be of any help. A doctor was called and nurses went back and forth. Little Dorothy cried in bewilderment, expressing the dismay and helplessness of everyone else (Crossman 235). With her quiet manner, Grace was a steady and calming presence during his final night of delirium, and by morning he was gone. It was September 25, 1938.

Grace stayed with Roxie for several weeks, helping her through the funeral and supervising the erection of his tombstone. The inscription was written in Lisu, Chinese, and English, and included the message for all to read, "Jesus said, I am the resurrection and the life; he that believeth in me, though he die, yet shall he live."

Roxie herself was stunned. Seven-year old Catherine was in Chefoo: how tell her the news, and comfort her? Roxie could hardly absorb it herself. And there was little Dorothy to care for, and the prospect of a newborn coming in just three months. It was almost too much. With quiet sympathy, Grace would sit on her bed and read passages of Scripture concerning heaven. "How I longed to go," Roxie later told her, "and how your very presence was such a help to me." She listened earnestly to Grace's frequent assurance, "God will never leave the wound open. He <u>will</u> heal it."

Eventually the wound did begin to heal. A routine helped. Together they resumed their study of Chinese, and each day they would go out for a walk, rain or shine. "She is very brave," Grace told her family, "but needs our prayers."

When word came that the Mission was sending nurse Dorothy Burrows to be with Mrs. Fraser, Grace prepared to return to Yuwang. In the end, however, it was she who remained and Mrs. Fraser who left. Since Mrs. Fraser wanted her new baby to be a British citizen, the child would have to be born on British territory. Consequently, plans were made for her to go to Burma, at that time a British colony. After the baby's birth, she would take five-year-old Dorothy and her new baby to Chefoo, to be with Catherine.

And so it was that Grace Liddell became the de facto hostess of the Baoshan Mission home. In addition to Mrs. Fraser and little Dorothy, the guests included Dorothy Burrows, and three missionaries returning to the tribes: Charlie Peterson and Mr. and Mrs. Fitzwilliam. "It will be very lonesome after having such a houseful," she mused.

As they left, it was especially hard to say good-bye to Mrs. Fraser. Grace had been her friend and confidant for ten weeks. At their first stop along the way, Roxie wrote appreciatively to Grace, admitting, "I am afraid <u>my</u> <u>whole</u> <u>heart</u> still longs to be in Heaven & not on earth." But earth was where she was needed, and she told Grace she was praying simply for the ability to stay focused, to rise to the claims of each day as it came, and to honor her Lord by following through on her commitment "until the Home call comes." (It would be thirty-four more years, and neither of them could know that Grace's Home call would come first.)

During this time Grace came to an important realization: she wanted to work among the tribes. The possibility had been on her mind since the fall of 1936, when she visited the Brownings' station in Salowu, but at that point she was not ready to forfeit the hard work she had put into Chinese. The study of Chinese had become "more or less of a little god," she explained in a letter to the general director, and it stayed that way during her six months of exile in Chefoo. She had thought she would lose ground at Chefoo, and wouldn't mind giving up Chinese to learn a tribal language. Instead, she had passed the fourth section, "and upon returning to Yunnan I discovered the little 'god' was still on its shelf."

Once settled in Yuwang, she had resumed work on the fifth section, but it was difficult to get any traction. "…I have seemed to be floating… unable somehow to get a rooting," she wrote. On the other hand, she had "the firmest confidence & assurance that the Lord has brought me [to western Yunnan]."

She recalled that Mr. Harrison in the east and Mr. Fraser in the west had both spoken of her as being "peculiarly" qualified for tribal work. These were men whose discernment and judgment she trusted. Furthermore, in Baoshan she had occasion to interact with many tribal missionaries—the Kuhns, the Fitzwilliams, Victor Christianson, Charlie Peterson, and others. In fact, Francis (Fitz) and Jennie Fitzwilliam had invited her to join them at their station in Longchiu. She found that she wanted to go.

Yet, it was an audacious request to make—that she, a single woman, be allowed to go to the tribes. The CIM had an unwritten rule against it, for obvious reasons—the physical hardships, rough living, brutality, isolation, and loneliness. At present there were no single women workers among the tribes in Yunnan, and in the past only one exception had been made. But Grace made bold to ask, though "only after much prayer & after having reached a place of rest in my own heart."

In her letter to Mr. Gibb, the general director, she addressed the hardship issue.

I have visited two of the tribes stations in the East, Salowu & Sapuhshan, and have heard varied descriptions of the life amongst the tribes out here. But I fear neither hardship nor loneliness & neither of these could or would cause me to swerve, having taken up the work.

Since she had never before indicated an interest in tribes work, she needed to put to rest any suspicion Mr. Gibb might have that she was being rash and impulsive. He did not know she had been thinking and praying about it for months. "I have always felt it better to keep such a matter between myself & the Lord until the time to make the move…" she explained. She did not want to make "bold assertions" that come to nothing, "which seem to me a reproach upon one's calling."

"I often have terrific struggles in coming to a decision…" she told him, "but having reached a decision, it has never been my experience to question it, or go back on it."

She even had a plan ready for him to endorse.

> Mr. and Mrs. Fitz are here at present & have given me a warm welcome to their station at Longchiu. It seems a very plausible plan to make my home with them for awhile, & then there is the Lisu station of [Palien] only ten li [four miles] from Longchiu where I could have an excellent opportunity of being alone for a few days at a time with the people to get the language.

The only drawback was that she would be leaving "my beloved co-worker Miss Embery" alone in Yuwang. She had written to Winnie about it, but perhaps the issue was moot. With Mrs. Fraser now gone, Winnie would likely return to undertake the work in Baoshan, where she would have the companionship of Miss Chiao, the Chinese Bible teacher who had traveled with them from Kunming.

Then she made a fair observation.

> My time in China has been more or less a game of checkers, there having been, in all, no less than seven

or eight moves in the four years on the field, but this is
the first move for which I have <u>asked</u>.

"I shall be eagerly looking forward to receiving your reply," she
concluded, "& in the meantime be praying that the Lord will direct you
aright in your deliberation & decision."

While she waited, she carried on with the work in Baoshan—
teaching, visiting distant villages, and studying for the fifth section
exam. When Winnie Embery joined her for Christmas, Grace was
satisfied that the last "drawback" was removed: Winnie had no objection
to Grace leaving her for the tribes.

They were four for Christmas dinner, 1938, including Miss Chiao
and the independent worker, Miss Hunter. "Winnie had made Xmas
candies & pudding, & with roast chicken etc. we had a good dinner by
candle-light…."

Chapter 20

A "Son of the Prophets"

While Grace was having a quiet Christmas dinner in Baoshan, twenty-two young missionary recruits were enjoying a more lively Christmas dinner at Chefoo School. The CIM men's language school had been evacuated from Anhui to Chefoo, where teen-aged students who had been studying the Old Testament prophets, Elijah and Elisha, dubbed the young men "the sons of the prophets." Most of the men came from Bible schools or college, but at least two were doctors, another had graduated from Oxford, and one was qualified to captain a ship in the British Merchant Navy. It was he who would eventually win the heart of Grace Liddell.

Eric James Edgar Cox was the second son of a lower middle class family in Kent, England. In 1921, he left home at the age of twelve to attend nautical school in Swanley, with his parents close by in South Darenth, where they served on the staff of a large orphanage called the Home for Little Boys. Three years later, at the age of fifteen, he embarked on his first voyage, serving as an apprentice on the *Northwestern Miller*, a grain ship which went across the Atlantic to Panama, up to Puget Sound, down the coast, and back to England.

For all the rough life of a seaman, he was a deeply spiritual man. For some time he had longed to go into the ministry of the Church of England, but the hard facts stood against him: his education was entirely nautical, and even if a theological college were to accept him, he would have no way to finance those years of study. His parents had four younger children still at home, with limited financial resources, so he made the decision to stay at sea and do what he could to help his parents.

In 1930, he joined the firm of Butterfield & Swire in the China Navigation Company, serving as second officer on six different ships before taking time off to qualify for his master's certificate in 1933. Interestingly, one of the ships on which he served was the *Taiyuan*, which Grace would take from Haiphong to Hong Kong on her way to Chefoo in 1937.

Once he had obtained his master's certificate, he was eligible to be a captain, and in hopes of achieving that longtime ambition, he left Butterfield & Swire and signed on with the Chinese Maritime Customs which, despite its name, was managed mostly by Westerners. The office of captain eluded him, but he was given second command (chief officer) of the *Haiyen*, a cruiser charged with hunting Japanese smugglers around the Shantung Peninsula.

Since the *Haiyen* was harbored at Chefoo, it was not long before Eric learned of the China Inland Mission, and a new avenue of service presented itself: he could serve the Lord as a missionary. One of his captains, Archibald Cook, was an earnest Christian who thought highly of Eric and did not want to lose him from the Customs. "All legitimate work is the Lord's work," he argued. The British Merchant Navy needed men who could be "light and salt," men who were not only capable seamen, but sterling in character. Eric could serve God as a ship's officer just as well as he could as a missionary. But he was not dissuaded. For him, the highest form of the Lord's work was evangelism, bringing the gospel to those who were without it, and he wanted to do it full time.

He was impressed with the caliber of the staff at Chefoo School. Their devotion to God resonated with what was in his own heart. Reaching the lost with the gospel was their passion, even as it was his. Consequently, in March 1935, he made the life-changing decision to leave the sea and apply to the China Inland Mission. Though it meant giving up a promising career and any hope of financial security, he resigned from the Chinese Maritime Customs and returned to England, without rank or title.

Since his only education had been nautical, Mission leaders advised him to acquire some practical experience before attempting missionary work. Consequently, for the next two years he did village evangelism with the Friends' Evangelistic Band in Essex and Suffolk. By that time he was twenty-nine, perilously close to the age of thirty, which was the CIM's maximum age for new recruits. But his application was accepted, and thus it was that in December 1938, three and one-half years after leaving Chefoo, he found himself there again, not as chief officer of a ship, but as one of twenty-two young men preparing to take the gospel to inland China.

It was just nine months earlier that Grace had been at Chefoo, and that wasn't the first time they had missed each other. When Eric visited Shanghai in December 1934, Grace had just left for language school. Now he was in Chefoo and she was in Baoshan in southwest China, about as far away as she could be. Their paths would cross only in the providence of God.

Chapter 21

Destination: Tribes Land

"We knew your heart was in tribes land," a friend wrote to Grace. She had received the coveted permission from Mr. Gibb to go, and she awoke eagerly the morning of April 1, 1939, ready to begin the long journey into the mountain ranges of western China.

But getting there would not be easy.

Friends accompanied her to the bus she was going to take, only to find it needed parts and would be delayed a week. A truck was going in two days, but word came that it had been delayed indefinitely. Finally, a week after she had first attempted to leave, she resorted to going by huakan. (At least there would be no stops for mechanical breakdowns and flat tires.) Ten others were traveling in the same direction, two of whom were young Chinese men from the Bethel School, which she had visited in Shanghai. The remaining eight were a Christian family of the Shan tribe: father, mother, and six children.

Known affectionately as Bethel Boys, the two graduates had just held a week of meetings in Baoshan, and Grace had been well impressed with their sincerity and zeal. Mr. Shen, nineteen years old, was known as *Paul*, and his older brother, Mr. Sha, twenty-two years old, was known as *Samuel*. Being Chinese, they were not as accustomed to mountain travel as were the Shan tribesman and his family. When the coolies asked the passengers to get out and walk down an exceedingly steep mountain, Paul and Samuel were tentative and slow, though they had the advantage of youth and were slight in build. Paul managed by leaping, but the Shan tribesman had to take Samuel by the hand and eventually carry him on his back.

After four days of this kind of travel, they reached Longling (Lungling), a tribal station where there was a CIM home, with Leita Partridge as hostess. "She was out visiting in the homes when we got here," Grace wrote, "but soon came home & we had a nice cup of hot tea & cleaned up a bit." The Shan family forged ahead to Mengka, their final destination, but Grace and the Bethel Boys stayed in Longling for several days while the young men held meetings. The response was not promising.

> Mr. Sha [Samuel] spoke & I felt awfully sorry for him. … Lungling is very anti-foreign & despises the Gospel. There are a dozen or so women who believe, but no men. It is very difficult. … The second evening it was better, the service was held in an outer courtyard nearer the street & more people came in to hear. One young man has expressed his desire to believe, and two lady teachers are showing unusual interest. It is our hope & prayer that they be true. It would be such a help to the church here.

At Longling – Spring 1939
L-R: Samuel Sha, Leita Partridge, Grace Liddell, Paul Shen

They were kindred spirits—the two missionaries and the two evangelists—and when Grace and the two young men pushed on to Mengka, Leita was bereft. "I wonder if you realize (you three) just how much sweetness & joy you brought into my life in a few short days..." she wrote to Grace. "I didn't know I was so hungry for spiritual fellowship—for the real thing...."

The two-day journey to Mengka was fraught with wrong turns and fractious coolies, but as they neared, a welcoming party of Christians came down the road to meet them, including CIM workers, Mr. and Mrs. Talmadge Payne, with their three younger children. Grace had hoped to find a Lisu tribesman with a horse there as well, to escort her to New Pool, where she knew the Fitzwilliams were temporarily working. She would join them for the remainder of their stay in New Pool, then go with them to her new home in Longchiu. But such was not to be. The Fitzwilliams had not received her message, and it would be almost a month before they could return and arrange an escort for her. She was stranded at Mengka, with Longchiu just one day away.

Earlier John Kuhn had written to her, "...Let me tell you something—the Devil is against our heading for Tribes' work—be assured of obstacles laid across our pathway. You already know this of course. Then too testing will be ordered of the Lord, and all for our profit."

He was right, and the stay in Mengka would present her with some of that testing. It wasn't the delay in getting to Longchiu; that did not surprise her. It was what she witnessed with respect to the two Bethel Boys. By now she had come to love them like younger brothers, and they returned the honor by referring to her as "big sister" rather than as *chiao-si*, "religious teacher." But not everyone was as magnanimous as she and Leita. In Longling they had listened with dismay as the young men recounted instances of prejudice. Coming from Shanghai, they were better educated and more refined than the Chinese in remote Yunnan. Also, three years of study with teachers who had traveled and ministered overseas had broadened them, making them seem more like foreigners than native Chinese. As a result, they had felt the cold shoulder from both Chinese and foreigner. They had expected rejection for the sake of the gospel, but not because of who they were.

At Baoshan and at Longling the young men had eaten with the missionaries, "just as one of the family," and Grace expected the same at Mengka. The Paynes, however, seemed not to realize that Paul and Samuel were cultured, educated, and could speak English.

> …So you can imagine my chagrin & dismay when I went down to breakfast here the first morning, to see them ushered into the kitchen to eat with the servants. Mrs. Payne said she didn't want them at our table because she wanted the children to learn to speak English & if the boys ate with us we would have to speak Chinese.
>
> I thought of the time that I was [treated like a slave] with Hardings in Chicago & remembered my own heartache even though our Lord gave me grace to go through with it. So I <u>would</u> that I could change places with them.
>
> After breakfast we came to morning prayers, & they both looked over at me & smiled. But when we sang our hymn I just couldn't keep the tears back. The little scoots were as cheerful as though they were eating at the king's table.
>
> For three days in succession I wept & prayed about the matter.

Presumably, courtesy and the importance of saving face precluded Grace's saying anything by way of explanation, but the Lord heard her prayer. Mr. Payne had taken note of the situation.

> On Sunday Samuel preached in the morning on "Children of God." He told of how when [his brother] was a child he would have a tantrum if his special dish wasn't on the table, but now since becoming a child of God he was willing to go a whole day without food just for the Lord's sake. Later Mr. Payne said, "He might have said, 'But now he is willing to eat even in

the foreigner's kitchen,'" [adding], "He is too much of a gentleman to say it with us present."

Sunday evening Paul preached on "Love of God." They both speak with old Methodist fervor & warmth & certainly know the Lord & their Bible. Well, that evening they, with Mr. Payne & me, were singing quartette numbers, & we sang one or two in <u>English</u>.

The next morning when we went to breakfast, can you imagine my relief when they were ushered in to eat with us?! Mrs. Payne said she didn't realize they could speak so much English. And I thanked our Lord for answered prayer.

It had been a time of testing for Samuel and Paul, too, and their sweet-spirited endurance prompted Grace to solicit prayer for them from her praying friends at home.

...Their love for our Lord, their zeal & fervor, their utter abandon to the things of God, and the life of Christ manifest in and through them, has been a source of real blessing to my own soul.

Never before has Western Yunnan had such [high] caliber Chinese workers to stay any length of time, and we are all truly praising our Lord for sending these two. They have come on faith and are looking only to our Lord for their support. They need your prayers too. Neither are strong, both having to guard against T.B., and besides this we know the enemy of souls will do his utmost to defeat in one way or another the work of the Spirit through these two. Will you also plead that if it is His will He will send more Chinese men and lady workers to this needy field? Oh, for an army of them!

As for the remainder of her protracted stay at Mengka, Grace took it as a gift.

The stay here is a very enjoyable one. I am taking it as
though our Lord said to me as He said to His disciples
of old, "Come ye apart----& rest awhile." It is good to
have just all the time one wants for prayer and reading
of His Word. Am getting some other reading done,
too: "A Philosopher's Love for Christ"—by Wrighton—
based on the Song of Solomon; "Sunrise Meditations"
by Mr. [Wendell P.] Loveless; & "Dynamics of Service,"
by Paget Wilkes.

Her day started at daybreak.

Each morning at daybreak we go to the church for
morning prayer with the twenty Christians or so who
care to come. The gong boomed this morning for the
first time at 4:30!!! The boys are taking turns leading &
are taking us through the book of Romans. ... So many
times I've thought of Mr. Fraser & of how thrilled he
would have been to know these two boys & to hear the
living messages they bring.

She also went on evangelistic trips, one where Paul and Samuel
spoke and "[Mrs. Payne and I] dealt personally with those who seemed
interested." On the way they stopped to see "a natural cave with
stalactites & a few stalagmites," but even a place of such natural beauty
and wonder had been co-opted by the Enemy. "Of course they have
made it into a place of idolatry."

On another occasion Grace accompanied Mrs. Payne and her
stalwart little boys.

[We] went eight miles into the country to tell the
Gospel to the people in a couple little villages. [They]
listened quite attentively, but they are so steeped in sin
& hardened. It is amazing how poor the people can be
& still spend money on opium. But He can break every
fetter, & so we carry on in faith.

Little Paul (5) & Titus (3 ½) walked <u>all</u> <u>the</u> <u>way</u>...& there was one very long & steep hill. Coming back Titus kept going down "ker-plop" as his feet slid out from under him, but he just wouldn't let me hold his hand. Time & time again he'd go down until one would think he was bruised, but he'd get right up without a whimper & refuse to take my hand. But when we were almost home his little old legs were just pretty tired & he began to fuss, so I put him on my shoulder for a little way. Paul not only walked but carried a thermos of water, attached to a strap slung over his shoulder. I thought they both did just pretty well.

Finally, the end of Grace's month-long wait at Mengka came into sight. She received word that Mrs. Fitzwilliam, at least, was back in Longchiu, and was ready to welcome her. It was May 1, 1939, when Big Fish, a young Lisu man from the Mission compound in Longchiu, came down the mountain to escort her "home."

Chapter 22

In Lisu-Land—Briefly

Grace had read about the Lisu in her *Handbook of the Lisu Language* by J. O. Fraser. Living in bamboo huts some 5,000 – 7,000 feet above sea level, they could be found throughout the mountains north and west of Baoshan, where they scratched out a living by farming, both men and women working all day on the steep mountainsides to raise corn and buckwheat for their families.

They were by nature a congenial people, friendly and hospitable to strangers, but living in constant fear of demons and evil spirits. Animism was all they knew until missionaries had come with news of the one true God. In back of a typical Lisu home would be a demon shelf, where they labored to propitiate evil spirits, especially those whose "bite" caused sickness. If the priest diagnosed demon possession, the family would sacrifice a chicken or even a pig, hoping for a cure. They knew no other way to live.

The twentieth century was not yet ten years old when J. O. Fraser ventured up into the mountains to reach the Lisu with the gospel. Gradually, other hardy CIM missionaries joined him until, by the time Grace came in 1939, it was considered an evangelized field. "There are one thousand baptized Christians in this district," she wrote, "[and] another thousand in the district to the south of us."

But being evangelized was only the beginning. It was the work of later missionaries, such as herself, to teach new converts the Bible. Thanks to Fraser and the other pioneers, the Lisu now had a written language, and major portions of the Bible had been translated into it, but it remained an ongoing task to teach them how to read, and how to understand the Bible's revelation of the one true God, and the amazing truth that he is Love.

So with Big Fish as her escort, Grace saddled her mule and followed him up the mountain to Longchiu. Mrs. Fitzwilliam would be expecting her, as would the tribes people who lived on the Mission compound to help the missionaries with the business of living in primitive circumstances. For example, besides going to market and being an escort, Big Fish milked the cow and acted as their mailman. There were also his wife and three young children, a cowherd, and a girl from the Kachin tribe, who helped with the cooking.

After settling in, Grace wrote happily to her family,

> Home at last! And I do like it here! It is just like being out in the country. It is so quiet & peaceful, with nothing to break the stillness but the chirping of the crickets. ... We are very high on a mountain side, & just as soon as we step outside the door we must either begin to climb or descend. ...
>
> There is a lovely view to the West as we look down upon the beautiful plain with the city of Chefang in the center and high, high mountains further on. The noted motor road [i.e. Burma Road] runs through this city just seven miles away, and we can see the road winding up the hills & lying on the ridges like a huge lazy snake.

But not all was lovely as she looked down on the plain. She could see "new corrugated tin roof buildings containing supplies of ammunition...." And Big Fish had heard disturbing news.

> When he returned from market last week he said they have a curfew in Chefang now, and all lights must be out by eight o'clock. He also reported that some are moving out of the city because of fear of air raids. Word comes that Paoshan is also preparing for raids.

For two years the second Sino-Japanese war had been plaguing the coastline and eastern China, and now the Japanese were at China's back door, just miles from Grace's new home in the west. But she settled in without demur.

Some of the Lisu in Longchiu

Grace loved the Fitzwilliams like her own brother and sister ("Mr. Fitz reminds me of Samy & Mrs. Fitz reminds me of Anita"). She loved their house, perched as it was on the side of a steep mountain. Unlike the house in Chinning, the roof, though thatched, was "so firm that dust & dirt don't fall down onto things even when the wind blows, & this morning when there was a [rain] shower, I enjoyed the grassy odor [of the thatch]." The house stood two or three feet off the ground because of ants, and it did not bother her that the whitewash on her bedroom wall covered a plaster of cow manure and mud. Instead, she marveled that the bedroom had a washroom with a curtain to draw across, "quite a luxury in tribes land."

In western Yunnan, tribes land consisted of at least two other tribes besides the Lisu: the Shan and Kachin. Longchiu had been reckoned a Kachin village until several Lisu families migrated from Palien, a village about three miles away, at which point it became an amicable mixture of both Lisu and Kachin. Although their languages were entirely different from each other, and from Chinese, a group of thirty or forty were meeting together for worship and instruction, with interpreters on hand to help make plain the missionary's meaning.

The first meeting Grace attended was in the home of the village official and his wife, a Christian Kachin couple. In tribes land, things didn't get underway until after nine o'clock in the evening, when everyone was in from the fields and had eaten supper. A gong summoned people to come, but that night Grace also heard gunfire. What did that mean?

It meant that demon worshipers were frightened. There was an eclipse of the moon that night. In Yangzhou the Chinese feared that a dog was swallowing the moon, but here the Lisu believed the demons were doing it, and attempted to drive them away with gunfire. So Grace and Mrs. Fitzwilliam went on undeterred, picking their way down the hill by the light of a lantern.

Being the new *chiao-sï* (teacher), Grace was the center of attention as each one came to shake her hand. Not knowing a word of Lisu, all she could do was return their smiles. When the meeting began, led by a Lisu believer named Aaron, she heard "the one phrase of the evening which was intelligible to me; it was *Li Chiao-sï*," as Aaron thanked the Lord for her safe arrival.

A congregation of two different language groups was a challenge. The first half of the meeting was in Lisu, then "other books were taken out of the bags slung over their shoulders, and the second half of the service was in Kachin." Understandably, there was considerable attention deficit. It was easy to fall asleep while the other language was being spoken, and it was hard for the women not to chat.

The Lisu were known for their ability to sing. Not only could they carry a melody, but they were naturals at singing in all four parts. Small wonder, then, that a hymnbook had been a priority with the early translators. In addition to the New Testament and some Old Testament stories in their language, they had a hymnbook consisting of 233 hymns and choruses, including a few of their own composition. Grace had been told not to expect much from the Lisu at Longchiu. Compared with believers in other districts, they tended to be listless and indifferent, and their singing was mediocre at best. But as she sat listening to them, she detected a good bass—it was the cowherd. And then a nice alto from a girl named Martha.

One evening after supper she glanced out the window to see the cowherd running up the steep incline. What had happened? Had one of the cows broken a leg? No, he had caught the strains of Handel's *Messiah* coming from the record player.

> Usually his countenance is very glum, and he has refused to give me a smile when I deliberately gave him one, hoping to break the cloud on his face. But as he listened to the choir singing the Hallelujah Chorus, his face was all animation, and such a smile! As his appreciation deepened his smile broadened until it was a grin from ear to ear. Music is in their blood, it is a part of them.

Even the language itself was musical. Like Chinese, it was tonal, and as Grace began to listen, she recognized the familiar *do, mi, sol* of the tonic sol-fa.

Mr. and Mrs. Fitzwilliam, who knew Lisu from their first term, were now learning Kachin, so the Lisu church at large was providing Tabitha, a Chinese-speaking Lisu girl, to be Grace's teacher and companion. Reserved and quiet, she was to live "right on the premises so her help may be had any time during the day, and for as long as it is needed." For Tabitha, it was an answer to a prayer of many years: that she be allowed to work "for the Lord." She was twenty-two years old, single by choice, and not doing this for the money, as Mrs. Fitzwilliam explained in a letter to prayer partners at home.

> [Tabitha has] refused all offers of marriage as she says married Lisu women have no time for the Lord's work. I am sure you will pray for her. The Pentecostal people have been trying to get her. Of course they offer her a much larger salary than the Lisu church can afford to pay. While I am sure money offers no temptation to Tabitha, it does to her father.

Her father was not sympathetic. If he could not dictate where she would work, he would use an illogical piety to avoid getting help for her very poor eyes. "The doctor in Burma says she can be cured," Grace wrote, "but the father disapproves of her using medicine and says she must trust to prayer."

Grace reasoned: "Is not medicine God's gift to mankind? I wonder if we should sit before a table of food and refuse to eat, saying we must trust to faith alone to satisfy our hunger, if the Lord would honor such conduct. My heart aches for her as it is such a handicap to her in her work."

But work she did, and with both Tabitha and Mrs. Fitzwilliam on hand to help—Tabitha with pronunciation and Mrs. Fitzwilliam with grammar—Grace began to learn Lisu.

As for the missionary work itself, it was "absolutely different" from what Grace had known among the Chinese. In tribes land no one was home to visit. Everyone was in the fields. So missionaries capitalized on the rainy season, when field work was impossible. Rainy Season Bible Schools, held for one or two weeks each in strategic locations, provided an opportunity for concentrated Bible study.

But the rain could make things interesting. For example, the clay road in Longchiu, trampled on every day by horses and cattle, became a quagmire with slippery edges and deep pits when it rained. The tribes people had grown up with it. "We marvel as we see them start home down a very steep grade with babies on their backs and with no light!" Grace wrote. And they were barefoot. As for the missionaries, they would just get into old clothes and enjoy it.

> It was fun going down to church last Wednesday evening. It was raining & very slippery. Sometimes we just put our feet together, brace ourselves & slide a couple feet or so & then—laugh! Even Big Fish fell down going down the hill. Coming home I was sliding backwards so he let me hold onto his hand & then if _he_ didn't start sliding backwards in his bare feet.

128

Three Bible Schools were scheduled for the fall of 1939. Accordingly, at the end of August, Grace, Mr. and Mrs. Fitzwilliam, Tabitha and two other Lisu set out to visit the Lisu villages of Ho-Liang-Ho and Muchengpo, where they would hold a two-week Bible school in each. They must have made a curious sight—three tall Americans and the three Lisu, each on horseback, traveling for four days along the mountain trail in the rain. One night when they could find no accommodation, they camped out, Grace in a tent that leaked. Another night they were glad for the upstairs room of a Chinese home, which Grace found "similar to a hayloft."

> Soon an open fire was built on a stone hearth & with poles etc. our bedding & clothes were hung up for drying. [We] all slept in the one room. We just kicked off our shoes & rolled in—the Lisu didn't even have shoes to kick off.

The next day they reached the first village, Ho-Liang-Ho.

> ...we reached here, feeling just fine. A group of men stood in line and sang a song of welcome as we arrived. ... After the customary shaking of hands we were ushered to a house beside the chapel. It is a little three room house prepared especially for the missionaries to live in when they come to hold Bible Schools. Much, much time and labor has been put into it, and it is much better than the homes which they themselves have.

Fifty-five had registered, and more were attending. There were Bible classes and music classes from morning until night, with time out for recesses and meals, and the students were eager. Grace was in her element.

> I am enjoying myself immensely. Even though I have to speak in Chinese while Tabitha interprets in the Lisu, it is a real inspiration and joy to teach a group so eager and open to the Truth. If they get one half the blessing from

the studies that I do myself, they are well worthwhile. I tell the story—give the character sketch—one day, then make the application in the next day & review, then they one by one repeat the Scripture verse memorized for the study. Even though much preparation was made before coming—outlines, maps, verses, etc, yet the days are too short.

After the two-week school had finished, the group took to the trail again, this time heading for Tabitha's home village, Muchengpo. There the attendance was greater—over one hundred—"but on a whole [they] do not seem to have the bright faces and spiritual response which we so much enjoyed in Ho-Liang-Ho." Yet there were baptisms at the conclusion of the school, and two men who had been at odds with each other were reconciled.

The third school would be at Palien, the village from which several Lisu families had migrated to Longchiu, but the little group separated for a few days first. Mr. Fitzwilliam and two Lisu teachers from Muchengpo went to visit some Kachin villages, and Mrs. Fitzwilliam, Grace and Tabitha began the long journey home, riding horseback by day, and finding shelter where they could at night. "The first night we slept in a barn loft over the horses & cattle. There were no walls, but there was a good roof, which is the most important thing in the rainy season."

Finally back at Longchiu, they received an enthusiastic welcome home.

> The Kachin girl met us first with a happy smile & a genuine hand-shake. Next was little Luke, then his daddy Big Fish with a grin from ear to ear. His little girl stood up on the bank by the gate & squealed her delight. Lastly came the mother & babe. Ma-t'u, the Kachin girl, had baked bread for us that day & had boiled vegetables for supper & RICE! [And we] did enjoy drinking all the tea we craved!

But Sunday was a let-down. "The coldness & indifference of the Longchiu group seems more marked after being out where there were those who were hungry for the Word." Yet, there were glimmers of understanding.

For example, although it was illegal to grow opium, and there were government orders to dig up any that had been planted, a Kachin Christian was not complying. Consequently, on Sunday he was admonished by means of an object lesson. The Kachin official in whose home they met "produced a dirty, broken bowl and, holding it up for all to see, told the offender that he was like that bowl, dirty and broken and no good as a Christian."

Another Sunday the young Lisu preacher, Aaron, gave a quaint description of what it means to seek, as in seeking the pearl of great price.

> If we have a louse in our hair or clothes and want to find it, we have to 'seek' for it. We part our hair this way and that, watching carefully all the while. We turn the seams of our garments back and forth looking closely to spot the louse. Thus we diligently 'seek' and are not satisfied until we find it.

But what had Gideon's little boy brought to play with during church? "Nothing else than a dead rat dangling on the end of a string tied to a stick. Not believing my own eyes I looked again more intently and had to believe what I saw! They say it is more fun when the rat or mouse is still alive!"

After the three-day respite, Grace, Tabitha and Mrs. Fitzwilliam left Longchiu to meet Mr. Fitzwilliam and the two Lisu teachers for the school at Palien. Since it was just an hour's walk away, Big Fish and his family accompanied them, along with the cows, "so we have fresh milk each day for our porridge and tea."

It was a shorter school (ten days) with smaller attendance (daily average of thirty), and "an indifference here akin to that in Longchiu." How the missionaries yearned to see lives change and hearts become eager to learn.

Grace had heard reports of this kind of response across the border in Burma, and she looked forward to January when she could see for herself. Two Bible Schools were to be held at White Fish Village, four days away, and she would be going along.

In the meantime, she was starving for mail. It is hard to imagine a world without instant communication, but missionaries in remote Yunnan could wait weeks for a letter from home, and Grace was being deprived even of that. Neither she nor the Fitzwilliams had received any mail for quite some time, not since they had changed their address from Mengka to Chefang, in fact. When Mr. Fitzwilliam left to do some more itinerating among the Kachin, "Jennie & I took a couple horses & with Tabitha went down to Chefang to see what was the trouble." But it wasn't that easy. "The postmaster said that letters were not coming through at all. So, very crestfallen, we went back home."

Grace and Jennie determined to try again, however, even if it meant catching a bus to Longling, which also was not easy. After waiting overnight, they rode on a hospital bus and then a truck before they reached Longling. There they learned that their mail was being forwarded not to Chefang, as they had asked, but to a town on the Burma border, two days beyond them.

If Grace could have known what was in that missing mail, she might not have been so eager to locate it. As she had expected, there were six weeks' worth of letters from home, but what she did not expect were two letters from Mission headquarters in Shanghai.

The first was actually welcome, a hand-written letter from Mr. McPherson, assistant China director, reassuring her about a sensitive issue he had raised earlier: her camaraderie with the young Chinese evangelists, Paul Shen and Samuel Sha. He feared lest she lose sight of Chinese etiquette, and so compromise her standing. She had written him a "kind letter" in return, but was frank to say that his letter had caused her some pain. The letter waiting for her was gracious and reassuring. "I just hate to think of my causing you sorrow of heart and I almost wish that I had not written that paragraph," he wrote. "I am glad that you felt you could write to me frankly."

The second letter was another matter. It was from Mr. Sinton, also an assistant China director, and it left her reeling. She was being recalled to Baoshan, for a whole year. Winnie Embery was in desperate need of a furlough, which meant there would be no one competent to supervise the three new women workers who had come to Baoshan, and Grace Liddell seemed an obvious choice. She was older, and she had already proved that she could handle the demands of the Baoshan Mission home. "We should be very glad if you would feel that it is the Lord's call for you to go to Paoshan and release Miss Embery just as soon as you can arrange to do so," Mr. Sinton wrote.

But how could she? How could she feel it was the Lord's call when she felt no such thing? She felt called to the Lisu people. Was not Longchiu where the Lord had put her, despite the many obstacles and delays? A much later publication of the Chinese Christian Mission in Hong Kong indicates how well-suited she was. Written in 1999 by Paul Shen, by then an elderly man, it told of the tribal ministry in western Yunnan. The accompanying translation is halting and incomplete, but it is clear that Mr. Shen remembered the "Li girl from the United States, (Iowa), farming for generations, able-bodied, [and a] most suitable co-worker" (ccmhk.org.hk).

Now, after only nine months, she was being asked to reverse course, to go back to Chinese work in Baoshan, keep the Mission books, and run the home there. For a *year* or so. By that time, Mr. Sinton told her, he hoped she could have a partner in the Lisu work.

Permission to do tribal work as a single woman had been hard won. Could it be that Mission leaders were still nervous about it? Was this an opportunity to get her back into a safer environment?

Whatever the reasons, she knew where her duty lay. She was to submit to those in authority over her, for the Lord's sake. That was God's will. Yet the questions would come.

Had she been misled about Lisu work? She knew she had not.

Had the Lord rejected her? That, too, she knew was false.

Like John the Baptist, she was being asked not to take offense at her Lord's dealings with her, not to "fall away on account of me" (Luke 7:23). And so, trusting God with the mystery, she made the necessary arrangements and went back to Baoshan.

As she settled in, a letter from Winnie Embery, en route to Australia, came as good medicine. Winnie knew the challenges of Baoshan, how unlike it was to the work Grace had just been doing, and she begged her not to go back. "I believe God cares more about what we are becoming than what we are doing," she wrote. "You can't understand God's way of reasoning—human reasoning [can't]. Nor because a place is hard & thankless does that mean God wants us to leave it. Maybe that's why we're there. He trusts us."

She was also helped by another letter from her dear friend, Pearl Galloway, suggesting that she, of all people, would be uniquely suited to train the three new workers in Baoshan. Hadn't she herself suffered at the hands of a senior missionary who was not well suited? And Roxie Fraser wrote, "I feel you are so suitable for new workers because you are so sympathetic & sane." Not surprisingly, the three young women—Wilma Tershee, Isabel Spence and Frances Flannigan—did find in her a companionable senior. In fact, they missed her when she was away. "Here I am counting the days till your return…" wrote one. "When may we look for you?"

The Baoshan Mission home was strategically located to be an oasis for travelers going west to Burma, east to Kunming, or to the tribes scattered in the surrounding mountains. How much of an oasis depended on who was in charge. It could be a place of refreshment and peace, as the Kunming home had been for Grace and Clare with the Arthur Allens in charge, or it could be less than that. For example, at another time a friend had written to Grace, "We are hoping we shall soon be able to [go to our post]. The Mission Home doesn't exactly lure one into wanting to stay on indefinitely." As for Baoshan under Grace's care, John Kuhn wrote, "It is a joy to come in and out of the Paoshan station."

When she first arrived, she was heartened to find that her Bilhorn folding organ had finally arrived. Her family had shipped it to her in July 1938, more than a year and a half earlier, and here it was, just when she needed to see a silver lining to the cloud that was Baoshan. "It certainly is a nifty little affair & as handy as anything to carry around," she wrote. They used it during a week of special meetings, "and it was a real asset."

After several weeks, since she was in need of dentistry and Dorothy Burrows was presently staying in Baoshan, Grace decided to leave the three new workers in Dorothy's care and attend to her dental needs. She did not relish the long journey back over the Burma Road to Kunming, and could ill afford the expense, but the work needed to be done.

As she made her way along, however, a grievous blow was befalling her friends back in Longchiu. Just eighteen months after J. O. Fraser had been taken with cerebral malaria, Francis Fitzwilliam was succumbing to typhus. He and Jennie and Allan Crane had been across the Burma border, holding the Bible schools at White Fish Village which Grace had hoped to help teach. Jennie had returned to Longchiu, and Allan Crane had gone on to another location the day Mr. Fitzwilliam took ill.

It was a Wednesday, with fifty new students in attendance, and only Fitz to teach them. Ill though he was, he persevered through the week, teaching two classes a day. Sunday he spent in bed; on Monday he was unable to walk. The Lisu carried him for the three-day journey home to Longchiu. There, within a week, the disease took its terrible toll in delirium, during which he spoke nothing but Lisu, and then death. "I thought I could not stand to hear another word of Lisu all the days of my life," Jennie confessed. It was Sunday, February 25, 1940, when he died, and one of the young men who dug the grave and helped to bury him was the Chinese evangelist, Paul Shen.

Roxie Fraser wrote to Grace, "I wish [Jennie] had had you there Grace, & yet—God let you go on to Paoshan & He knew."

Jennie struggled for answers. Was it the sovereignty of God, as Roxie suggested? Or was it chance? Was it just nature taking its course? Was it inevitable? She could see that, humanly speaking, chance had been against him: no medical care, poor food, the strain of teaching, plus the difficult journey home. "I have nearly gone crazy thinking of the human ifs," she wrote. Yet she bowed her head to the sovereignty of God, and eventually it was that fact—that a gracious God was in control—which gave her peace, despite her heavy heart. "...the Lord has given me an assurance that it was all of Him & from Him so that now I have a peace of heart, but can't say I have much joy there yet," she acknowledged.

The Mission leaders recommended she go to Chefoo to be with their son, Jack, and rest, but the Kachin sent a delegation to implore her to stay. She opted for Chefoo, writing to Grace from Rangoon, "Now that I have gotten away, I don't feel that I ever want to go back there...."

Eventually the Lord gave her "a quietness" about it, and she reached the place where she was willing to go back if the Lord wanted her to. Roxie Fraser, herself still at Chefoo, even suggested that at some point she and Jennie and Grace might all work together, "seeing that Tribes stations <u>need</u> three."

Grace would not learn of Fitz's death and Roxie's suggestion until after she reached Kunming, and during the brief time she was there, an entirely different possibility came into view.

Chapter 23

Climbing into Love

It had been two years since Grace was last in Kunming. Now, as she returned for dentistry, she was pleased to find friends from former days at the familiar Mission home, and new acquaintances as well.

When she arrived on Saturday evening, February 24, 1940, Fred and Dora Hatton were still in charge. Her friend, Irene (Barberini) Allen, had come with her husband and two little girls. Also, Mr. Porteous, who had escorted Grace and Clare Lassen to Chengkiang, had stopped for a few days. Around the corner, the Harrisons' home would normally have been vacant, but the Harrisons, too, were in Kunming. They had come from Chengkiang, where they had been senior missionaries for three new men workers—Hector Goodall, Norman Charter, and Eric Cox—and all five were staying at the Harrisons' home.

The next morning, Sunday, Mrs. Hatton asked Grace to substitute at the organ for the English-speaking Chinese service. "That was when I first saw her," Eric recalled, and he was smitten. As for Grace, "I didn't even see him."

That afternoon Mrs. Harrison invited Grace and Mr. Porteous for tea. Being fond of the Harrisons, Grace was glad to accept. The three young men staying with them were of no particular interest to her, aside from what they might have in common in Chengkiang, but Mrs. Harrison noticed with quiet surprise that Eric Cox was taking an interest in Grace. Other single women missionaries had crossed his path, but Grace was the first one he seemed to notice. When they sat down for tea, he chose a seat that would put him directly across from her at the table.

Another day she dropped in for tea, hoping to confide in Harrisons her continuing concern for the Bethel Boys. There was still tension at Mengka, and she empathized, remembering her own difficult days at Chengkiang. She knew the Harrisons would understand and offer good counsel, but Eric "sat on and on" until Mr. Harrison had to leave, and she never did get the opportunity she wanted. "I thought it strange," Grace reflected, "but nothing more."

On the next Sunday, March 3, she was asked to speak, and Eric was asked to lead the service. Grace innocently obliged, but "had I known then what was going on in his heart I should have been too embarrassed to open my mouth!"

Grace suspected nothing, but Eric faced the dilemma of how to declare himself to a young woman in the circumspect society of a Mission home not far removed from the mores of Victorian England. When could he ever see Grace alone without causing premature talk? Furthermore, there wasn't much time. The dentistry she had come for would soon be completed, and it was imperative that he talk to her before she started the long journey back to Baoshan.

Recognizing the bond that existed between Grace and Mrs. Harrison, Eric decided to take her into his confidence. She was a wise and competent person, warm and generous, but still it was with some caution that he broached the subject. What would she think?

He found, with relief, that Mrs. Harrison was not at all surprised, much less disapproving. She and Mr. Harrison had already noted how the reserved young Englishman, heretofore indifferent to single lady missionaries, seemed fascinated by Grace. She was willing to help him meet privately with her, but she could not be encouraging. Eric wrote to his mother,

> She said from all she knew of Grace she thought she had no particular objections to marrying, but that in all the time she had lived with them, she had shown quite an indifference to all the young menfolk around. I gathered...that once or twice Mrs. H. had tried to

do a little match-making for her, & had been very disappointed by her lack of response!!

The plan was that Mrs. Harrison would invite Grace to supper. The others would be there, of course, so Eric would write her a note, "telling her something of what was in my mind," and ask if he could talk to her afterwards. But Grace was out, and the servant came back with the note still in his hand. Undeterred, Mrs. Harrison herself went to the Mission home with it, and waited for Grace to return.

As she read the note, Grace was stunned, but not dismissive. She could see it was not a scheme contrived by Mrs. Harrison. Eric had initiated it, and she reread his note with care. He said he wanted to talk with her, and he told her why, though he feared she might think ill of him. She warmed to his candor and courtesy.

In her return note she suggested a compromise. She would not come for supper, but she would come around for a few minutes afterwards. She also assured him that she respected his letter and in no way disparaged him for writing it.

It is not hard to imagine the questions, the wonder, the tumult of speculation that must have raced through Grace's mind as she made the short walk to the Harrisons' home that Tuesday evening, March 5. Neither she nor Eric was given to small talk, and Eric didn't waste any time. "I told her I had felt strangely drawn to her on first meeting her," he recalled, "and that in prayer and in seeking guidance from God's Word, it had seemed confirmed that I was being guided by the Lord in the matter."

But Grace would need more than that. She needed to know her own heart. "I told him I could in no wise encourage him, and that although I would pray about it, he must be just as ready for a 'No' as for a 'Yes.'" As she had told Mr. Gibb in her request to do tribal work, she was cautious about claiming to know the Lord's will in a matter until she really did, and this would take some time.

The next day, Wednesday, March 6, Eric followed up with a second letter, telling her about himself and his family. Grace read the letter with interest, but made no reply. Finally, after a day and a half had passed, he wrote again on Friday, March 8, telling her more about his life and background. But he assured her he would not presume on her any more. He would not write again unless he heard from her. "Then I was sorry," Grace wrote to Pearl Gallagher. "I <u>wanted</u> another letter." She wrote that afternoon.

> Dear Eric,
>
> Please do not think that the reason I failed to answer your letter was because it was not appreciated. For one thing, I would rather talk than write, & for another, felt that I dare not do anything which would add to your suffering in some future date. For as yet, I do not know my own heart.
>
> To me, in a matter such as this, the Lord's will includes a deep, abiding love in the heart of each for the other. Apart from this, I cannot believe it to be His will. I have seen hearts & health broken because of friendships which did not culminate in marriage; & on the Mission field worse tragedies still—unhappy marriages. And I dare say these same people <u>thought</u> they knew the Lord's will in the matter, in fact one told me that she did. – As one has put it, there should be a 'climbing into love,' not a 'falling in love.' …

Eric's reply came that evening. "This letter began with a 'My,'" Grace confided to Pearl, "but was crossed out with the explanation that he could not properly use it as yet. And I found myself wishing tremendously that he could!"

The next day was Saturday, March 9, and Grace decided to reply in person. She found Eric at home, working on a hymn sheet for the English service the next day. Harrisons' home was private and quiet, and they were able to talk together for about an hour.

On Sunday, March 10, they both attended the English-speaking Chinese service, but not together. Time together came in the form of a walk that afternoon, which Eric described to his mother.

[Grace] is very sensitive to what others say & feel, & anxious that at this early stage, the other folk at the Mission Home should not be aware that there is anything between us. So we went out of the city by one of the holes cut in the big walls for times of air raid alarms, & so were soon in the country, where we were not likely to meet any other foreigners. Our conversation was just about the work here, & the things of the Lord, but I think it drew us closer together. At present we are just on good terms as Christian friends, with a real interest in one another. But I feel quite confident that the Lord Who has led thus far will draw us ever closer together in the bonds of His own true love.

Two days later, on March 12, there was a picnic. The two households (Harrisons and the Mission home) joined together and went across Lake Dian to Haishan Mountain. Grace related simply, "The two of us went off together and it was settled that p.m." Eric was more expansive in writing to his mother.

I shall never forget that time. We sat high up on the hill face, in a sheltered grassy spot, overlooking the beautiful blue lake. We just talked, but it was there, I think, that the Lord really confirmed to both of our hearts that this love that had come to our hearts was truly of Him....

He had his camera and took a picture to enhance the word picture he had given his mother earlier: "She has a very sweet face, & a very merry twinkle in her eye oftimes. Her voice is very low & soft & I don't think you would recognize that she has an American accent."

If Grace had an American accent, Eric certainly had an English one. The difference in nationality was significant. He was proudly English, and Grace was just as proudly American. He had been raised with the customs and manners of an English home. Grace came from a farming family and shrank from the rigid rules of etiquette which governed the English missionaries. In her introductory letter to Eric she had written,

> ...Coming from the farm, I naturally enjoy a life of
> freedom & simplicity, & formalities terrorize me—
> that was one of the difficult things at Chefoo, for the
> atmosphere of the Girls School was extremely stiff.

There were other differences, too. Grace was older than Eric by two
years and four months: she was thirty-three and he was not quite thirty-
one. Eric had a master's certificate in the British Merchant Navy. Grace
had an academic degree, a BA from Western Union College, though
she discounted it. "Do you know what it means to me?" she asked Eric.
"Ba-a-a-a." In fact, even as a new worker she had asked that her degree
not be placed after her name in the Mission directory. "I once asked her
why," Leita Partridge recalled, "and her answer was, '[Does it] make me
any better than others who have none—definitely not!'"

Both were in their first term in China, but at different stages. Grace
had come four years ahead of Eric, putting her that much farther along
in Chinese. And she was within two years of furlough, whereas Eric
had six years to go.

Physically they were well matched. Each had blue eyes, and both
were tall. Grace was about 5 feet 11 inches, and Eric, at 6 feet 3 inches,
was usually the tallest of a group. What he wasn't used to was a woman's
hand as large as his—a feature he noticed in Grace the first time they
shook hands.

But these things were all incidental. What mattered was who they
were spiritually, and in that they found no disparity. Each was devoted
first and foremost to Jesus. Each had left a promising career in order to
labor, by faith in God alone, in China. And each believed that the Lisu
tribe was where God was calling them to work. Eric had declared as
much as a new recruit, long before he met Grace. Not surprisingly, then,
they wondered if the Lord might be providing a married couple—the
Coxes—to augment the depleted Lisu team.

Grace summed up their engagement in her letter to Pearl Galloway,
"...after looking much to Him we both had peace and rest of heart that
it was His will." It had taken a mere sixteen days! Eric reflected on that
remarkable fact in a letter to his mother.

It seemed to happen very suddenly, but as Ray Joyce said when I told him about it, situated as we are here in Yunnan, with stations many days journey apart, & very infrequently meeting one another, the Lord must work things in these seemingly sudden ways if they are to be worked at all. If Grace hadn't needed attention to her teeth, & come in as she did, we might not have met for years, if ever. As it is, I know the Lord just synchronized our movements, enabling us to meet here as we did & learn to love one another.

They had one more day together before Grace began the return journey to Baoshan. She left on March 14. "I went down to the bus with her & saw her off," Eric wrote, "& when she was gone, it seemed to leave an awful blank."

Chapter 24

It's Hard to Keep a Secret!

The Burma Road hadn't improved, but the wonder and glow of Grace's new status made the breakdowns and overnight delays seem of small account as she bumped along towards Baoshan. Even when she had to run to catch the next bus, she could see some humor in it. "The passengers were all sticking their heads out like chickens in a coop, watching & waiting for that 'foreigner' to get there & get in."

The trip took five and one-half days, but when she arrived on March 19 she kept her news a secret from the household of four women for three more weeks, telling them only that there would be a surprise in a couple of weeks (i.e. April 9, Eric's birthday). But that was all they needed. They guessed that she had met somebody, they guessed it was one of the new workers, and they even guessed which one—Eric Cox, to be exact. Still, Grace gave nothing away until his birthday.

> Early that morning [April 9] as I sat on my bed
> with my Bible on my knees, I heard steps coming up
> the stairs & soon three mischievous faces appeared over
> the partition between my room & Dorothy [Burrow]'s
> as they stood on her bed. In a short time the fourth
> face—Isabel's—came through a small 2 feet square
> window. [S]he had climbed up on a ladder! She climbed

on through the aperture & let the others in at the door & they began teasing for their surprise. I told them they would be guests—I had invited Richard Tseng, Samuel Sha, and Lydia Chiao to come over for a cup of tea & cookies that p.m. So they concluded that Harrisons would be coming & Eric would be coming with them!

At breakfast, still acting on supposition, Isabel presented me with a valentine with two silly poems on it. It was made of red card-board & with a heart-shaped opening in the center. She had swiped Eric's picture from my desk & Dorothy gave her a cutout snap of me & she had our two faces in the opening! Then Frances presented me with a bouquet of artificial roses—[supposedly] having arrived just that morning by airplane from Eric's mother!! Then Dorothy & Wilma each made a little speech & presented me with a Ladies Magazine having articles in them about brides etc. During all of these pranks it was up to me to appear innocent. The nearest I came [to] giving myself away was when the two pictures appeared—my face must have been a study, as they said afterwards that it was. ...

At afternoon tea she revealed her secret by means of personalized cupcakes—initials on the bottom of the paper liner, and a handwritten announcement, carefully wrapped in oil paper, which she had baked inside the cupcake. "It was all good fun & I think everybody enjoyed it."

Good wishes were not slow in coming from friends farther away. Isobel Kuhn voiced something Grace herself must have noticed: her unwelcome reassignment to Baoshan was but the precursor of something wonderful. Addressing her as "Dearest Grace-girl," Isobel wrote, "God never asks a hard thing of us without a handsome reason for it tucked out of sight so that we might exercise our faith. ... I surely am happy for you, and would like to tell Mr. Cox how lucky I think he is."

Olive Simpkin, hostess at the Mission home in Dali where Grace had just stayed on her way home from Kunming, exclaimed, "Well, what a 'dark horse' you are to be sure!" She reported that a couple of the young men staying there seemed crestfallen at the news, but "the English boys say [Eric] is a splendid chap, and all agreed that he would need to be, to be worthy of you."

Grace's dear friend, Pearl Galloway, wrote from Chefoo: "What perfectly thrilling news!! ... What a jolly lucky man Mr. Cox is. ... I can just see you two trudging off to Tribesland together!"

A friend of Eric's at Chefoo wrote, "How very happy we are, dear Eric, to hear of your engagement! I have become knit in heart to Mrs. Fraser & I hear from her just what kind of a girl you have chosen! How glad I am."

Grace lost no time in writing to the Mission directors in Shanghai. It seemed obvious to her that she and Eric should go to the Lisu, after he finished the necessary sections in Chinese, of course. Now that the Fitzwilliams were gone, the entire southern Lisu field was left in the care of one couple—Allan and Evelyn Crane—who had not yet learned the Lisu language. At present Eric was visiting the tribal districts in central Yunnan with his senior missionary, Tom Mulholland, but surely the directors would recognize the critical need in the west and agree that she and Eric would be the logical ones to go there.

It was Mr. Sinton who replied, reminding her of the importance of seemliness. After congratulating her for "having won the affection of a good man, for whom I have much respect," he cautioned her against assuming Eric could go with her to the Lisu. "While we must not be too bound by precedent, it is usual rather for the woman to follow the man," he wrote, but promised to discuss her suggestion with the other directors in Shanghai.

To their credit, the leaders realized that the first thing the young couple needed was to spend some time together, regardless of where they would be stationed. They had known each other for only a scant two weeks by the time Grace returned to Baoshan.

Since Eric was visiting the tribes in the area east of Baoshan, the Mission arranged for them to meet in Tsuyung at the home of Miss Cornelia Morgan, the independent American missionary with whom Grace had stayed on her return trip to Baoshan following her engagement. The only other guests would be Tom and Iza Mulholland, giving Grace and Eric more privacy than they would have at the Mission home in Baoshan, with its resident single women.

They were to meet in June, but on May 28 Grace received a sobering summons. She was asked to come to the aid of two men from the International Red Cross whose truck had overturned on the Burma Road. They were Mr. Ridley, an engineer from Glasgow, and Mr. Mitchell, the transport director and a pastor with the Canadian Mission. Both had sustained head wounds, and one suffered a rib broken off the backbone, but because Mr. Ridley had no identification, the doctor at the hospital where they had been taken refused to attend him. Helpless, the Red Cross asked the CIM in Baoshan to intervene, and Grace obliged. She arranged for coolies to take both Mr. Ridley and Mr. Mitchell to another hospital, where they were successfully admitted and cared for. The hospital did not provide meals, but Grace did, and arranged for the men to be guests at the Baoshan Mission home after their release. "We brought all of their things down to our premises to take care of them & will take them their food [in the hospital]," she explained. When she left on June 13, they were still in the hospital but "doing nicely."

"May the Lord take me safely to Tsuyung & back again!" was Grace's heartfelt prayer as she herself set out to travel the Burma Road to Tsuyung. Her companions on this trip were Harry Wang, a Bethel Boy, and Chu Chia-lin, a ten-year-old orphan girl. The little girl was badly carsick, and travel was exasperatingly slow—engine burnout, a two-day wait for another vehicle, a delay for wet spark plugs, yet another delay while drivers located missing passengers—and she was in a hurry! Finally, on the fifth day, they arrived in Tsuyung at noon, where Eric was waiting for her. "I could only greet [him] with a handshake, but he was wise & quick enough to take my baggage to my room for me!" she reported.

Then followed "a happy two weeks together." The weather was "splendid," they had the leisure and privacy they had hoped for, and in their Father's kind providence, they were together when weighty letters from Shanghai arrived.

Mr. Sinton was making the bittersweet proposal of an early furlough for Grace, and he had written to each of them about it. She had served five and one-half years of her seven-year term, but it was Mission policy that when she married Eric, their years of service would be combined and furlough would have to wait until the total equaled fourteen. That would extend her first term from seven years to nine. An early furlough would, of course, delay their wedding until after her return, but if she accepted the offer to go now, she was to respond by wire and the Mission would book her a passage.

The dilemma was agonizing, but it would have been worse had she and Eric not been together.

"It was the Lord's goodness that the letters came while I was with Eric," she wrote home. "It would have been awful to have received [this offer] when I couldn't talk it over with him, & pray it through together."

One of her considerations was Eric himself, whose home country was now under assault by Germany. The Home for Little Boys, the orphanage where Eric's parents lived and worked, lay directly on the path followed by German bombers approaching London. Eventually an errant bomb did destroy the house where they were living, but providentially, no one was injured.

"I know I need Eric—for ever so many reasons," Grace wrote, "& if ever he needed me he does now, when England is facing such peril." The prospect of declining this opportunity to go home was excruciating. "Of course I'd love to see all of you," she wrote, "but I'd rather see you when Eric can come with me." Besides, she added bravely, "I am strong & feel perfectly fit in every way & don't mind an extra two years." But there were tears as "we both prayed together about the matter & felt that before Him the thing to do was to decline the proposal. So we both wrote letters to that effect & mailed them by air to Shanghai."

Not lost in the turmoil of that decision was some encouraging news from Mr. Sinton: "[He] said the prospects of our working in the West are good. So although that word is not final, yet it makes us very happy."

When the two weeks in Tsuyung were over, they began looking for a ride back to Baoshan for Grace. And each day, when they returned to Miss Morgan's guest home to say there was none, she and the Mulhollands would laugh, "because they knew we weren't sorry!"

As it turned out, they needn't have made the effort. The day after Grace had arrived, Mr. Mitchell passed through Tsuyung. Surprised to find her there, he informed her that a contingent from the Red Cross would be traveling that way in another ten days, and he would have them stop for her. But Grace had dismissed this possibility as unlikely—until a telegram arrived, followed shortly by a truck with three Red Cross workers. They had heard of her kindness to Mr. Mitchell and Mr. Ridley, and they were glad to take her along free of charge. As a further kindness, they delayed their departure until the next morning, to give her another evening with Eric. "In so many ways the Lord just showered kindnesses upon us," she exclaimed. Even though tire trouble and a landslide made the trip two days longer than they expected, the Red Cross men "wouldn't take a cent for the ride, & besides paid for all my meals along the road...."

Chapter 25

Wedding Bells and Air Raid Sirens

Once back in Baoshan, Grace resumed her life as hostess of the Mission home, now at the half-way mark of the "year or so" which Mr. Sinton had asked her to stay. In anticipation of someday returning to Longchiu, she had again taken up her study of Lisu, on her own. She also finished out the Bible School she had been teaching, continued visiting in the homes, kept the household accounts, and wrote to Eric almost daily. "There are 56 letters from him tucked away in the drawer here beside me!" she told her family. The thought of him sweetened her household chores. "Yesterday I put up a lot of plum jam, & wondered, when I was doing so, if Eric would be here this winter to help eat it!"

They were planning to be married in the fall, but by August they still did not know definitely where they would be stationed, and mail was not coming through: the Japanese had bombed the railroad, and the Burma Road was impassable. Finally, a telegram from Eric arrived. It "was like an oasis in a desert," and its message was exhilarating: "Good letter, Sinton. Designation West. Wedding October."

Grace left it to Eric to find a suitable date since he was preparing for his fourth section exam in Chinese and hoped to take it before their wedding. The location would be Kunming, in the chapel of Mrs. Carson Cox, the Quaker missionary from America who had been "Aunt Vercia" to Grace since 1936. Loving hands at home were busy making a wedding gown and trousseau, but if the gown did not arrive in time, the white dress she had worn for her graduation from Moody could be a back-up. She would send for that from her things at Longchiu. And Isabel Spence, one of the three new workers who had by now become a dear friend, would be her maid of honor.

The date Eric settled on was Thursday, October 10. Consular regulations required that Grace be in Kunming three weeks before the wedding, and since the journey from Baoshan would take the better part of a week, she did not have long to wait before it was time for her and Isabel to start out. Amazingly, they made the trip in just two days, and they rode in style.

> … [A] Mr. Clayton who works for Vertannes Transport Co in Lashio [Burma] brought a convoy of eleven spanking new sedans through to Kunming from Rangoon: 1 Buick, 2 Pontiacs, & 8 Chevrolets. So he gave us free ride to Kunming in a cream colored Chevrolet. The <u>whole</u> trip, including a $5.00 tip to the chauffeur, cost me only $9.05, & my food is included in that too!
>
> We left Sat. noon [Aug. 31] & arrived here Mon. eve [Sept. 2] about 8:00. We'd travel half a day & then wait half a day for the truck carrying the 'gas' to catch up with us. The first day Isabel & I sat in the back & both were "ILL." I had him stop the car eight different times! The next two days we sat in front with the driver & fared <u>much</u> better. It was riding so fast over these mountainous roads. On a straight run he'd sometimes get up to fifty per hour, & once we timed him & for an hour according to the mile posts he averaged 40 per!

So the bride had arrived, but to her dismay, the wedding dress had not. She had hoped it was with Mr. and Mrs. Will Allen, who were returning to Yunnan from furlough, and she began sending telegrams back and forth to Shanghai, trying to locate it. Finally, she received the news, "Allens have dress, departure uncertain." So at least it was in

China, and with that encouragement she and Isabel went shopping for accessories.

But the vagaries of war kept the Allens' departure date uncertain. The same blown-out railroad bridge which made mail delivery impossible was likewise making passenger travel impossible. "...so <u>how</u> will Allens get to Kunming is the question in my mind," Grace wrote. Even if there were some other way to travel, could they possibly get to Kunming before October 10?

The dress was not the only thing missing. The wedding ring Eric had ordered months before had not come, nor had the water-color announcements Grace had commissioned from a friend in Baoshan. Even her back-up dress had not arrived from Longchiu, and Eric himself was questioning if he could get his language exam done. A stubborn head cold and nine hours of study a day were taking their toll. Grace urged him to postpone the wedding rather than jeopardize his health, but in the end it was the exam he postponed, not the wedding.

He set out on the two-day walk from Wuting ten days earlier than he had planned, and Grace met him on the way, happy to be taking along the ring, which had finally arrived.

> Isabel and I prepared some tea in a thermos & took milk & cookies & walked out about 45 min. along the Wuting road to meet him.... She went right back home as soon as we saw Eric coming. So he & I scampered up onto the bank & found a nice secluded spot among the groves & enjoyed our tea. I took the ring along.... Of course we tried it on there and found it to be a perfect fit.

It was September 24. Six days later the air raid siren sounded, and they fled the city in what was to be the first of several Japanese bombing attacks.

> The siren blew about 9:30 in the morning as a warning to get out of the city. Eric & I were in the home of Mrs. Carson Cox at the time, and as her home

is near the North Gate we made our exit from the city through the gate and waited in a big garden belonging to the British Consulate.

After waiting for nearly three hours we saw a squadron of twenty-seven bombers flying toward the city. Without lowering or changing formation they dropped their bombs and flew away quite undisturbed. … Anti-aircraft guns were firing all around us but to no avail.

The aftermath was terrible—craters more than thirty feet in diameter, and gruesome carnage. "Some people were blown over walls of compounds and picked up in pieces. Pieces of human flesh were seen sticking on the wall of the East city gate."

The next day the alarm sounded again. As it turned out, those bombs fell on a city farther down the railroad, but the peril was all too clear. If the bombers returned to Kunming and Eric and Grace had to flee permanently, when and how could they be married? If they became separated from their consuls, there could be no legal declaration of their marriage. The safest thing to do was to move their wedding date forward to Friday, October 4, just two days hence.

It was four years earlier, on October 1, 1936, that Grace had helped with the wedding of her dear friend, Irene Barberini, right there at the same Mission home in Kunming. The celebration included a surprise shower, artistic decorations, gifts arriving from various parts of China, fragrant pine needles on the walkway, and the bride wore a beautiful white dress and veil.

Now, in wartime and with just two days to plan, there could be very few of the traditional elements. The wedding cake was ready. Grace and Isabel Spence had helped "Aunt Vercia" make it two weeks earlier. Two other things were definite: the wedding would be in the evening, when there was less chance of an air raid, and, sadly, there would be no white wedding dress. The dress was still in Shanghai, with no promise of it reaching Kunming for another five or six weeks. "It was not without tears that I decided to forego the pleasure of having the beautiful dress which you dear ones so lovingly prepared for me," a disappointed Grace wrote to her family. Since her back-up dress had not arrived either, she settled on "a blue georgette from Pearl Galloway (a trade for my blue velvet when I was at Chefoo)."

Yet some things would be reminiscent of her friend's wedding. Mr. Hatton would give her away, as he had Irene. Like Irene, she would enter to the traditional wedding march. And the Rev. J. David Harrison would perform the ceremony, as he had for her friend.

At three-thirty in the afternoon, on October 4, 1940, Grace and Eric attended the Friday afternoon prayer meeting at the Mission home, where Mr. and Mrs. Eugene Crapuchettes were now in charge. At five o'clock, the bride and groom, with Isabel Spence and Eugene Crapuchettes as witnesses, went together to the British Consulate for the civil ceremony, where an American consular witness was also present. Grace wore a new dress for the occasion, "a navy blue net dress with a slip & red belt to wear if I chose." It was a gift from Mrs. Archibald Cook, wife of Eric's sea captain friend in Hong Kong. Since mail could still get through from Hong Kong, she had sent it when she learned that Grace's wedding dress from home would not arrive in time.

Grace retained her own passport and her American citizenship, but by virtue of marrying Eric, she also became a British subject and was included on his passport, a fact which crystallized her loyalties. Because of the Japanese offensive, the US State Department had forbidden women to travel to China. Consequently, if and when she returned to the United States, she might face a ban on her return, as other wives were facing. Their husbands could return, but they must wait. As fiercely loyal as she was to the USA, she determined that she would forfeit her citizenship, if necessary, to avoid that dilemma. She would travel with Eric on his passport. She belonged with him, and they both belonged in China.

Supper was at the Mission home, where a surprise greeted them which no amount of planning could have arranged. "A big home mail was waiting for us." Since they had only just set the date, no one in Iowa or England could know to congratulate them and give them their good wishes, but just the coincidence of hearing from family on this particular day was a gift in itself.

The wedding proper, the religious ceremony, was a candlelight service at seven-thirty in the evening, in the Quaker chapel. There had been little time to think of flowers, but because a Chinese couple had been married there the day before, the chapel was still adorned with "an abundance of fragrant lilies, chrysanthemums and various other flowers." Isabel Spence attended Grace as her maid of honor. There was no best man, so Eric and Mr. Harrison waited together as the bride walked to the front. The ceremony went as planned, using the Church of England service and two hymns: *Love Divine, All Loves Excelling* and *O Perfect Love.* Grace was especially pleased that one of the guests was Mr. Ridley, the Red Cross engineer whom she had helped after the truck accident he and Mr. Mitchell had suffered on the Burma Road.

The reception afterwards was in Mrs. Cox's home, with about thirty guests in attendance, an equal mix of Chinese and foreign. Mrs. Arthur Allen (Mabel), who had come to the capital for dentistry, helped Isabel serve. "We had nice sandwiches with sweet pickles, two kinds of cake besides the wedding cake and two kinds of candy—fudge and homemade marshmallows." They had music. "Some Chinese young fellows played the phonograph with a radio transmitter attachment while we ate." And an unplanned "extra" was a live performance by a violinist who had played for King George VI. She was a French woman from London, married to a Chinese, who was staying with Mrs. Cox at the time. "It was a real treat to hear her play."

Most of the wedding gifts were cash—another concession to wartime—but not all of them.

> Harrisons & Hattons gave us a beautiful Chinese set of dishes for rice & tea. A couple ladies from another mission gave us half a dozen glass sherbet dishes. Mr. & Mrs. Joyce gave us a linen tea set & the German sisters a small table cloth. Crapuchettes gave us a thermos bottle, Mrs. Arthur Allen a towel & wash-cloth & a couple of dishes. Mr. Arnold of the Y.M.C.A. gave us candles & candle holders.

Mr. and Mrs. Eric J. Cox – October 4, 1940

As the war had curtailed their wedding plans, so too it curtailed their plans for a honeymoon. Eric had hoped to take Grace to Hong Kong, especially since her furlough was being postponed for two years, but fighting in southeast China made that impossible. His second plan was to rent one of the cottages across Kunming's beautiful Lake Dian for a month, but with bombs dropping on Kunming, the owners had moved out from the city to use the cottages themselves, and none was available. Their only other option was to stay right where they were and honeymoon in the annex of the Mission home. Isabel and Mrs. Allen did their best to turn what was a common guest room into a bridal chamber, keeping it locked until Grace and Eric arrived. "They had borrowed rugs, bedspread, etc. & have everything as nice as possible, & Isabel even had glasses of milk & cookies spread on a small table for us!"

Whether by design or coincidence, the Mission home was unusually quiet. The local secretary, Eugene Crapuchettes, left after the wedding to join his wife and children in Wuting. Mrs. Allen returned home. The

Hattons remained, but were "living in the flats & have only breakfast & supper here with us," leaving Isabel as the only other guest.

It was a working honeymoon. In the absence of Mr. Crapuchettes, they helped maintain the local secretary's office: cashing checks, transmitting news reports, and generally keeping things up to date—a déjà vu for Grace, who had managed the same office in 1937, when Mr. Hatton was ill. In the absence of Mrs. Crapuchettes, the Mission home hostess, it also fell to them to provide hospitality for missionaries passing through, and Grace found that she had a chivalrous husband.

> One evening…we were just preparing for bed when David Johnson arrived from Chengkiang. Eric wouldn't listen to me getting dressed again, but he himself got out the linen & made the bed & prepared the room for David & got him some supper. In so many ways he is a jewel.

"We are enjoying ourselves immensely," Grace assured her family.

Three days into their honeymoon, the squadron of twenty-seven Japanese bombers returned, wreaking new havoc on the beleaguered city. From their place of safety between the motor road and the railroad, the newlyweds watched as the planes made their ominous approach, flying at about 7,000 feet over the south of the city, which they had ravaged a few days earlier, and coming straight for the northwest, where the Mission home was located. "For the first time fear came into my heart," Grace wrote. Then, as the planes roared directly overhead, "my heart failed me and I didn't want to watch." But Eric watched, and before long they were in the middle of it.

> There! The explosions at last. Whizz! A bullet went past us. A succession of "booms" with terrific clouds of dust…caused the earth to quiver where we were crouching about a quarter of a mile away, and we could feel the force of the concussion in a draft of air that swept over us.

Once their ruthless mission was completed, the twenty-seven "drifted peacefully away despite the barking of the anti-aircraft guns."

When the all-clear signal finally sounded, Grace and Eric made their way back into the stricken city. A crater in the road alarmed them, being perilously close to the Blind School run by the German sisters associated with the China Inland Mission, and they hurried to check. It had sustained several direct hits, and they were aghast at the destruction, yet no one had been killed or even harmed.

Only a few days before, all of the blind girls had been moved to Anning as it was almost impossible to run out of the city with them every time an alarm was given. Both of the sisters who had been staying there had gone to Anning for the week-end and knew nothing about the disaster until their return on Monday afternoon.

Grace and Eric spent the next two days helping the sisters salvage what they could from the ruins. Sister Kuningunde, the dentist who regularly cared for Grace and other missionaries, retrieved enough of her equipment to set up shop in the Slane Girls Home.

On the heels of the raid over Kunming, Eric received word that his parents' home in England had been bombed. The irony of it was profound. They had just been helping German missionaries recover from a Japanese bomb, while it was a German bomb that had destroyed Eric's home in England. "How precious the bonds that unite us in Christ!" Grace reflected. "The love of Christ and our heavenly home and citizenship is stronger than any earthly ties."

The alarm would sound two more times before their honeymoon was over. The next one began to wail just as they were finishing breakfast, leaving barely enough time for them to clear the city before enemy planes were upon them. By starting from a base in nearby Indochina, the bombers had come in record time, and to make matters worse, a sleeping sentry had failed to warn that they were on the way.

People were panic-stricken. Some huddled in gutters, others tried to hide in weeds, a nicely dressed gentleman flung himself into a pit where a rough coffin had been placed. "He lay there holding his nose and gazing up at passersby."

Despite machine guns ripping the air, Grace and Eric kept steadily on until they found a hiding place on top of a hill covered with grave mounds. From that vantage point they could see the city and surrounding plain. They witnessed the downing of a Eurasia passenger plane, which had just taken off for a place of safety, when the enemy spotted it and made it "their special target for that morning." The four men on board (two German and two Chinese) managed to escape.

Eventually the all-clear sounded, and they returned home—until next morning when again the siren sounded. But this time they were prepared. Breakfast was early and their kits were ready (reading, writing, sewing) for what could be a long wait out on the hillside. They hurried into the street with the rest of the city.

> Trucks were jammed so full of people they were too heavy and swayed from side to side, and more than one went into the ditch. Buses, private cars, motorcycles, bicycles, rickshaws, muleteers and hostlers with their litters and pedestrians of all ages and sizes. Old, old women with tiny bound feet, mothers with children on their backs, hawkers with their wares carried in baskets hanging from the end of the carrying pole on their shoulders, and beggars of all descriptions who were loathe to leave the world despite their terrible destitution.

Police were on hand, taking special notice of foreigners.

> Three times the police reprimanded me because of the color of my dress, even though I was carrying a raincoat to put on if the planes should come. ... Mr. Harrison was told that his dog barked too much! ... They didn't like for us to talk when the planes were near for fear they would hear us. One day they held the secretary of the American consul at the point of a bayonet for four

hours because he had a white suit on and they thought
he was a spy.

Amazingly, it was during this chaotic time that word of their field
designation came through. They were to live and work in Baoshan until
Eric finished his six sections of Chinese.

What a remarkable year it had been! Leaving Longchiu had not
been Grace's choice, but she could hardly now regret it. She had left as
a single woman whose existence in a tribal ministry was tenuous, given
the Mission's policy about single women working among the tribes.
Now she was returning as a married woman, blessed with a husband
who shared her love for the Lisu and her commitment to them. And
he was taller and bigger than she. Whatever would the coolies and the
diminutive Bethel Boys think!

In mid-November Eric and Grace joined Mr. and Mrs. Hatton
and their little girl, Margaret, as passengers in a convoy of seven Steel
Brothers trucks bound for Burma, on a trip fraught with more than the
usual delays. They spent one night cramped together with the driver in
the cab of the truck, waiting in vain for a gasoline truck to refill their
tank. In the morning, when help still did not come, they walked ten
miles to spend the next night at the Mission station in Dali. Finally on
their way again, they narrowly escaped a mishap on the approach to the
Lancang River gorge, which Grace described.

> Going down the mountain side of the Mekong River,
> our driver became ill with malaria. ... We noticed his
> eyes protruding, his jaw shaking & his flesh looked like
> goose flesh. Finally he lay his head back on the back of
> the seat. I grabbed the wheel thinking that a nose-dive
> into the bank would be better than a nose-dive over the
> precipice. But he roused and kept the truck going at
> normal speed until we reached the bridge.

As the Burma Road was the only motor route west, unsafe bridges
were the only way across the Lancang River. There were four: the
suspension foot bridge, which Grace and Winnie Embery had used

three years earlier; a treacherous wooden bridge, which was used for emergencies; the old Gongguo bridge, a suspension bridge that had been bombed and repaired; and the new Gongguo bridge, made with steel girders, which was still under construction (Montsma, "Bridges"). The latter was preferable, but since it was passable only at certain times, they headed for the old Gongguo bridge, only to find that a disabled truck was blocking the farther end. It was now dusk, and their driver confirmed their fears: they would have to wait until morning. They walked across the bridge, past the disabled truck, hoping to find a place to stay in the village on the other side. Instead, they found the village had been obliterated by bombs, and the sentry, seeing they were foreigners, ordered them to clear out.

Their only choice was to return to the truck, where they found their malaria-stricken driver stretched out on the front seat. In spite of the aspirin and quinine which Eric and Mr. Hatton had administered earlier, he was in no condition to move, much less oblige the sentry who was ordering him to move the truck. When it became apparent that the truck lights were not working, the sentry relented, and the four stranded missionaries stood in the road and prayed. In particular, they asked that the other trucks in the convoy not pass them by, assuming they had gone on. Then, having cast their cares on God, they prepared to spend the night. Grace pinned her watch and new wedding ring inside the neck of her clothes, in case of marauding bandits, and Eric cleared a place on top of some boxes in the back of the truck where they could lie down. But it wasn't long before their desperate prayer was answered. The rest of the Steel Brothers convoy came by and stopped, and the four thanked God and took heart.

Next morning, when attempts to move the disabled truck proved futile, the bridge engineer directed them to return and cross at the new Gongguo bridge, and do it quickly. It was twenty minutes after seven, and because the bridge was still under construction, trucks would be prohibited from nine o'clock in the morning to three o'clock in the afternoon. The bridge area was a prime target for Japanese bombers, but in daylight they could see that the damage was not as extensive as it might have been. "The deep gorge of the river & the high mountains surrounding make bombing very difficult & the Japs have dropped hundreds of bombs to do the little damage that they have," Eric observed, as they made their way across the uncompleted bridge.

Back on the road, with the river behind them and Baoshan not far beyond, the fuel pump broke. After an hour or two of waiting for it to be repaired, Grace and Mrs. Hatton with little Margaret boarded another truck. The men eventually followed in the disabled truck, but only as long as the head driver sat on the front mudguard and poured gasoline into the carburetor to keep the engine running!

Chapter 26

At Home, but Not Alone

Since the war had played havoc with their wedding plans and sabotaged their honeymoon, the newlyweds, in search of some privacy, asked their superintendent, John Kuhn, if they could be in quarters of their own for at least their first year. He was sympathetic and seemed hopeful, but in the end, the only position was as temporary host and hostess in the Baoshan Mission home, a role all too familiar to Grace. Their home would be the two small rooms over the chapel, accessible by means of a ladder. The number of guests at the Mission home varied, but even if only one was in residence, Grace and Eric were obliged to host that person for meals. Not surprisingly, they cherished the times when they could "have a bite to eat up here in our own little room, just the two of us."

As for the rooms, they were "scarcely bigger than a ship's cabin," Eric wrote, and "without all the convenient furniture of a cabin." One room they made into their bedroom, where Grace was glad to stay put for a day after their grueling six-day journey from Kunming, and Eric arranged the other to be a study and sitting room. "He is good," Grace wrote home appreciatively. "It is not much to look at but we have our own things in it & to us it is home." She ventured to use the embroidered dish towels her mother had given her. "I never put them out to be used [before] because I knew they'd soon be gray. But Eric & I use them up here to dry our cups when we have tea etc. & enjoy using them & seeing them hang on the wire in our room." Another item she could now utilize was her father's big "Husband" cup.

They hadn't been in their first home a full week before their hospitality skills were put to the test. Eight travelers arrived one day and five more the next, all with their luggage and two with "three tons of stuff between them" (literature, foodstuffs, and other supplies for remote mountain living). However, one piece of luggage had Grace's name on it. It was her wedding dress and trousseau, carefully packed in a lightweight, tin-covered suitcase, carried through Burma by fellow-missionary, Allyn Cooke. "We both had pangs of regret as we pulled out one lovely thing after another, and remembered the love and thoughtfulness and time and labor that went into it," Grace wrote. But her regret was not for themselves. "We felt most sorry for those at home."

Remarkably, almost everything fit. The simple, two-layered white dress needed to be taken in at the waist and the veil needed to be enlarged, but the undergarments, the white shoes ("good old Selby's arch preservers") and stockings fit, and even the white kid gloves. "Where did you ever find a size to fit me?" Grace marveled. There were silk nightwear and a kimono, toiletries, and a going-away dress made of "greeny-blue silk, with tiny white stars figured on it," which she took as a reminder not to forget the Stars and Stripes!

On the day it all arrived, she wore the going away dress to afternoon tea. "John & Isobel Kuhn, Mr. Cooke & Mr. Willis of the Christian Book Room in Shanghai were there & also Orville Carlson. They clapped their hands and made fitting remarks," she wrote her family. Later, as promised, she and Eric engaged a photographer to come and take "wedding pictures" in the garden of the Mission home.

As a new homemaker, Grace was now missing the things she had left in Longchiu. Perhaps she had not had the heart to bring them when she first came to Baoshan, but now, happily married and in her own little space, she missed them. Would they still be usable? After all, the house had been vacant for the eight months since Fitz had died and Jennie had gone to Chefoo (March 1940).

On December 1, Grace and Eric celebrated her thirty-fourth birthday by asking Superintendent John Kuhn for permission to visit

Longchiu. Permission granted, they set out the next day in the back of a truck going west, taking with them the tombstone for Mr. Fitzwilliam's grave, which Grace had designed and commissioned from a stone mason in Baoshan. Eric estimated it weighed "at least 3 hundredweight" (336 pounds).

They crossed the Nujiang River on the Huitong Bridge (Montsma, "Bridges"), spent the night in Longling with Kathleen (née Davies) & Gilbert Moore, and traveled on to Chefang, where they spent the next night "on the floor in an empty room of a compound belonging to the Rockefeller Foundation for Malarial Research," because they could find no coolies going up to Longchiu.

The following day they pushed on to Longchiu, wading across two streams on their way. When they reached the second stream, "Eric carried me across on his back!" Grace reported delightedly in her letter home. They met a number of Lisu coming down to market and arranged for them to bring the luggage they had left at Chefang—all but the tombstone. That remained for another day (actually two days), when eight Lisu and Kachin carried it to the hilltop where Mr. Fitzwilliam had been buried. Normally it would have been a three-hour climb.

Grace had designed the stone to bear his name in English, Lisu and Kachin, with a Scripture text in each language. It was good they had come when they did, as the site would soon have been obscured by undergrowth on the hill. Nearby Grace noticed another grave. Big Fish's wife, Phoebe, and their little three-year-old boy, Luke, had both died since Grace was there.

It was a solemn task to oversee the placement of yet another fallen comrade's stone. Just two years earlier Grace had done the same thing for J. O. Fraser. Now, with Mr. Fitzwilliam's death, the western Yunnan field was bereft of not just two, but four workers, since the widows were at Chefoo indefinitely. No one was left to undertake the large Kachin field, and Grace wondered if the Coxes would be designated there. "I love the Lisu," she wrote, "but Eric and I both feel that the greater need is among the Kachin."

She had three brief days to spend among her Lisu friends, introducing Eric and sharing meals in their homes. They had a meal with Big Fish and his infant son, whom he was raising on cow's milk from a bottle.

They had a meal with Aaron, and another with Gideon, and then at last came the opportunity they had craved—to be alone by themselves.

> We had ever so much fun finding my things & "showing" & explaining them. Eric had his little primus stove with him so we could without difficulty make us a cup of tea & boil us some eggs. It was a real tonic just to be there alone with Eric for the first time since we were married. He had a small tin of cheese & a tin of sardines left over from the stores he brought from Shanghai & we had those for a treat.

They packed up Grace's belongings in three trunks and several small boxes, and began the hazardous trip back to Baoshan. Once down the mountain, the next step was to wait in Chefang for a truck with enough room for them and their baggage. To their delight, the one that came not only had enough room, but room for them to sit in the cab, where they would suffer less motion sickness on the steep and winding mountain road. They themselves suffered no mishap, but within twenty-seven miles they witnessed no fewer than six other trucks that had come to ruin. "Two trucks had four wheels in the air & two were on their noses. One had plunged from one meander to the next & its engine & hood were smashed to bits."

They reached home by evening of the second day, grateful to get into clean clothes and a clean bed. And, being mistress of the Mission home, Grace informed the cook that they would have breakfast in bed at eight o'clock the next morning. Much to her surprise, Eric did not demur. "We just had ever so much fun reading the umpteen home letters…and devouring the lovely snaps [of nieces and nephews]."

To celebrate their first Christmas they had their own tree, decorated with "icicles" of red, green and silver paper, and two pieces of tinsel that had been around the mirror of their "bridal suite" in Kunming. Three single ladies joined them for Christmas dinner, featuring roast rooster, and for dessert Grace favored Eric with three plum puddings and two fruit cakes. "First I made in my life," she acknowledged, "but they weren't too bad."

Shortly after the dawn of the new year, 1941, they were plunged again into the cat-and-mouse existence of a war zone. The peace of their little living quarters was shattered by the familiar wail of air raid sirens, and the ominous roar of airplane engines in the distance. Nine Japanese bombers were on their way to Baoshan and within minutes were raining death on the city. With no time to flee, they took refuge in the back garden, where they would be free of buildings. "As soon as we heard the air sizzle we prostrated ourselves on the ground & both listened to & felt the explosions that followed." It was a terrible déjà vu as they walked through the city afterwards. The devastation in Kunming had not inured them to the sickening sight, once again, of demolished buildings, clouds of dust, dismembered corpses, and families left bereft as the bombers callously flew away.

After that initial raid they made a dugout where they and the single ladies could sit and wait for the planes to pass, as they usually did, en route to the Gongguo bridges. "The dugout is a protection from shrapnel and flying debris only," Grace explained. "It would be no good at all in case of a direct hit."

Three months later they nearly did receive a direct hit. Three planes dropped a succession of bombs along the north wall of the city, where the Mission home was located. Grace had just lain down for a rest, but quickly jumped up and ran to the dugout.

> Three of us were inside but Eric stood at the opening peering up at them and keeping us posted as to their progress. When they were directly overhead he thought he heard a whistle so ducked inside. He was no more than seated than the bombs began to burst. We waited. In about two minutes it was all over. Before leaving the dug-out, Eric led us in prayer thanking the Lord for protecting us.
>
> When we came out the air was full of dust and the smell of gunpowder was strong. Some of the window casings [of the house] were blown out of alignment but none of the panes were broken. A door was blown down, and several pictures were on the floor. Our rooms

were filthy with the dust which had been shaken down. But we were just very, very grateful that it was no worse. Fortunately the bombs were all small ones or our rooms would have suffered badly from concussion. Eric helped me clean our rooms, then with the use of a hammer and some nails he soon had things righted.

Others had not fared as well. When they went for a walk to see what damage had been done, they found that two houses in their neighborhood had been demolished, and at least twenty people had been killed.

Chapter 27

A Momentous Year

They were to be in Baoshan for five months, and Grace was glad for the end date. Though she and Eric made a good team—she with her thoughtfulness and care, he with his physical strength and ingenuity, and both with a willing and gracious spirit—Grace found it wearing and stressful to keep house for a large, ever-changing household.

Yet there were advantages. For one thing, she was there when her dear friends, Mr. and Mrs. Bosshardt, came through en route to their old province of Guizhou. She also met new friends, particularly Miss Mabel Soltau, who "is just gold itself, so sensible & sane."

In addition, she and Eric took it as no coincidence that two other guests, Dr. Jessie McDonald and Dr. (Miss) Powell, were medical personnel who had come to Baoshan to establish a hospital. Early in the new year, Grace and Eric had discovered that they were to be parents, and Grace had questions by the time the "medicals" arrived. How convenient to have them living right in the Mission home!

Not surprisingly, the five-month assignment stretched into a year. About the time the five months were up, four new men recruits had managed to come through from England, despite war conditions, and a telegram from Mission headquarters arrived, asking Eric to meet them in Rangoon, Burma, and escort them back to Baoshan. It would be a round trip of four or five weeks, which Grace fully intended to make with him. After all, she was no stranger to rough travel, and she was still early in her pregnancy. But the Mission directors discouraged it, and the doctors advised against it, partly because of the insufferable heat in Rangoon at that time of the year. So they were facing their first separation.

Eric, conscious of young people being asked to leave loved ones behind to fight for England, reasoned that he and Grace "ought to be more than willing to do it in the Lord's service." Grace might have agreed with her mind, but her heart was not so easily mollified. Tears came easily and often for a while. Yet, there was an upside. "It will be a fine opportunity for him to get a lot of things [in Burma] which we need, & also which the hospital needs," she explained bravely.

Once the parting had taken place, she could count off the days until Eric's return—just two days short of five weeks—and she could write letters. "I wrote to Eric every day he was gone with only one or two exceptions," she told her family. And Eric kept pace with her. "Just for fun I counted the number of pages this size [8½ x 11] that Eric wrote to me while he was gone & there were only eighty!!"

She was still mistress of the Mission home, so there were housekeeping chores to tend to, tomato plants to coax along, and preserves to put up. (She wished she had ordered more jars from Shanghai when she could.) She contracted with a Chinese tailor to make Eric a new pair of khaki trousers as a surprise, and she herself made new curtains for their bedroom. On Sundays she taught the adult Sunday school class, and during the week, if it wasn't raining, she walked two or three miles to outlying villages to teach and encourage the Christians living there.

So the days went by. Eric heard rumors that Baoshan had been bombed, but had no way of verifying it, and Grace could not know that his trip home was taking longer than it should have because of heavy rains, bad roads and customs delays. As the time drew near for him to return, she found herself "constantly on the 'qui vive' at night, listening at the gate, & during the day [glancing] out every time the gate squeaked."

Finally it happened. She had just returned from a walk with Dorothy Burrows and Miss Chiao and had gone upstairs when she heard the familiar squeak of the gate, looked out, and saw Eric coming through it alone. "I dashed down the stairs—I guess my feet touched the steps—unhooked the gate into the outer courtyard & met him there quite free from the curious gaze of any," she wrote. Eric completed the picture: "Grace…was in my arms before I had crossed the courtyard…and we talked half the night."

As she heard of the reverses and setbacks and difficulties he had endured, she could only be thankful and recognize her heavenly Father's care. "In so many ways, both in small things & big, our Lord very definitely undertook for Eric during his absence."

Among the things he brought home was material for three maternity dresses and items for a layette, all of which they had ordered ready-made weeks earlier from Shanghai, but now could not receive in time because of the war. There was "flannelette, some silk & cotton material, rubber sheeting, diaper material (gauze for inside nappies), mosquito net on a folding framework, some bibs, white wool & thread…." And he brought a piece to repair Jennie Fitzwilliam's sewing machine, which they had retrieved from the house in Longchiu. Unfortunately, the repair did not work.

The account of how they "set to, to make the little garments ourselves," is a testament to the thrift, ingenuity and resourcefulness of missionaries stationed in that remote area. Grace, not being a seamstress or a knitter, found the prospect daunting. "But just taking my time & having someone to help & another someone to admire & express his delight over a tiny finished garment has deflected, as it were, any nervous strain, & I really enjoy it."

- There was no table to work on, so Eric made one by stretching two planks across the space between their two desks.
- They had no pattern for baby clothes, so they used an older child's size and cut it down. They had no "practice material," so Grace surrendered one of her old dresses.
- Dorothy Burrows undertook to teach both Grace and Eric how to knit, "and we are each working on a little inside vest."
- Blankets would be relatively simple to make, but out of what? Eric contributed an old white sweater, which Miss Soltau unraveled and knit into a blanket trimmed with blue, and Dorothy Burrows made one out of some heavy brown material she had on hand.

- Grace removed the down from a cushion to make a "tiny pillow," turning some of Eric's old white shirts and pajamas into pillow cases.

- The sewing machine was broken, but a student at the Bible School who needed work came in her spare time to do long seams and hemming, while Miss Soltau hemmed most of the thirty gauze diaper liners.

- They had no outing flannel for the diapers themselves but, unexpectedly, a package arrived from Grace's friend, Kathleen Moore, containing enough for at least twelve diapers, plus "several pairs of little wool socks old & new, a little knit wool dress of greenish blue & several other knit garments & wool garments."

- Then, just in time for Grace to make herself a second maternity dress, Eric fixed the sewing machine by using a bottle top, a spirit lamp, and induced rust. "The casting that clamped the needle rod to the crank was broken and there was no means of gripping the two together. I finally fixed it by inserting a piece of thin sheet lead from a bottle top between the rod and the casting and then fusing it in with a spirit lamp. To make it more sure, I poured water on, hoping that it would seep down in the crevice and in process of time rust the two together!!! [It worked, and] in the course of a day or two Grace had another very nice dress to wear."

- It is doubtful they had a dresser for their own things, let alone anything for the baby's, but Grace saw the potential in an old basket of Eric's. "It is nothing in itself," he wrote, "and a number of times I nearly threw it away. But Grace has lined it with pretty blue material and made little cardboard pockets in it... and covered them with the same material." Watching her labor over the basket and the layette reminded him of Freckles, the orphan boy in Gene Stratton Porter's novel by that name, who yearned for proof that his mother loved him. "Our little baby, please God, won't need any proof, but if he does, it will be there for him," he declared.

- They had nothing for the baby to sleep in, probably not even a dresser drawer, but Grace's dear friend, Miss Chiao, presented them with a cradle. She "had it made for us and then wouldn't let us pay for it, and said that she was giving it to the baby to have the right to be called 'Auntie.'... It has a big soft mattress of Kapok which grows in Yunnan...."

So it was that he who clothes the lilies of the field provided for Grace and Eric's babe in the hinterlands of China. And it would not be the last time.

As Grace's pregnancy advanced, Eric was concerned that she be on the ground floor, not climbing a ladder to their little rooms above the chapel. Consequently, they moved into the "main house," into what Eric described as "the nicest bedroom I've seen in Yunnan."

But where would the baby be born? Unable to secure suitable premises for a hospital in Baoshan, Dr. McDonald and Dr. Powell, with Miss Soltau, had removed to Dali at the end of August. Grace and Eric had expected to go with them, although it would mean Grace bumping and lurching along the Burma Road in her eighth month. Then they again saw their heavenly Father's intervention. Just days before the staff left, Dr. and Mrs. John Jeffrey—he a medical doctor and she a nurse—arrived back from furlough. They had expected to go to Dali with the other medical personnel, but the Mission home in Dali was full, Mrs. Jeffrey was ill, and they were compelled to remain in Baoshan, along with Eric and Grace. "We did enjoy having them here," Eric wrote. "He is a quiet and very humorous Scotsman, and she a very vivacious American from New England." A quiet Scotsman with a good sense of humor suited Grace fine. And as an added boon, Leita Partridge, her dear friend and "a splendid nurse," came from Longling to care for her.

Their first baby, Miriam Grace, arrived early in the evening of October 2, 1941, weighing seven pounds and measuring twenty-one inches. "She is a dear little pet, & we never tire watching her," Grace wrote. As for herself, Dr. Jeffrey prescribed the customary fourteen days of bed rest, and Eric was glad. She was "dreadfully tired and washed out" before her confinement, which he attributed to "housekeeping for such a big household," and then "the birth took a lot out of her." By the end of the two weeks little Miriam had regained her birth weight plus another half-pound, and Grace was receiving visitors, and writing home, though she could never be sure the letters would arrive. When news came that the Japanese had captured Hong Kong and bombed Pearl Harbor, she despaired of writing any more. "Perhaps it is for a similar reason that we have had [no news] from you," she mused. Almost a year later she would write, "Our little Miriam was born on Oct. 2nd. We have not yet heard that you received the news."

After being up and around for a period of time, Grace suffered a "slight hemorrhage." Dr. and Mrs. Jeffrey had gone on to Dali, but nurse Leita Partridge was still with Grace and recommended another ten days of bed rest, though she herself had to leave before the ten days were up. When Dr. Jeffrey heard about it, he was ready to return to Baoshan and care for Grace himself. But Dr. McDonald was in charge, and she could not see the point. What help could he be? she reasoned. Grace would have to go to a hospital.

But where? wondered Eric. Dali was not yet prepared for inpatients, and to go to Burma would be prohibitive. "...we should be spending about ten times more per day there than we are here, and here we can barely make ends meet," he explained in a letter to his mother.

Gradually Grace did recover, in time for another trip on the Burma Road. She and Eric were finally going to leave Baoshan and take up the work in Longling, where Gilbert and Kathleen Moore had been until they left for furlough, and where Leita Partridge now waited to welcome them.

It had been one momentous year since they had limped into Baoshan with the driver of their truck pouring gasoline into the carburetor to keep the engine running, but it would pale in comparison to the next year.

Chapter 28

What Time I Am Afraid

Longling was located seventy-five miles west and south of Baoshan, along the Burma Road and beyond the Nujiang River with its formidable 13,000 foot gorge. If Baoshan was remote, Longling would be even more so. Eric and Grace would have to think in advance of everything they would need—canned goods, preserves, flour, sugar, medicines, gasoline, disinfectant, clothing, books, personal belongings, the cradle, and the little hanging chair which Dr. Jeffrey had made for Miriam—about a ton and a quarter of goods in all. "It took me about ten days to get packed up," Eric wrote. After packing the breakables in straw, he fit everything into forty wooden cases, nailed them shut and bound them with metal strapping.

They had been praying for some time about how they would travel and who would take them. It would have to be a truck, and because they had been praying, Eric was not surprised when he "happened" to meet an official with Watson & Sons, a truck firm in Burma, whom he knew. The result was that they were given "a free pass to use one of Watsons trucks to take ourselves and our goods to Lungling," he wrote, and that included a tip for the Burmese driver, despite the fact that he put them all at terrible risk.

> We left Paoshan on Monday Dec. 15th. ... I sat next to the driver and Grace next to the door and we had a pillow on our knee and little Miriam lay on that.

We thought she mightn't like the new experiences, but on the contrary she seemed to enjoy them and was wonderfully good. We had to keep a handkerchief over her face most of the time because of the awful dust but she didn't mind it too much. She slept a good deal of the time....

We had one very nerve-racking experience, which gave us to know that the Lord had indeed given His angels charge over us. We were beginning the descent to the Salween River, which was a thousand or more feet below us, and on rather a steep stretch of road the driver let the truck gather too much speed. We came to a very bad piece of road and the truck started to bounce and I was so concerned to keep Miriam on our laps and not have her jumped up to the ceiling of the cab, that I didn't see what happened in the next second or two. But suddenly I was conscious of the driver reaching frantically for the handbrake, and looked up to see that the truck had swerved on the road and we were heading for the precipice edge. Even as I looked the brakes had pulled the truck up, but only just in time, for the front wheel was only a foot or so from the edge. [It gave] the driver an awful scare, and the perspiration just stood out on his face. ... Evidently when the truck bounced he lost control of the wheel, and the truck swerved before he knew what was happening.

Crossing the Huitong Bridge over the Nujiang was typically halting and slow, but just before midnight they finally reached Longling, tired, hungry, cold, and very ready for Leita's warm welcome.

Conditions were primitive compared to their quarters in Baoshan, "as primitive as they were in England in the middle ages," Eric told his mother. But the church was thriving: self-supporting, self-propagating, and eager to learn. It concerned them that the members were all women, but men were attending services, and the women prayed earnestly for their husbands to believe. Each week there were cottage meetings, a prayer meeting, visits to homes or the jail, a Bible class, and the regular meetings on Sunday. Eric and Grace reveled in it because there was "far more opportunity of active Christian work than we had in Baoshan." Eric had caught up to Grace in his study of Chinese, so he, too, was working on the fifth section, hoping that by the fall he might begin a tribal language.

They still wondered which tribal language it would be. Grace had resumed studying Lisu, but with the Fitzwilliams gone, no one was learning Kachin. The Coxes would be the obvious ones to take it up, though Kachin bore no resemblance to Lisu. "I don't know why the Lord gave me those nine months with the Lisu," Grace mused, "but perhaps His purpose, all unknown to anyone, was accomplished in that time."

In February 1942 they took to the Burma Road again, this time traveling 500 miles to Kunming and back. On the way they attended a field conference in Dali, where Grace also visited the new CIM hospital, and received assurance that all was well. After the conference, it was 165 miles farther east to Kunming, for dentistry. Eric had worn dentures since his early days at sea, but Grace was dependent on the good services of Sister Kuningunde, the one dentist available in that remote area.

After they returned to Longling, Eric embarked on two trips with Fred Hatton to visit outlying districts. The first was to check on believers in Longchiu, left on their own for a year since Mr. Fitzwilliam had died and Jennie had gone to Chefoo. Eric had last climbed that hill at the time of Grace's birthday in 1940, almost eighteen months earlier. Now he and Mr. Hatton found the path blocked with felled trees and the village stockaded. It was the work of the Kachin, desperate to save their opium crop.

The Chinese government had outlawed the growing of opium, but the Kachin had resolutely planted their crop anyway. When Chinese soldiers were sent to dig up the plants, the Kachin blocked the path, then fought them as they commenced to dig. The soldiers retaliated by burning the entire village, including the church. The house where Grace had lived with the Fitzwilliams had been stripped.

Eric's second trip was to visit Chinese villages near the Lisu village of Muchengpo. "The coming week is going to be long—oh, so long,"

Grace wrote to him. "And I wonder if you'll come by noon, or will it be later in the day." She was expecting him on Saturday, May 2, but the week of waiting was fraught with distress.

It began on Saturday, April 25, when she and Leita were called on to attend three different members of the church who were suddenly near death, one of stab wounds, and two others of a sudden illness. "We began to wonder if some plague had broken out in the city," Grace wrote.

A few days later, a young telegraph operator, a Christian, brought the ominous news that in Burma, Lashio had fallen to the Japanese, bringing the dreaded invaders within 150 miles of Longling.

Grace wondered if Eric knew. She had no way to reach him, and no one to send to look for him. He was to return to preach on baptism on May 3, then have baptisms through the week, before the rains began. But where was he now?

About midnight "an awful wailing began," indicating that someone had died. It was the young man next door, who had succumbed to a bronchial ailment.

As the strain of the long day took its toll, both Grace and Leita suffered what would become all too familiar in the days ahead—nausea. But by the next morning, Sunday, April 26, the situation had eased. The two women who had suddenly been taken ill were better, and one even came to church. Since Eric was away, Grace took the service "and it did me good, as it took my mind right off everything else and the nausea left me, so that I really enjoyed dinner." But not for long. It returned that evening and through the week. "[We] couldn't even enjoy a cup of hot tea."

They began to pack. If the Japanese had taken Lashio, it would be just a matter of days before they reached Longling, prompting Grace to see a hidden hand behind their scheduling of the baptisms. "...this was God's way of getting Eric home in time. But for this arrangement he would probably have stayed out longer."

For her part, Leita began to question the wisdom of packing anything. She had been reading the account of Paul's shipwreck in Acts 27 and was stunned by verse 22: *But now I urge you to keep up your courage, because not one of you will be lost; only the ship will be destroyed.*

It seemed such a clear forewarning of what was to come that she told Grace she didn't see any point in packing. Grace did not demur, except to observe that it was not beyond the devil to use Scripture. In her mind it was better to keep packing, to take what they could, "and if we lose it—it won't matter." As it turned out, Leita was right. They needn't have bothered packing at all. But not knowing that, they continued, always with an eye on the calendar. Eric was due home on Saturday, May 2.

"On Friday evening I was sitting in the bedroom feeding Miriam when I heard Eric's voice! A day early! Was I glad?!!"

As Grace expected, he was unaware of the Japanese advance, but he had begun to wonder what was happening when he saw crowds heading into the hills. Then, when he stopped in Mangshi (Mangshih) at the home of their missionary friends, the Foggins, he found it boarded up. That was enough to make him very accepting of the ride offered by two men from the American Volunteer Group (AVG), thus getting him home a day earlier than he had planned.

The AVG was a group whose presence they would welcome often in the coming days. They had first met them in Baoshan in the person of Mr. Miller, a radio operator who kept them informed of news from the outside, such as the Japanese attack on Pearl Harbor the previous December. As its name indicates, they were a group of volunteer flyers and support personnel that came together before the US declared war on Japan. Eric described them to his mother as "a regiment of several hundred American aviators and ground personnel formed...to assist China in her war against Japan.... They have been doing good work down in Rangoon, fighting the Jap raiders, and the accounts of their exploits read like those of the RAF over England in the Autumn of 1940." In time they would become known as the Flying Tigers for the ferocious teeth painted on the cowling of their P-40 fighter planes.

The Royal Air Force (RAF) was also a welcome presence in Yunnan, along with the American Technical Group (ATG), mechanics who had been recruited to help China with truck repair stations along the Burma Road. Still another outside military unit in the area was the China Commando Group (CCG), formed in the summer of 1941 as a joint project of Britain's Special Operations Executive (SOE) and the Chinese government.

It was from the AVG men that Eric learned that Lashio had fallen, and that the airport at Mangshi, on the other side of the Burma Road from Longling, was even then being evacuated. Grace invited the men to stay for supper, and in further conversation they learned a piece of good news: bridges had been blown up between Lashio and Longling, meaning the Japanese advance would be hampered considerably. The men estimated it might take them thirty days to reach Longling.

Eric sent a telegram to Mission officials asking for advice, though there was little hope of an answer before they would be compelled to leave. Mission headquarters had been temporarily moved from Shanghai to Chongqing (Chungking) in Sichuan province, putting them that much closer, but communication was still unreliable at best. Realizing they were on their own, they decided to leave as soon as possible and head for Muchengpo, the Lisu station higher in the mountains. But they had no means of transportation. With everyone else preparing to flee, no more horses were available for hire.

The day after Eric arrived was Saturday, May 2, the last day they would have any sense of normalcy. He updated monthly accounts, and they started sorting through their belongings. But at prayer meeting that evening the telegraph operator had alarming news—"the Japs had already crossed the two rivers which our AVG friends had assured us would hold them up for three weeks."

Sunday was anything but a day of rest. Eric went out on the street to see what he could learn, only to find an RAF man attempting to ease a terrible traffic jam on the Burma Road with his tommy gun. "Get out as soon as possible," he told Eric, suggesting they might find a ride with the RAF convoy that was coming through that day, *if* they could limit themselves to a bedding roll and one suitcase apiece.

"The town seemed mad," Grace wrote. "The very atmosphere was panic. Sometimes it seemed the strain was too much to bear, and I'd ask Eric just to hold me a bit. It helped a lot to weep a little."

Grace and Leita took a break from packing to go onto the street and look for the RAF trucks, but they found none. They did notice a line of Jeeps in front of a hotel, and discovered they belonged to the American Technical Group. As Grace and Leita explained their plight, two of the men, including the leader, Mr. Bowman, returned home with them to see what they had. After looking it over, Mr. Bowman assured them they had a truck that could take everything they really wanted, and they wouldn't need to leave for two or three days.

"We were full of praise to God for this marvelous provision for our needs," Grace wrote, "and perhaps more for the clear guidance that the offer provided, for before this we had been very undecided whether we ought to venture on the motor road since the congestion was so terrible and the panic so intense."

Eric had planned to hold morning worship as usual, but those who came arrived early, before he and Grace could break free from the chaos of events to meet with them. A Chinese refugee pastor from Rangoon had come by, asking if he and his family could take shelter there for a day or two, "and we readily consented." But by the time that was settled, they discovered to their chagrin that the Christians who had come early for worship had returned home, so they could have no service at all. "We were very sorry, feeling that we hadn't put first things first."

With the prospect of taking more of their belongings, they began to repack. Delightedly Grace included the "Merrill book" she had been keeping as a surprise for her sister Flora. There would be room for all the letters she and Eric had written to each other, and her Bilhorn folding organ, and the suitcase with her wedding dress and trousseau in it. They took all their provisions, grocery and medical, not knowing if or when they would return, and such supplies were fast becoming irreplaceable. The price of powdered milk had inflated to two hundred dollars per pound, so they took all thirty-seven pounds of that, and a case of condensed milk which George Soderbom of the China Commando Group had given to Miriam. They took some of Grace's homemade preserves, giving the rest to the ATG men. Other foodstuffs (flour, sugar, lard, salt) they gave to the Chinese staff officers who visited that afternoon to ask if they could have the use of the house after the missionaries had gone. "We were glad to [oblige], feeling that it was much better to have officers there than soldiers, who would probably start to loot as soon as we left." They took a trunk full of clothing and bedding. Things they couldn't take—extra bedding, dishes, curtains, pictures—they packed away in Leita's rooms, which were easier to lock. With hindsight, Grace realized the futility of having done any of that. "But we didn't realize it then, and it was awfully difficult for us to reconcile ourselves to leaving even half our stuff behind, still less to losing it."

"While we packed, little Miriam sat in the hanging chair that Dr. Jeffrey made for her. It hung from the porch ceiling and she sat in it for nearly two hours watching all the hustle and bustle and having the time of her life. Later we packed the chair to take with us."

Mr. Bowman returned in the afternoon, bringing with him the driver of their truck, Mr. Bartley, but also the unwelcome news that the situation had grown more urgent. They must be ready to leave at daybreak the next day.

They were ready by dark that evening, except for things they would load on the truck in the morning: a folding spring bed, Miriam's little folding bed-box, a small pressure stove, and a few personal things. But sleep was hard won.

> ...though we were tired out we couldn't sleep. That awful nausea!! Then too, we could hear tanks and tractors going along the motor road, it seemed, all night long. And the awful thought was constantly at hand, 'Suppose the Jap tanks should suddenly come rumbling along too.' It seemed a foolish thought, and one to reprove oneself for, but actually the enemy tanks were much nearer than our worst fears supposed.

Finally they gave up trying to sleep. It was Monday, May 4.

> We got up soon after three, whilst it was still pitch dark and very foggy.... The old servant woman we had had for about six weeks prepared tea and porridge for us. For Miriam's sake I forced the porridge down, but retched with every bite. Leita felt the same. Eric said he would begin taking the things to the truck, and then finish his porridge. Some days later he told me it was because he was having difficulty in swallowing too!!

The poor servant couldn't take it in that we were leaving so much stuff behind. We gave her the rice we had gotten in for the month…and a big piece of salt, and Leita gave her a length of material. To her it was too good to be true. We told her that she mustn't stay after we left, but must go to her home, a town some distance away and off the motor road. She said when we came back we must let her know and she would come and help us again.

Eric carried most of the things himself, Chinese fashion, using a pole with a load on each end. It worked well until the last trip. It was an awkward load, with the folding spring bed on one end and the little folding bed-box on the other, packed with flour, cornmeal, and two bottles of kerosene for the pressure stove. As he set it down beside the truck, one of the kerosene bottles broke and ruined the flour! "We thought we could make ourselves cornmeal porridge along the road, using the little stove, but it was not to be."

Their Christian friends were leaving too, traveling on foot and taking only what they could carry to the hills, but all—missionaries and Chinese alike—were coming to the grim realization that when they returned, their homes would be gone.

As day began to dawn, "we stood together in the courtyard whilst Eric prayed, thanking the Lord for the happy home He had given us there and praying that in due time He would lead us back." Knowing firsthand the treacheries of the road even in peacetime, they took as their watchword, "What time I am afraid, O Lord, I will trust in Thee" (Psalm 56:3 KJV). They also agreed they would not be separated, however expedient it might appear. Then, leaving the house to the refugee pastor and the Chinese staff officers, they joined the congestion on the Burma Road. Eric climbed into the back of the truck. Leita and Grace, with seven-month-old Miriam, sat in front, with Mr. Bartley driving.

Later that same day Longling was indeed bombed, and occupied by the Japanese.

Chapter 29

Grace on the Burma Road

Historians would be careful to document and analyze the Japanese march up the Burma Road into Yunnan, and the Chinese would erect a memorial at the point where the Japanese were stopped, but when Grace sat down to describe it in a letter for her family, she was careful to record not only their experience as refugees, but the grace of God to them in their desperate plight.

The road near Lungling, and, indeed, near all the cities along the road, seemed just a bottle-neck, and the jam of trucks, all packed to, and beyond, capacity with pitiable refugees from Burma and the cities down the road, was quite indescribable. Many of the trucks had been parked alongside the road for some of the hours of darkness, and as the refugees daren't leave for fear of losing place, they had in most cases just had to stand there all night with perhaps only an umbrella to keep the rain and fog off them. This kind of suffering became a quite common sight to us as we went along, and in fact suffering abounded in every form, until it almost ceased to impress us. It seemed that anything that stirred up compassion in my heart also stirred up nausea. I'd look at these poor people and then a wave of nausea would sweep over me.

Before traveling very far, it was necessary to rearrange the seating. With three in the cab, Mr. Bartley was having difficulty changing gears, so he asked Leita to transfer to one of the ATG Jeeps, which she and Grace had seen parked on the street in Longling. Eric could have done the same. He was "yellow with dust" from riding in the back of the truck, but remembering their agreement not to separate, he declined. "We had prayed much that we mightn't get separated, and it was of the Lord that he didn't change to the Jeep," Grace wrote, realizing later how grim her situation would have been without him.

Travel was painfully slow (two and one-half miles in three hours), but eventually the congestion eased and by noon they had reached Lameng, the stopping place mid-way between Longling and the Nujiang River. Much to their delight, they met up with Leita. They purchased something to eat and had lunch together, but that would be the last food they would find for sale for two weeks.

The long and winding descent into the Nujiang River gorge brought them to the Huitong Bridge at six o'clock that evening. "We praised God from our hearts when we were across the bridge and had the comfort of feeling that we had the Salween River between us and the Japs." Baoshan was fifty-six miles away. If only they could get there, they reasoned, they could leave the Burma Road and go north to the Lisu village where the Kuhns were stationed.

We started the climb up from the river, but when we had gone only 10 kms [6 mi] or less, the engine broke down. One of the cylinder head gaskets had broken and as we had no spare and no tools, we just had to stay there. Mr. Bartley knew that there were several A.T.G. Jeeps coming along behind us and said we must wait for them. Eric lit the Primus stove and Mr. Bartley produced a tin of coffee, so we made coffee and had some bread and butter we had brought with us.

It was dark now so Eric opened up the spring bed we had brought with us for just such an occasion as this, and spread it beside the truck. We put Miriam's little bed on the ground between the bed and the truck and we lay down under the stars. Mr. Bartley sat in the cab, waiting for the Jeeps to come past.

The Jeeps did indeed come past, but they were of no help. The drivers had no tools and were unwilling to take on more passengers. However, they promised to send tools out from Baoshan the next morning, along with the spare part. Mr. Bartley thought these things might reach them by nine o'clock in the morning, so they settled down to sleep.

It was a nightmare of a night! I couldn't sleep. Cars zoomed past us continually, and on the upgrade made a tremendous roar. Zoom, zoom, zoom, they flew past us, and we would we were going with them. But there we sat, and the Japs were coming near and nearer.

Occasionally there was a traffic jam, some quite lengthy, and then the line of trucks would be stopped close to ours and people would get out and come prowling round us. One fellow came right up to our bed, but went away again when Eric asked him gruffly what he wanted. Another fellow was on the opposite side of the truck, but I was lying so that I could see his legs under the car. As Eric went to the front of the car to see what he was after, he would go to the back and vice versa.

Many of the trucks were loaded up with defeated Chinese soldiers and once during the night when there was a stoppage, three of them got out of their truck, slipped past our bed, and slid down the declivity on the side of the road. Soon an officer came calling for them, but there was nothing he could do except peer down the bank into the darkness and then go back to the truck. They had deserted.

When dawn finally brought an end to the nightmare, it was Tuesday, May 5. They made coffee, had some more bread, and Grace was able to take care of the baby. "I washed Miriam and rinsed her nappies, hanging them on an improvised clothes line—a rope stretched from end to end of the truck." And they continued to wait.

Cars kept whizzing past us, and now we noticed that many of them were empty; a bad sign, because it indicated that they hadn't had time even to collect loot. Nine o'clock came, nine-thirty, ten, and still no sign of the Jeep, and for me it was nausea, nausea, nausea.

From where we were, on the far side of a long hairpin bend, we couldn't see the bridge. But now, getting on for ten-thirty, we saw great excitement at the lower curve. People were frantically running up the hill, and when they reached us they shouted that the Japs were coming, i.e. the first enemy soldiers. Mr. Bartley said we would wait till we heard shots before leaving the truck.

Eric cherished a hope that we might get on a passing truck, which were now few and far between, and started getting out our bedding rolls [from our truck] and also Leita's two cases, in one of which she had $2,500. Then he attempted to stop a truck which was tearing frantically up the hill. He stood in the middle of the road, but a man on the running board, who was flourishing a revolver, leveled it at him, and so he quickly got out of the way, and we knew that that plan was hopeless. In such a panic they would shoot on little provocation, and I have thanked God that Eric was spared then.

It soon became clear that they would not only have to leave the truck, but also abandon much of what they were carrying, as travel on foot seemed inevitable.

… I asked Mr. Bartley to open the bedding roll so that I could get out my walking shoes and put them on. He just cut the ropes! and we unrolled the bedding and left it on the side of the road. I put on my "rubber tire" soled shoes, and then threw the others down the bank. This all takes time to tell, but it happened in minutes, if not seconds. Just then we heard two terrific booms and knew that the bridge had gone, blown up by the Chinese guards. This was followed immediately by heavy gunfire from the Japs, who were evidently still high up on the other side of the gorge. The shells whizzed, or whined, over our heads and then exploded higher up the gorge on our right.

It was time for us to go!! I picked up Miriam and Eric took her little case and our two rain coats, expecting that we should have to sleep out, and we started off along the motor road. There wasn't even time to open Leita's case and take out her money, for nothing was of any value then except our lives. All the time over our heads was that long drawn out Whiz-z-z-z-z and then the Bo-o-o-o-om of the shell as it exploded.

Mr. Bartley took to the road with them, but climbing the steep ascent of the Nujiang gorge was exhausting, especially for Grace with a baby in her arms. "I asked Mr. Bartley [who was empty-handed] to take Miriam for a bit, and he did. But I took her again after a couple of rods or so, when I got a second breath."

The next meander of the road would put them in the direct line of fire from Japanese artillery, so Eric and Grace left the road and began to climb the bare mountain side. Mr. Bartley, however, took his chances with the road. He could make better time by himself, and once he got to Baoshan, his intention was to bring a Jeep back for them. Meanwhile they inched their way up the steep side of the gorge.

A lot of Chinese were with us, both civilian and soldiers, many of whom had had to leave their trucks in the jam on the other side of the bridge and run across on foot before the bridge was blown up. The mountain side was so steep that we would walk about 10 paces and then flop for breath, and of course, everybody else had to do the same. It was so hot, and many of the civilian refugees were "office" men from Burma and down the road, and they weren't in nearly such good trim for walking as ourselves.

It soon became evident to us that we couldn't go on loaded as we were, so Eric opened up Miriam's case, which we had packed with what we thought was the bare minimum of necessities for her, in case we did have to leave everything else, and took out a few nappies and a little woolen coat and abandoned the rest on the hillside, together with our raincoats. My watch which Samy gave me and which I've carried for 19 years was in Miriam's case because the bracelet had broken a few days before. But we never even thought of it, though I greatly wish we had, for it would have been so easy to slip it into Eric's pocket. We made a little bundle of the nappies and coat, and I carried it whilst Eric carried Miriam.

You must realize all this as happening whilst shells were constantly screaming overhead and bursting somewhere just up and beyond us, we couldn't tell where. Some Chinese told us to follow them and they'd lead us to the motor road higher up the side of the gorge, so we did so, tho at first our thought had been to get to some little village or hamlet as far from the road as possible, for we fully expected that the Jap troops would soon be coming along the road at our heels.

Everyone was very friendly and kind and we kept along a little mountain path which presently brought us to—a pig sty! But why mention this? There was a pail of water there, and what everyone needed just at that moment was water. Some drank, but we didn't dare, but I took one of Miriam's little vests and wetted it and we used this to wipe our faces as we went along, and were much refreshed by it.

The sound of planes overhead forced them to take refuge in a deep gully. "We had quite a job to get into it. Eric jumped down a drop of several feet and then I handed Miriam to him and climbed down too, and by repeating the process we got down." As they had hoped, they found water in the gully, but one look told them it was not a clear mountain stream. Yet, because of their intense thirst, they drank it. "It was a risk we had to repeat over and over again as we went on, but each time it was with the inward prayer that the Lord would protect us from harmful effects."

The gully was deep enough that they felt safe from machine gun fire, but not from the fighting overhead, where an AVG P-40 had engaged a Japanese fighter plane. "They were very high, but clearly visible and circling rapidly round each other, firing noisy bursts of machine gun fire."

> We have wondered since what that Jap fighter would have done if the American hadn't been there to fight him. It is pretty certain he wouldn't have missed up the opportunity of machine gunning the hillsides when they were so covered with refugees.

Grace wondered if those at home would be disappointed to know that at times she was afraid. "It doesn't bother me a bit," she assured them. She had reasoned it through. Their own watchword was David's admission that at times he was afraid, "What time I am afraid, I will trust in Thee." She also came to see that it wasn't cowardly to try to escape. After all, Paul escaped his enemies by being let down in a basket over the city wall, and Jesus escaped a crowd of would-be murderers, his time having not yet come. "Personally I think there is no shame in being afraid if fear doesn't become your master," she concluded. "I know now what David meant when he said, on being given a choice of three punishments, that he would rather fall into God's hands than man's." They might be running from men, but they were in God's hands.

> Previous to this we had practically given up hopes of escape, and talked about it between ourselves, and were

both quite ready and happy to go if we <u>all three</u> could go together. It was then that the strain seemed to lift and the nausea left me. Now as the planes fought overhead I could glance up and watch them and not be afraid at all.

When it seemed safe, they made the torturous climb back up out of the gully and, in a short distance, came out again on the Burma Road. The filling station they remembered from previous trips was demolished. "Half of the main building had collapsed, but whether as a result of shell fire we couldn't say. We saw two corpses lying here, one very badly mutilated and stripped of clothing. It looked as tho it was the result of shell fire, but no shells fell while we were there."

As they returned to the old Silk Road, "hope of escaping began to well up in us again." Baoshan was now about forty miles away. Could they make it?

When the Silk Road again paralleled the Burma Road, they came to a place where they had stopped for lunch in easier times, only to find it deserted. "We had hoped to find some boiled water for drinking, but the people had fled and taken everything with them. It was the same thing in every village we came to." Consequently, since the Burma Road wasn't as steep, and the artillery fire seemed farther away, they kept to it.

There were many broken down trucks and cars deserted along the roadside, and presently we came to one that was being looted by refugees. Eric said that if there was anything edible in it he was going to take some, and noticing that the people were all getting packets of cube sugar, he too climbed into the truck and got us a couple of packets. This was a great help to us, both then and later on, and we were able to share some with others who were exhausted. It made us more thirsty perhaps, but from time to time we stopped and picked wild raspberries, and these helped to quench our thirst.

Walking on the motor road was much easier, so occasionally I would carry Miriam to give Eric a rest.

Going up one grade we met a group of Chinese from the Aircraft Manufacturing Plant at Loiwing on the Burma border, near Wanting. They were drinking water from a washbasin and putting condensed sweetened milk in it, and invited us to have some. For Miriam's sake Eric accepted their offer and put some of the condensed milk in my water. They said the water was boiled, but I doubt it. However, I dropped on my knees to drink, and we both drank some, and were most grateful to them for it. This was only one of many kindnesses shown to us that day by people who were perfect strangers to us, but who were the Lord's messengers.

How we praised God that Miriam was such a good little baby. She was just the best little dear, and couldn't have been better. For some little distance we made a hammock of Eric's coat and carried her in this, each holding one end. But it was uncomfortable for her and she couldn't get used to it, so Eric let her sit in his hands with her back against him and she liked this much better. And it was much easier for Eric, and she rode like that most of the way to Paoshan. ...

We kept steadily walking, pausing for rest as we needed it. Sometimes we were on the motor road and sometimes on the old horse road since the latter, tho' generally more steep and difficult, often offered a good short cut, and saved us a mile or two. We couldn't do this after dark though, but had to keep to the motor road. Once or twice as we walked it sounded as though the cannon fire was getting closer again, and the old nausea would return. But this was likely due to the winding of the road occasionally bringing us closer to the Salween gorge again.

About five o'clock Miriam was hungry and I had nothing for her. A Chinese man heard her crying and said, "If we grownups are hungry it doesn't much matter, but it is too bad when the little ones cry with hunger."

Then he pulled a tin of condensed sweetened milk from his pocket and gave it to us for her.

There was scarcely any wheeled traffic on the road. Mechanics were tinkering with some of the deserted trucks and occasionally would get one going. Then it would groan past us, incredibly overloaded with refugees, people sitting, standing, or clinging in every available position. Needless to say, we weren't tempted to try for a ride, and on the whole we made as good time as these trucks, as we walked steadily and the trucks were constantly breaking down. Some small Chinese tanks were also running away up the road, and they kept breaking down too. Once a small private car passed going [the other direction] towards the Salween, and shortly after we saw it returning, carrying military officers. Eric signaled it for a ride but they waved a refusal.

Toward Tuesday evening—their second full day on the road—they themselves broke down. Exhausted and hungry they sat at the edge of the road to rest. Eric, realizing all too well the precariousness of their situation, broached a subject which had no doubt been on Grace's mind as well. In the gully they felt they would be happy to perish, if only they all three could go together. But what if, like John and Betty Stam's baby, Miriam was left alone?

"Have I ever told you, Eric asked, his voice faltering, "that if anything should happen to us, I would want Flora and Sherman to have her?"

The thought of "the little mite without her daddy & mummy" was too much. They got to their feet, tenderly situated Miriam, and once again set out for Baoshan.

It was now getting dark, but we pressed on to reach a place…where we knew there were a few restaurants. It was pitch dark when we got there, and we found that it was deserted too. We were tired out and very hungry, and we decided that we must rest there anyway until the moon rose, whether we could find food to eat or not. There were quite a few soldiers there, and we felt our way into one place where we could see a fire glowing and asked if they could let us have rice or boiled water. They had neither but some of the soldiers said we could have some of the water left from the preliminary boiling of the rice. But when we tasted it, it was so hot with red pepper we couldn't drink it. There were also some kind of dough balls in it which I couldn't eat, but Eric managed to force one down.

We went across the road to another house. The owner of this inn was still there but everything was gone except some rice. This he had dumped in a big heap on the floor and told the soldiers to help themselves. They were then cooking it and said that when it was done we could have some too, all we wanted. Eric then busied himself trying to boil some water. While he was hunting for a container, I sat on a "sawhorse" bench holding Miriam. Soon I began to feel sick and could feel weakness creeping over me. I was afraid I might faint with Miriam in my arms, so called out for him to come. When he arrived I was vomiting, but could bring nothing up—likely due to exertion, strain and hunger. I soon felt better.

When the rice, with peas in it, was cooked the soldiers told us to help ourselves. We found a couple of old cups and each ate three cups full, putting some of the condensed milk on it. We had no means of giving the milk to Miriam, having no clean boiled water, so we dissolved some in our mouths and gave it to her. Eric then found some planks and rested them on two benches and we lay down, with Miriam between us on Eric's coat. We fitfully slept for a couple of hours, and about 11:30 got up again. Some more soldiers were cooking rice and shared it with us, and we got a little boiled water, and so were strengthened and refreshed.

When they took to the road again it was midnight of Tuesday, May 5. They had been walking and carrying Miriam for more than twelve hours, and now, as the calendar turned to May 6, there was just enough moonlight to keep going as they began the third day of their harrowing escape.

> Many other people were on the road too. Occasionally a truck would pass us, loaded to beyond capacity. We longed for a ride, and since we were now meeting trucks going to the "front" carrying soldiers and artillery, we hoped that presently one of these returning might have space to give us a lift. But we kept walking on.
>
> At one place we could see an overturned truck down the bank at a bend in the road. We could hear a man saying the equivalent of "Oh dear," but could not see him. We pitied him, but his voice didn't sound weak, and as we had no light, no medicine, no tools, we decided not to go down to him. It seemed hard, but it was wise.

One consideration was the money they were carrying, not only their own but Longling church funds and Mission funds as well—a total of about four thousand dollars—half in Eric's pocket, the other half in Miriam's bundle. Amazingly, no one attempted to pick Eric's pocket or wrest the bundle, and they wished they could have retrieved Leita's money before abandoning her suitcase with the rest of their own belongings. But Leita had the key, and there would have been no time to break it open as they fled for their lives out of the Nujiang gorge. Wearily they trudged on in the light of the waning moon.

> After walking about 10 miles I held out my hand to stop [a passing] truck and, wonder of wonders, it stopped and picked us up. It was already packed like a sardine tin, and the people all loudly protested at our attempting to get on, but somehow we managed to scramble up over the side and force a place for ourselves

in the crowd. After getting in we couldn't locate Miriam's little bundle and supposed it lost. I soon felt faint and had to squat down, much to the annoyance of those around, but whilst in this position I found the bundle right at my feet.

The truck swayed terribly and we had to hold on for dear life. Eric was holding Miriam in one arm and trying to keep his balance with the other. And when the arm holding Miriam got so tired he hardly knew how to bear it, he stuck her feet and legs under his suspenders (braces) and held her that way. It was a desperate ride, but how thankful to God we were for it.

We had hoped to get right into Paoshan, but the truck stopped when still 7 ½ English miles from the city, and the driver said he could go no further. He took no money.

It was a weary business taking to the road again, and we hardly knew how to put one leg before the other. Each of my toes felt like a boil, and I was so tired I kept stubbing my feet on the stones in the road and hurting them the more. Then I'd cry a bit and feel better! (Since that walk one of my toe nails has dropped off.) I now tried hailing every passing truck, but none would pick us up.

"We were disappointed," Grace commented, in typical under-statement.

They had heard that the Chinese armies were concentrating to make a stand at Baoshan. If only they could get there, they could get some supplies and head north to Pade, the Lisu village where the Kuhns were stationed. It would be a six-day journey, but at least they would be off the Burma Road and out of reach of the Japanese invaders. The prospect kept them plodding on and, as if to cheer them, they began overtaking many of the vehicles that had passed them back at the Nujiang gorge, but were now stuck in a traffic jam about three and one-half miles from Baoshan.

As day dawned, the sight of an AVG car gave them fresh heart: maybe they could still get a ride. Eagerly they approached the driver, but he declined even to offer one.

On they trudged for the last weary miles, but still more disappointment awaited them at Baoshan. The city was deserted, having suffered "two days of terrible bombing," and the Chinese army was nowhere to be seen.

> As we neared the South gate that morning, Wed., we could see that the section outside the city was burnt out. It was a dreadful sight. Such utter destruction, and corpses and portions thereof lying around utterly uncared for. I was too faint to stand, so sat down on a rock by the roadside. It seemed the last straw.

Mr. Bartley had left them just the day before, hoping to find a Jeep in Baoshan and return to rescue them. Now they saw that he had not had a chance. Baoshan was bombed on the same day they left Longling.[5]

With the city in ruins there was no hope of turning north. Supplies were non-existent, not to mention coolies to carry them. Besides, they themselves were "utterly exhausted." Trucks were moving along the road, but they were packed beyond capacity. While Eric stayed at the South Gate to watch for a possible ride, Grace went to check on the Baoshan missionaries.

---

[5] The destruction of Baoshan was part of Japan's retaliation for the first American bombing of Tokyo two weeks earlier, when Eric and Grace were still at home in Longling. This daring raid on Tokyo took place on April 18, 1942, four months after the Japanese attack on Pearl Harbor. Commanded by Lt. Col. James (Jimmy) Doolittle, sixteen pilots in their B-25's took off from the aircraft carrier, USS *Hornet*, dropped their bombs over Tokyo, then were forced by a communications error either to crash land or parachute out over southeast China. As intended, the daring raid did embarrass Japan, and it did improve morale at home, but when sympathetic Chinese were found to be helping the downed American pilots, Japan became enraged, striking with a vengeance wherever it could; hence the vicious bombing of Baoshan on May 4, 1942 (Tow, "Doolittle").

The Swedish Pentecostal missionaries have a house just inside the S. Gate, whereas ours is across at the N. side, so I said I would go in and see if they were there, tho' we had but little hope of it.

Inside the gate all was desolation, and when I got to the alley leading to their house I could see that it had had a direct hit. Looking up the street it seemed that all was ruins, and at the main crossroads a big fire was shooting flames high into the air. It seemed incredible that our missionaries could still be in the city, and we didn't go to see. We heard later that they had left at daybreak the previous morning.

The biographies of God's people are replete with accounts of his intervention and deliverance, just when their situation seemed most dire, and so it was to be with Grace and Eric and baby Miriam. As Grace returned to Eric at the South Gate, Eric spotted a truck being driven by a foreigner.

The foreigner was Pilot Paul Greene from Clarendon, Texas, a flight leader with the AVG's third squadron. The squadron had been nicknamed "Hell's Angels," but on that day, May 6, 1942, Pilot Greene came as an angel from heaven. He was leading a convoy of AVG vehicles, and on the back of his truck was an Oldsmobile sedan.

> Quite desperate, Eric asked if we might ride up on top of it, for one couldn't get in as the truck was too narrow to permit the doors to open. [He] hesitated because of the risk it meant to us, but finally said we could.
>
> But meanwhile I saw [an] A.V.G. sedan just behind, with only three people in it, and I asked if they would let us ride with them to get clear of the city, for one of our fears was that soon there might be further air raiding. The driver asked, "How far?" and I thought, "The farther the better," but didn't answer quite so bluntly. He gave permission, so just as Eric was calling me to come to

the truck I called him to come to the car, and of course we rode in the latter.

As we got into the car, and sank back into the cushions, the relief was just overwhelming. Eric buried his face in his hands and wept. It was harder for him, having Miriam and me, than had he been alone. It seemed almost too good to be true after all we had been through, and we couldn't thank God enough.

It took us hours and hours to cover the two kilos [1.2 miles] round the city but then progress got a little quicker. The A.V.G. men were all tired and hungry, as they had left the [Baoshan] airfield at ten the night before and it had taken them until 6:30 that morning to cover the 6 kilos to the South gate where they picked us up. So when we were clear of the Paoshan plain we stopped for breakfast. It was by a stream, and we were so thankful to get a wash, and to get Miriam and some of her things washed. I bathed my feet in the cold water and they felt much better afterwards.

As soon as we stopped, Pilot Green[e] came and talked with us and made us feel thoroughly at home and quite members of their party. They had only tinned foods with them, and we [did get] tired of them after a few days, but you will guess how we felt that morning when Pilot Green[e] brought us plates on which were asparagus, sardines, pineapple & soda crackers. Later he brought us coffee, and that tasted best of all.

This Pilot Green[e], whilst in Rangoon, shot down two Jap planes and then had his plane shot to pieces. He baled out at 9,000 ft. and 2 Jap planes flew back and forth trying to machine gun him as he came down but without success. He didn't tell us this of course, but some of the others did. He was leader of the convoy, and treated us with the greatest kindness and courtesy.

Whilst stopped for breakfast, a wave of panic swept over the road as word was shouted from one to the other that the Jap planes were coming. It was possibly a false alarm, but that day Jap parachute troops did attempt a landing at Paoshan, and it may have been at that time.

We soon got going again, and our next stop was Wayao, a little place about twenty miles from the Mekong bridge. Our car wasn't running well, and they thought it needed oil. It was very difficult to get some, and we were delayed quite a while. Everyone was very nervous for it was rumored that the Japs had already got Paoshan and we couldn't but believe it. Most of the convoy went on, leaving two Jeeps to escort us. Meanwhile I tried to get some boiled water, for it was very hot and we were desperately thirsty. But the same conditions prevailed here as in other stopping places, and finally all I could get was some water rice was boiling in.

We finally got going, but soon the engine heated again and we had a further stop. Upon investigation it was found that the radiator had boiled dry. So we had to get water from the river to fill it. Eric went for the second lot, as the Chinese interpreter who got the first was so slow, and we were desperately anxious to get on, fearing that at any moment we might hear the rattle of the Jap tanks in our rear. The atmosphere was eerie. Nausea! that is hardly the word for it. And we weren't the only ones feeling it. Mr. K., one of the tough A.V.G. men with us, was saying nothing but nervously working his lips back and forth and thus showing pretty plainly how he felt.

At last we got off again and pretty soon we [came upon] the Mekong bridge traffic jam, tho' we were still some ten odd miles from the bridge. It was the worst yet. But our cars being small we were able to get along much quicker than the main body of trucks. The Jeeps are very easily maneuvered, and ours had very skilful drivers. So one went ahead of us alongside the trucks, and when there was a move, would motion the driver to pull over and so make room for us to follow. It became a real game to them but it showed excellent teamwork and marvelous driving. If the trucks wouldn't move over our driver would fire his revolver over their heads, and that usually made them move. We passed miles of cars in this fashion, and I really enjoyed the fun of it. But finally the traffic got too thick and we could only creep along at a snail's pace.

And so, in addition to the blowing up of the Huitong Bridge, they became witnesses of yet another historic ordeal—the Lancang River traffic jam. While thousands in France and Poland had fled from the German army, they fled on foot, since all vehicles had been commandeered, and they had a choice of roads. But as refugees in China fled from the advancing Japanese, they were in thousands of trucks and cars, trying to navigate a narrow river valley with no alternate routes. "It must have been the densest and longest traffic jam that has ever been."

About 8:00 pm we got into the bridge area, and it was now pitch dark. Suddenly there was a scare that the Jap planes were coming and all lights were ordered out. This but added to the panic and of course brought everything to a standstill. But soon a light here and there came on again, and we could begin creeping forward once more.

The bridge area consisted of two bridges over the Lancang and one over the Pi, a tributary of the Lancang. Grace and Eric's car was directed over the bridge that could handle lighter traffic, but in order to return to the Burma Road they had to drive north, where they soon encountered the mass of heavier vehicles from the other two bridges, which were also trying to do the same thing—return to the road.

Trucks and cars were there in thousands. The R.A.F. convoy [which Eric had seen before leaving Lungling] was there as well as the AVG and ATG, and all were trying to keep the road open and liquidate the awful jams. Most of the truck drivers would, it seemed, take no notice of anything but a gun, and so pistol shots were reverberating through the gorge all night long.

It was midnight when they finally stopped for a rest. The AVG drivers had been behind the wheel for twenty-four hours, and no one had eaten since the morning meal by the stream. Their rations were in the trucks that had gone ahead, except for some "tinned things," but at least the Lancang was now between them and their pursuers. At the pace they were moving, a stop for some sleep would only cost them a few inches of progress.

> The drivers just slept at the wheels of the cars. Had we not been in the car our driver could have stretched out, and that made us feel a bit badly for him. But Pilot Green[e] had made it clear he wanted us to go all the way with them, and he was leader.

The RAF convoy also was traveling without food. Their ration trucks had halted near Baoshan and the cooks were lighting fires to make a meal when an officer found them and told them to "get going and keep going." With the Japanese in hot pursuit, the cooks were only too glad to keep going, all the way to Kunming, but it left the rest of the convoy to travel on empty stomachs.

During that troubled night the RAF also had to bury one of their own. He had been shot and killed in the traffic jam at Baoshan, "probably by Chinese traffic soldiers for some offence or other," and was left sitting in the cab of the truck until the driver dumped his body along the roadside in the congested Lancang gorge.

> There it might still have lain, but an officer on the rear trucks chanced to see it, and at two in the morning, whilst the traffic was at a standstill, they hurriedly scratched a grave by the road side and buried him.

When day dawned it was Thursday, May 7, the fourth day on the road for the weary refugees. The AVG drivers rejoined the snail-paced traffic, and by mid-morning finally reached the point where traffic from the three bridges converged. Traffic soldiers holding pistols were allowing five vehicles at a time from each direction access to the road, and it didn't pay to argue. An RAF man was shot through the arm. For Grace "it seemed as though our turn would never come."

When it did come and they were back on the Burma Road, they began to encounter some of the RAF trucks. Knowing they were without rations, the AVG men shared their tinned food, but for some of the Burmese refugees with the RAF, relief came too late. If they had brought food, it was gone and they were literally starving. One young man had opted instead to bring looted cigarettes, as they found when they opened his bedding. No doubt the loot would have brought a good price on the black market in Kunming, but he didn't live to find out.

Eventually they also came upon the AVG trucks that had gone ahead the day before, when Grace and Eric's car was stopped for radiator trouble.

> [Their drivers] had stopped and slept at the wheel too. We were all desperately hungry, and the food was in these trucks, but of course there was no time to stop to prepare anything. Panic was still very rife because very circumstantial rumors were circulating to the effect that the Japs were only just behind us. If they had been, the mass of jammed cars would have been easy prey to them, for there was no way to move except ahead, and the rate we were traveling was only two or three hundred yards an hour at that time. On one side of us was the river and on the other a sheer mountain wall so there would have been no escape for anybody.
>
> I was sitting with my head in my hands when I heard someone say to Eric, "Would she like this?" and looked to find Pilot Green[e] standing there holding a tin of pineapple he had just opened. He knew, for we had told him, that Miriam was dependent on me for her

milk, and would be alright if I had food. So we knew why he brought this along, and were most grateful to him. Later they managed to get out some canned meat and vegetables, but the first we knew of it was when they handed me a plate of it through the car window with the remark, "We want to see that you are well fed." There was some for all but they served me first.

We were all desperate for something to drink and would have given anything for some tea or coffee, but of course there was no time to make it. If we could have done the 2 or 3 hundred yards per hour that we were making all at one stretch, then there would have been time, but it was more or like 2 or 3 yards per stretch. And if one didn't move immediately there was a gap ahead, and there was terrible scolding from the cars behind.

Another time when Miriam was crying from hunger, it was a Chinese airman who took pity. "He came to our car holding a tin of condensed sweetened milk in his hand saying, 'Can you use this? I don't want it.'" For Grace and Eric it was more evidence that an "Unseen Hand was touching hearts here and there."

As they gradually left the Lancang River behind them, Grace marveled that they had been unharmed. It would have been such an easy thing for enemy planes to machine gun and bomb the concentration of defenseless refugees waiting to get out of the congested bridge area. "We can't thank God enough that we were spared this further horror," she wrote.

They were indeed across the river and back on the Burma Road, but the climb up out of the Lancang gorge was exceedingly steep and traffic was still heavy. "Our drivers would go miles ahead in their little Jeeps trying to clear the jams, but invariably had to do it with their guns in their hands."

They witnessed what their drivers called the appalling "waste of war." Trucks that broke down or could not make the grade were pushed to the side of the road and tipped over the edge.

Some good trucks went over too. Once we heard a dreadful crash just ahead of us and found the RAF had just pushed over an almost new truck. It had a leaky radiator which they couldn't repair, and they had no spare, so over it went. They took one or two essentials off it, and then one of our men drew his gun and shot up the gas tanks etc. etc. so that the Japs couldn't easily salvage and use it. ... As we passed the broken down trucks, mostly packed with miserable refugees, my heart just ached for them. We knew from bitter experience just what it meant to be stalled by the road side and watch other trucks streaming past towards safety.

Their progress was halting and slow, but that very fact allowed them to be found by their friend, Mr. Miller, the AVG radio operator whom they had met in Baoshan before moving to Longling. He was going against traffic, driving nonstop from Kunming to evacuate the Baoshan airfield, when he came upon the Lancang gorge traffic jam and learned from some RAF men that the AVG convoy was somewhere behind them. Knowing the Coxes were with the AVG, he left his truck and worked his way back on foot until he found them. He assured them he had seen Leita, who by then was traveling with a group of ATG men. When they informed him that Baoshan had been bombed, he returned to his truck, turned it around—while drawn guns held up traffic—and joined the AVG convoy back to Kunming.

By mid-afternoon we were still climbing slowly up out of the gorge, but getting along a little faster. We came to a place where a stream of water was cascading down over a cliff and Pilot Green[e] decided to stop there and have the cook make coffee. While it was making, we were glad to get a wash as the dust was awful and our car had no windshield.

The food didn't taste quite so good this time, tho I was hungry. They had smeared butter over the meat and vegetables (tinned, of course) and it was a bit rancid.

I was having a job to get it down when an RAF man passed us and as he did so called out, "The Japs are only 30 miles behind! Did you know??" And immediately I began retching, quietly but surely. But I tried to veil my feelings, especially when asked, "Does it taste good?" The others were disturbed by the news too, and the pilot was heard to remark, "They said that P40 (Tomahawk fighter plane) on the Paoshan field couldn't be repaired. But if I'd known we were going to get caught like this I bet I would have fixed it."

Immediately I began wondering what we'd do if overtaken. There was only one recourse, take to the hills, and this would be terrible for little Miriam, as I would be unable to feed her. The villages near the road were all deserted, and it might be days before we could get food or proper water. The thought was terrifying, to say the least, and finally, being unable to contain myself, I spoke to Pilot Green[e]. I said I knew I was only a passenger and had no say in the matter, and that the fatigue of the drivers had to be considered, but if a vote was taken, mine would be in favor of traveling all night. His answer was very kind as he explained that there was only one thing worse than a drunken driver and that was a sleepy one, but if the drivers could stand it we would certainly keep going all night. ... They all loved Miriam, and were always inquiring about her and marveling at how well she was standing the trip.

In the end they did keep going, into the wee hours of their fifth day on the road, Friday, May 8. By the time they stopped at four o'clock that morning to make coffee, they had gotten ahead of much of the traffic, and progress became more heartening, in spite of occasional alarms. In the village of Yangbi (Yang Be), which used to be a welcome stopping place, they found machine guns positioned all down the main street. Still, there were a few shops open, giving them their first sign of normalcy since leaving Longling.

The next goal was Xiaguan (Hsiakwan), supposedly under the protection of the Chinese army. But that was supposed to have been true in Baoshan, also.

We got there about three and found it deserted because of an air alarm. But we pressed on through nevertheless, and were relieved to notice that apart from the alarm, things looked pretty normal there. Our drivers were just desperate with tiredness, but they kept on, as they wanted to get to the airfield at Yunnani, where the [AVG] has a Hostel. This was some fifty odd miles from Hsiakwan, and before we had covered half the distance our driver stopped because he kept falling asleep at the wheel. We waited until Miller overtook us and then he changed with our driver and trusted a Chinese to drive his truck.

Our car had been giving constant trouble, and they were debating whether or not to "ditch" it, to use the current word. Both back springs were broken, and had been for days, and now the gas tank was punctured by hitting a big stone in the road. Should we ditch it or not? Some were for and some against, but it was decided to attempt to patch the tank with soap. If it worked we would go on, but if not, "over she goes" as they expressed it. Well, it worked, and so we limped into Yunnani that night at about 7 o'clock, just before dark.

You would hardly have recognized us had you seen us. Travel stained wasn't the word for it, and weary! Why, we just felt like sleeping where we stood. We had only the things we stood in, and Eric didn't even have a shirt. His had split across the back on the walk to Paoshan and we tore it up for handkerchiefs. We hadn't had a proper wash since Wed. morning and Eric hadn't shaved since leaving Lungling, and had no means of doing so.

To their relief, such luxuries as "hot baths and showers and nice clean beds" were waiting for them at the hostel in Yunnanyi (Yunnani). After a bath came "a good dinner—roast beef, roast potatoes and peas, followed by hot cakes and <u>real</u> maple syrup." And then came bed with clean sheets and room to stretch out. Furthermore, all this was by kind courtesy of Mr. Miller. "We wanted to reimburse him, but he wouldn't take a cent."

A fairy tale would have it that they had a wonderful night's sleep that night and were quite themselves the next morning. In reality, Grace's sleep was disturbed by what she thought was distant artillery fire. It turned out to be the cabin walls vibrating in the wind, but it was similar enough to make her "tremble from tip to toe." And in the morning (May 9) she found she couldn't enjoy breakfast, "feeling rather off color."

May 9 was Day 6 on the road, and they still had 200 miles to go to reach Kunming. They started at five o'clock in the morning, riding with Mr. Miller in the cab of an International truck, and he was in a hurry. Add to that a fairly level road and a truck in good condition and the result was a happily uneventful trip, with arrival in Kunming, at last, at six o'clock that evening. On the way they had passed their AVG friends, Mr. Bowman and Mr. Bartley, riding in a Jeep, which allowed the men to see for themselves that the rumor they had heard was true: the Coxes were safe. Later the men paid them a personal visit at the Kunming Mission home. Their plight had touched others as well, as they learned that "one of the ATG men broke down and cried when he heard we were safe."

Mr. Miller's destination was the Kunming airfield, so he dropped his passengers off at the West Gate and went on to the airfield with his load of Chinese assistants. Mercifully, the city was still normal, but Eric and Grace felt distinctly abnormal, "like two scarecrows." Though they were cleaned up and fed, Eric was still shirtless and people smiled at their bedraggled state.

When they arrived at the CIM home, they found that Leita had preceded them by just an hour or two. "Leita," Grace said, in reference to their conversation back in Longling about the apostle Paul's shipwreck, "we are all here, but the ship is gone!"

Part of the "ship," of course, was Leita's suitcase with her money in it. But there were no hard feelings or regrets. "She has a heart of gold," Grace declared, and they were glad they could give her "a third of our personal cash."

After supper the three of them went shopping for essentials "like tooth brushes, underwear, stockings, etc., and talcum powder and things for Miriam." Other things came from the kind hearts of compassionate missionaries.

> Our friends from Mangshi, the Foggins, had arrived a day or two before us, and they were more than kind to us. He gave Eric a shirt, pajamas and a tie, and she gave or lent me things for myself and Miriam. And later they gave us $500 and Leita $200. They are not CIM workers but independent Brethren missionaries. Other friends gave or lent us things, especially Mr. & Mrs. Crapuchettes, who run the CIM home in Kunming, and we soon had enough things to carry on with. Receiving the kindness, love and sympathy of so many dear friends, we felt that we were indeed "As having nothing and yet possessing all things."

Given the amount of unboiled water they had been obliged to drink, plus the "tinned food eaten at very irregular intervals, hard travel, [and] the tremendous strain," it is not surprising that they were two rather unwell missionaries. Both had developed dysentery, but in God's mercy they could now stay in one place long enough to receive proper medical attention. The Kunming hospital treated them at no charge, giving them shots not only for dysentery but also for cholera, a new menace coming in with the influx of refugees.[6]

During that week they heard only hazy and contradictory news from the west. No one knew for certain that the Japanese advance had been stopped at the Nujiang. If not, it would be only a matter of time

---

[6] Cholera and bubonic plague had been unleashed by the Japanese during the attack on Baoshan, which included both bombing and germ warfare (Tow, "Heroic Battles").

before they reached their goal of Kunming, the capital city. Or perhaps they would advance from the south, coming up from the Indo-China border in a pincer movement. "People in Kunming were pretty scared."

It is understandable, then, that Eric and Grace and little Miriam were among those urged to move on. The consuls "strenuously agitated" for foreigners, particularly those from the west, to join an RAF convoy going north to the province of Sichuan. Eric inquired about going instead to one of the hill stations in Yunnan, but the consul had already ordered people in those stations to evacuate to Kunming. Grace's concern, which she kept to herself, was "to get going, and the further we went the better!"

For a fleeting while they had a chance to join a party of missionaries who were flying out to India on a transport plane. From India they could take a ship home. As Eric reasoned, since they were having to leave Yunnan anyway, they could be of little help in a province where they didn't know the dialect. They had no belongings, and who knew when the Japanese might even reach Sichuan, given their rapid advance thus far?

But they themselves were part of an army tasked with bringing the gospel to all of China. They were under authority. "If we could have gotten Mission permission we might have done it, but without it we didn't really consider it," Grace explained.

Chapter 30

New Life in Suyung

Given the urgency of the consul's order, it was only a week after their arrival in Kunming that Grace and Eric and little Miriam took to the road again. It would be some time before anyone would know that they needn't have hurried, that when the Chinese blew up the Huitong Bridge, they did indeed stop the Japanese advance at the Nujiang River. Only with hindsight would Eric and Grace realize that in those terrifying moments and the chaotic aftermath, they had been a part of history. The Huitong Bridge is now an historical landmark, preserved by the Chinese to mark the spot at which the Japanese advance was halted (Montsma, "Bridges").

The CIM had temporarily assigned them to minister in Suyung, a town to the north in the province of Sichuan, where Mr. and Mrs. Ben Tweter had been sidelined by illness. Since an RAF convoy was preparing to travel north to Chengdu (Chengtu), the provincial capital, and Suyung was on their route, the Coxes could have safe travel to Suyung.

Compared to their experience of just a week earlier, this trip was easy. No one was pursuing them with gunfire. They were well supplied with provisions for the road, thanks to Mrs. Crapuchettes. And there were friends traveling with them, including Leita Partridge, Kathryn Harrison, and Isobel Kuhn. Even some of the RAF men were familiar to them from their ordeal in the Lancang gorge. Eric was amazed to discover that another, Eric Marks, knew him from home. His grandmother and Eric's mother were good friends, and in delight at this discovery, he gave Eric and Grace nearly five pounds of powdered milk, an item which could no longer be purchased.

Dysentery was still an unwelcome companion, but an RAF doctor was with them, "named LeFrenais, but a good Scotsman," Grace observed. He charged them nothing for four more shots of emetine. And there was Flight Lieutenant Wean, the RAF version of Pilot Greene, who made them his special charge. "A real gentleman and most kind and considerate," he was the only one of the company not shy of Miriam, although by the end "even the Cockney cook was carrying her around in his arms."

Also in contrast with their previous journey, the ration trucks traveled with them, so the convoy could stop and enjoy a meal. Grace and Eric had their own provisions, but the RAF men urged them to join them, courtesy of the British consul. In return, Grace and Eric gladly shared their honey and marmalade "and they enjoyed it."

> Stops were made in open country, well clear of towns and villages, and usually near a stream or lake for water supplies. The cooks soon had a big fire going and a boiler of water heating for tea and another for porridge, rice pudding or stew as the case might be. There was no panic now, and traveling was leisurely, so this trip was more like a picnic. ... We went but slowly, and with the delays caused thro' cooking our own meals, it took us nine days to do what could have been done in five. But we didn't mind.

At night they slept in their vehicles: Leita in the front seat of a ration truck, Grace and Miriam in a small private car, and Eric in the cab of a breakdown truck with his feet sticking out the door. But at least there was no artillery fire in the distance, or fighter planes overhead, and they thanked God they could sleep in peace, if not total comfort.

Although the Coxes' destination was Suyung, they ended up going with Leita beyond Suyung to Luhsien, a change of plan which Dr. LeFrenais welcomed for the Coxes' sake, as they were still suffering from dysentery. He knew of a German Jewish doctor in Luhsien, a specialist in dysentery, who could give them the treatment they needed. But first they had to take a ferry across the Yangzi River, three vehicles at a time. It was a slow and tedious process, but finally across, the CIM home in Luhsien was easy to identify by the genial missionary standing at the gate to welcome them. Arnold Lea invited not only the missionaries, but the drivers and the cooks as well, to come in for tea.

As the RAF convoy moved on to Chengdu, they left behind three rather lonesome missionaries. After nine days of roughing it together on the road, sharing stories and comparing experiences, they had become friends. Although the airmen were battle-hardened, they had spoken frankly of the "nasty feeling it gave to be chased by the Japs, and of the strain of the Mekong gorge experience." Grace warmed to their humanness. She hoped they would take the missionaries' advice and connect with the CIM home in Chengdu, finding there what she herself would give them if she could: a welcoming home, so far away from their own homes.

The week in Luhsien had not been on their itinerary, but it was exactly what they needed as they continued to recuperate from the adversities of the last three weeks. It gave them time and leisure just to live. Arnold and Jeannie Lea were English, with three little girls—Rosie, Helen, and a thirteen-month baby girl "with a mass of red curls"—and the Coxes soon found them to be warm-hearted and generous, "extremely kind to all of us." Miriam made the transition to solid food, and Grace and Eric received the medical attention they needed. Indeed, by the end of the week, the dysentery specialist had pronounced them "free of germs," and on June 2 they made the day-long trip back to Suyung, while Leita went to fill a vacancy in the neighboring station of Chihshui.

The CIM station in Suyung had been in existence since 1920, but presently it was a station in flux. With the Tweters absent on account of illness, the Mission had sent a young couple, Don and Irene Cunningham, to be in charge while they waited to move to their appointed post of Fuhinwan, a Miao tribes station in the hills. Also in residence was Dr. Parry, a missionary statesman of eighty-two years, who had come to hold Bible classes and speak on Sundays.

It was a large compound with a main house, a gate house where the cook and his family lived, a dilapidated church building and manse combined, an abundance of fruit trees, and a vegetable garden. "I did something today which I've never done before in my life," Grace wrote. "I picked some figs!" And not only figs. There were loquats, apricots, lemons, peaches, grapes, pomelos, oranges, strawberries, apples, persimmons, pomegranates, greengage plums, cherries and oranges. Truly the Lord had brought them to a spacious place, but Longling was never far from their minds and hearts.

> We are both glad to be here, as it is so peaceful and quiet. We like the Cunninghams very much and enjoy fellowship with them. Eric has been able to get a teacher, and is continuing his study of Chinese. The loss of all our study books and note books is a big handicap to us both, especially our Chinese study Bibles.
>
> I am not only glad but G L A D we came; but we shall both be glad to go back when it is safe for us to do so. … We often wonder about the dear Christians in Lungling, and constantly commit them to the Lord's grace.

A week after they arrived in Suyung, Grace sat down to write the story of their escape for their families at home. They had lost their typewriter with the rest of their things on the Burma Road, but Eric found one to borrow, and began to type Grace's longhand original. By using carbon paper, he made two copies besides the original. Single-spaced on thin, legal size paper, with minimal margins, the account reached sixteen pages. Since mail service was erratic at best, they registered the copies sent to Iowa and to England, and kept the third for themselves. Even so, when Grace wrote home four months later she asked, "Have you received [it]?"

The Cunninghams moved to Fuhinwan about five weeks after the Coxes arrived, allowing Grace and Eric the luxury of being by themselves once again. Mr. Parry was there, "but he is such a dear old gentleman, that it is just as nice to have him as if he was a very close relative," Eric wrote. He even asked if he might call them by their first names. He had been in China early enough to know Hudson Taylor, and inspired them with firsthand accounts of the early days of the CIM.

Miriam continued to thrive. "I am still able to feed her," Grace wrote, "and we are thankful indeed to Him Who has made it possible." She had also branched out to porridge and cow's milk, but did not much like "the spinach water and egg yolk which she has at noon." Then she contracted a strange illness. The symptoms indicated dysentery, but when Dr. Mi, trained in Shanghai, examined her, he assured Eric and Grace it was not dysentery.

> It is her first illness in eleven months and it just doesn't seem like our little frisky girlie when she is so languid & lifeless. Before when we'd put her in bed with us she was busy pulling hair, noses and ears and not still a minute, but now she just snuggles up on my arm and lies still. Her eyes look so tired and her little face so pallid.

Grace was no stranger to child mortality on the mission field. She had felt keenly for Arthur and Mabel Allen when they lost little Geraldine to whooping cough, and for her friend from language school, Grace Weir Rockness, when she lost a baby to dysentery. She knew they could be no exception, but the thought of losing Miriam was almost more than she could bear.

> ...she is all we have and all we can think about now & naturally all I can write about now. When all our things were lost we just praised God that he spared our lives and that Miriam stood it without harm. And as we can only wait before him and bow in submission to his will, it will be easy to rejoice and be thankful if our request [for her recovery] is granted, but if it is not, then he will carry us through, as otherwise we could not endure.

In the end their request was granted, though it was almost two months before Miriam was fully herself, and they never did know for certain what the trouble was. A visit to the specialist in Luhsien ruled out amoebic dysentery, but not bacteria, so they could only conclude that it was a bacterial infection. At about the same time, they learned of two more CIM children being lost to dysentery. "We feel that God has been so good to us," Grace wrote, "and we are so undeserving."

The work in Suyung was familiar to them: Bible classes, prayer meetings, evangelistic services, visiting in homes, prison visits, and a full day on Sundays with two preaching services, children's Sunday school, and a ladies Bible class. But interest was flagging, and family feuds persisted. Paul Shen, Grace's friend from former days, was preaching in a neighboring town, and the Suyung church invited him to come for three months of evangelistic services. But what concerned Grace and Eric more than the unevangelized were those already in the church. "They stay away from services on the slightest excuse," she wrote. She found that preparing for classes was a chore, compared to the pleasure it would be "if only the people were hungry for the Word."

Yet they were glad not to have the strain and pressure of managing a Mission home, and the weather was cooler. "I feel ever so much better than I have since leaving Longchiu," Grace wrote. "My back seems better too but still aches if I get over tired." And in spite of the apathy of the Suyung Christians, she could say, "I have been happier here in the work than any time since I left tribes land."

The daily task of living in primitive conditions was itself time-consuming: water had to be fetched and carried; kerosene lamps had to be lighted; warmth came only from heavier clothing and more blankets. A Chinese girl came in to help, but otherwise, missionaries did the daily maintenance chores on top of their weekly round of classes and meetings and visiting. As fruits and vegetables came into season, Grace canned them or made preserves. Sugar was scarce because the government was appropriating it to make alcohol for truck fuel, but she was able to acquire some made by tribes people in a neighboring province. "It is in little cakes, a yellow brown colour, & is quite sweet," Eric explained.

Clothing continued to be a challenge, because everything had to be made by hand. Grace managed to make dresses for herself using Mrs. Tweter's hand-cranked sewing machine, and she recycled garments left by non-returning missionaries to keep Miriam and Eric warm in the winter. Mrs. Tweter had left some knitting instruction books.

> I unraveled a red wool cap of Miss Carpenter's & am knitting Miriam a pair of red socks. It is my first attempt. … I have made Miriam some little vests out of a moth-eaten nightie from one of Mansfield's trunks in Kunming. … I must make her some woolen nighties too & petticoats. Eric says there is a woolen shirt which I can use to make into petticoats.

She fashioned a pair of shoes for Miriam, using a leather glove for the soles, blue serge for the shoe itself and white flannel for the lining. Then, by using other pretty remnants, she made several more pairs: "little soft shoes like the Chinese wear," Eric explained to his mother, "and Miriam loves them." Other material she transformed into a garment for Eric.

> I made Eric a wadded waistcoat which is very warm, & which he wears underneath his regular waistcoat. It is invisible. I covered it with some cloth in the things which Cliffs sent to us & which had been used to cover a quilt. To have bought it would have cost several hundred dollars, but the whole thing complete cost only around fifty dollars.

For six months they shepherded the Suyung church in a temporary capacity, expecting Tweters to return and resume the work. But Mrs. Tweter's health was fragile and her recuperation was slow. Meanwhile, the consul had given missionaries from Yunnan permission to return. The Coxes and Leita were the only ones still displaced, but with Longling still under Japanese occupation, it could be a long wait before their turn came. Consequently, at the field conference in Luhsien in January 1943, the Tweters were assigned to a station less strenuous for her, and the Coxes were officially designated to Suyung. It was good to have their designation made official, and it was probably good for them to stay put. As they were to find out, the trauma of their recent escape was still affecting Grace.

On the way home from the field conference, they traveled part of the way in a truck that had been converted to burn charcoal for fuel, since gasoline was unobtainable. Using charcoal for fuel reduces efficiency and, therefore, power and load capacity. Hence the driver's request, before they crossed a bridge, that the passengers get off first. However, instead of allowing them back on after he had crossed the bridge, he took advantage of his lighter load to climb the next hill. They ran "at breakneck speed" to catch up, Eric carrying Miriam, only to see the truck disappear around a bend in the road. In reality the driver had stopped to wait for his passengers, but they could not know that, and for Grace the sense of abandonment was too reminiscent of the Burma Road. "When we got in and sat down I had to cry," she admitted. "I was afraid he wasn't going to stop."

The little church which was now their designated charge consisted of about ten families plus some elderly and single people. All but the elderly were employed—two as doctors, others as merchants, radio operators, railway workers, gatekeepers, and caretakers. Some had remained steadfast and devout over the years, but after twenty years the church was still not officially organized.

Grace and Eric soldiered on, but Eric too was suffering. At the field conference, the first signs of "rheumatism in the back & sciatica" appeared, and when they returned to Suyung his schedule of twelve meetings a week, plus visiting and trying to finish the fifth section of Chinese language study, did not help. "The pain lets up at times & then again becomes very severe, nauseating him," Grace wrote to her family. A Chinese doctor in the church recommended a series of seven milk injections, to which Eric submitted, though each one caused "a dreadful reaction—fever and pain." Dr. Parry advised bed rest for ten days, but Eric doggedly persevered. "I heard him tell Dr. Parry that it would mean too much for me to do," Grace wrote. "But I wish he would [rest] for his own sake."

The news that a Chinese fellow worker would soon be joining them was welcome indeed. Mr. Tiao was a Bible School graduate coming for four months—from the first of May to the first of September—under the auspices of the CIM. As a native Chinese, he was fluent with the language and at home with the people. As an educated Christian, he was not only devout but knew his way around the Bible. After he had worked with Eric for a month and held a week of evangelistic meetings, encouraging things began to happen. Signs of new life appeared. Ten people gave their testimonies and were baptized. A communion service was held, and the church agreed to hold one monthly.

A week later, over twenty attended a church meeting to elect deacons. Furthermore, the deacons took responsibility for restoring the old church building. They wanted to rededicate it to the Lord. The congregation followed by contributing the necessary funds, and even those who had been feuding for years dismissed their quarrels and began to help.

At the second communion service there was a dedication of babies, including Miriam, with Dr. Parry officiating. They began home Bible classes, and new families joined the church community.

September marked the end of Mr. Tiao's four-month commitment to Suyung. He had a fiancée waiting for him in Chengdu, and the wedding date was set. Also, he had an invitation to work in Chengdu. But the Suyung church wanted him to stay, and since his bride was a Bible School graduate, highly regarded in her own right, they promised to provide a salary for both if they would come to Suyung. Much to the delight of the church—and the Coxes—Mr. Tiao and his new wife chose Suyung.

It was well they did, as far as Eric was concerned. The pain in his back continued unabated. He persevered with teaching and visiting, even adding a new Bible class out in the country, but Dr. Parry was concerned. They were due for furlough, and when he realized that they were deferring to those whose furloughs were overdue, Dr. Parry wrote privately to headquarters: it was imperative that Eric get rest and proper medical attention. But autumn was approaching, and Eric knew from his days at sea that the fall months were no time for an ocean voyage. Besides, war still raged worldwide, making travel of any kind more perilous.

Meanwhile, they saw the Lord supplying needs they had hardly had time to recognize. Miriam fell heir to clothing from Ruthie Tweter that would outfit her for the year. In the "box room" were containers belonging to Mr. and Mrs. Frank Meller, whose return from furlough had been delayed. Mellers urged Grace and Eric to open them and use what they could. Although moths, moisture, and rats had gotten to the boxes first, they salvaged bedding, clothing, books, curtains, and even pantry supplies, "enough to make us truly rejoice."

With chagrin Eric recalled in a letter to his mother what he had been thinking just a year earlier.

> I said that I didn't want to come into Szechwan, but dallied with the idea of flying out to India, because we had lost everything & most of it would be irreplaceable in inland China in time of war. Well, that was a year ago, & here we are today, in a little city in inland China, with everything that we need, of clothing for ourselves, & our little Miriam, for summer, winter, & between seasons, of household necessities of bedding, etc. etc. And in a fully furnished home, much nicer, I expect, than we should have if we were living at home [in England] at this time.

Grace also found some "foreign toilet soap" and talcum powder. They themselves had been using laundry soap ("It hasn't hurt us any"), but there was a baby on the way, and Grace gratefully put the bath soap and powder away for her newborn. It was a secret whispered in Miriam's ear from time to time, and shared with a select few at home, but if others could have looked in on them, they would soon have guessed. Grace had found some knitting wool. Even though moths had chewed the wool into pieces, "I just tied it together and used it anyway" to knit a little outfit of coat, hood and booties. The wool was "a beautiful sky blue."

What would have excited Miriam more, could she have known, was that a new baby meant another trip to Luhsien, where she could play with Helen and Rosie Lea, and have the fun of a boat ride across the Yangzi River. The trip was not Grace and Eric's preference. They had hoped the baby could be delivered at home, but no doctor in Suyung had midwifery instruments, and Leita Partridge, who had attended

Miriam's birth, advised against it. So they made the journey to Luhsien, where Eric left Grace and Miriam in the care of the Leas and Leita Partridge, while he returned to Suyung.

They were separated for about two weeks, writing each other daily with candor and affection. "I can visualize you coming across the tennis court at tea-time & meal time," Grace wrote, "but to an empty house. Wish I could step out from behind a door or crawl out from under the table & give you a BIG surprise!"

Before Eric had left Luhsien, however, an incident had arisen which caused Grace a great deal of anguish. What was an act of charity on Eric's part had seemed like pointless extravagance to her. She was frugal, and Eric could be resolute, and it troubled her that they had differed.

> I do love you so & it grieves me that I let you down so often. .... Your attitude is the right one, I know it. Of course it was the Christ-like thing to do, to give the nicest & best hot water bottle to the old gentleman, & I'm sure that He was pleased with your suggestion about giving the material to the school. It was only I who, through perversity, contrariness or an over practical turn of mind, opposed it. I want to be one with you in all things that please Him.... I want to be a fragrance of Christ to you no matter what the circumstances, no matter what the test or trial, no matter what the physical or nervous strain.... Please pray for these longings which He has put into my heart, & I shall pray for you, my beloved Eric.

Her letter took almost a week to reach him, and he was quick to respond in kind. He knew all too well his own failures of spirit.

> Gracie darling, I know how you felt as you wrote, but you don't let me down, dear. If anything it is the other way round, & how often & often I have felt rebuked & cut to the heart by your sweetness & patience when I

have been so cross & disagreeable. I began to despair of ever being anything else but the latter, but the Lord has blessed me & given me again the peace of abiding in Him, looking unto Him, the Source & the Completion of our faith. … I love you more than I can say.

A week later he was telling her so in person at Luhsien. He had seen to it that "the obstetric books for Leita" had been sent ahead, and when he arrived, all was ready. A room had been designated as the confinement room, Grace and Leita had assembled the bassinet, and when the time came, Eric would go for the doctor. In the end, Philip Eric came on his own, with help only from Leita and Jeannie Lea. Eric had gone for the doctor, but when he arrived with his instruments ten minutes later, the baby was already born. It was Grace and Eric's third wedding anniversary, October 4, 1943.

Although Miriam had seemed to resemble no one, Grace saw in baby Philip a clear likeness to her father. With time, however, it was Grace whom he resembled more than any one.[7]

A radiogram took the news to Grace's mother in Iowa, including the baby's weight (9 pounds) and the fact that Grace was recovering better than when Miriam was born, but four months later they still had no word that it had arrived. As for Eric's parents, not even radiograms could be sent to war-torn England, and mail service was capricious at best. However, in December the CIM was able to get the word through to its London headquarters, and Mr. Fred Mitchell, Home Director, personally passed it on to Mr. and Mrs. Edgar Cox in South Darenth.

For Grace's sake, they waited a month before undertaking the return trip to Suyung, with its journey across the Yangzi in a "small boat" (low enough that Miriam could drag her hand in the river), and another punishing ride in the charcoal bus with makeshift seats. Once at home, Eric plunged again into the life of the awakening Suyung church, and Grace reveled in her little family. "Our baby boy is the dearest little

---

[7] When Philip was old enough to talk, his Uncle Virgil, Grace's youngest brother, came to visit. "I bet you don't know who I am!" young Philip announced. With a chuckle, Virgil replied, "How could I not know? Your mother's face gives you away!"

cherub," she wrote, "quite as bonny as his big sister. We think we are wealthy now, having them both to love."

But Eric's back was not improving, and Mission leaders were taking seriously Dr. Parry's recommendation that the Coxes go on furlough as soon as possible. Consequently, in February 1944, almost two years after their arrival in Suyung, they were prepared once again to travel, this time with a two-year old and a nursing infant, and Eric with persistent back pain. It would be a journey of 20,000 miles before they reached Grace's home in southwest Iowa.

The parting was bittersweet. Although Grace and Eric's heart was in Yunnan, they had grown to love the Suyung Christians, and left them only with reluctance. The church held a special service in the new building to say farewell, presenting Grace and Eric with the gift of a group photo, a simple black and white snapshot, costing twenty-five dollars in US currency. "I don't know who felt the goodbye most," Eric wrote, "they or we."

PART THREE

✠

GOING HOME

"Isn't it wonderful at <u>all</u> times to know Him, to trust in Him, to hide in Him, to love Him with all our hearts! How sweet too, to be given the grace at <u>all</u> times to say, "Thy will be done."
(Letter to her mother, Lucy Liddell, October 1945)

Whate'er my God ordains is right; here shall my stand be taken;
Though sorrow, need, or death be mine, yet am I not forsaken.
My Father's care is round me there; he holds me that I shall not fall:
And so to him I leave it all.

Samuel Rodigast 1675

Chapter 31

Flying the Hump and Crossing the Seas

In normal times, missionaries going on furlough would travel to the CIM headquarters in Shanghai and board a passenger ship for the voyage home. But times were not normal. The Japanese controlled Shanghai and its harbor, putting travel by sea out of the question, and Japanese armies had blocked the Burma Road, making the route southwest through Burma impossible. These same circumstances were preventing the Chinese army from receiving supplies and reinforcements.

In search of an alternative supply route, the China National Aviation Corporation (CNAC) moved their headquarters to Assam, India, a point from which they hoped pilots could fly supplies over the Himalaya Mountains into Yunnan, though no one had yet ventured over them. Their snowy tops were the "roof of the world," unseen by human eyes.

In 1941, two Americans, Captain Hugh Woods and his co-pilot, Captain Frank Higgs, made an exploratory flight. With only primitive instruments, no weather forecaster, little protection against the massive icing at such high altitudes, and an unpressurized cabin, they successfully flew the uncharted 530-mile route and landed in Free China (*Wings*). Thereafter, that route over the eastern Himalayas was known as the Hump, and became a lifeline for the Chinese army, though at tremendous cost. By the end of the war the CNAC and ATC (Air Transport Command) together had lost nearly 640 planes and

1,100 men. In the opinion of General Albert C. Wedemeyer, Chiang Kai-shek's American chief of staff, "Flying the 'Hump' was the foremost and by far the most dangerous, difficult and historic achievement of the entire war" (CNAC).

The route had also become the lifeline for evacuating missionaries. Planes coming east to Chongqing with their payload had room to take passengers west. Consequently, when the Coxes left Suyung, the Chongqing airfield was their first destination. Taking the barest minimum of luggage, they made the 130-mile journey in two stages: first on the notorious charcoal-burning truck, and then by river steamer, which they assumed would be the easier part of the journey. Instead, it recalled more painful memories of the Burma Road.

The ship was seriously overbooked, requiring that they wait two days just for tickets, and another two days for a departure date. They found lodgings, but on the night before they were to leave, Eric camped out on the wharf with the baggage to secure a place in line. Grace got up in the pre-dawn darkness, gathered the babies, and "picked her way through the dark muddy streets" to join him, only to have the ship—just twenty feet out in the river—move upstream to the next wharf.

Desperately, the waiting passengers grabbed their baggage and raced up the bank, leaving Eric and Grace with their little ones to bring up the rear. By the time they arrived, all the deck space had been taken, but as Chinese soldiers had come to their rescue on the Burma Road, so they did now. They "helped Grace scramble over the rail just outside some officers' cabins," Eric wrote, then he quickly handed her the children, threw the baggage across and climbed over himself, just seconds before the steamer pushed off.

Their "accommodation" for the next day and a half was a narrow space on deck, four feet long and eighteen inches wide, except that they were spared this indignity during the night hours. When the boat stopped that evening, they recognized it as a place where CIM missionaries were stationed, whom they knew. Ralph Toliver had been a "son of the prophets" with Eric, and he and his wife, Becky, gladly took them in and made them comfortable for the night.

Morning found them once again squeezing into their hard-won deck space for the remainder of the trip, and by mid-morning they were at Chongqing. CIM staff had reserved space for them on a CNAC cargo plane, but the long walk from the wharf, followed by an uphill climb to the CIM home, had aggravated Eric's back condition, and Grace was ill with nervous exhaustion. They were in no condition to fly. A week at the CIM home, with its hospitable and caring staff, provided the respite they badly needed. It also gave them the opportunity to update Grace's passport to include the children. George Bolster, another "son of the prophets" who was staying at the Mission home, took note of what he later described to Eric as Grace's "quiet depth and rich consecration."

On March 16, 1944, exactly one month since leaving Suyung, they boarded the cargo plane—unheated and unpressurized—which would take them over the Hump to Calcutta, India. Ten years earlier, Grace could hardly have known, when she marveled at the Rocky Mountains on her way to China, that she would return home over a range that would dwarf them. Eric described their trip.

Our route took us over our old home at Suyung, but to our great disappointment it was so cloudy that we could see nothing. When we got over our "own" province of Yunnan, the atmosphere was so bumpy that most people in the plane were sick, and some of us who were novices wondered if the plane was out of control.

A stop at Kunming [airfield] was a welcome relief, but we were soon on our way again, and meeting, as the pilot had forecast, very strong head winds. Long before we got to the famous "hump" we were flying in dense cloud, so it was not for us to see the beautiful snowcapped Himalayas which some had talked of. Instead we were shut up to our misery. Nearly everyone in the plane was very sick, and evidences of it, in the paper bags provided, were painfully obvious.

It was bitterly cold and the rare air made one conscious of breathing, and induced a strange kind of sleepiness. From time to time one of the pilots would look in, as I found out later, to see if anyone needed the oxygen apparatus. We were so glad when after a few hours of this, it began to get warmer and we began to get glimpses of jungle clad hills.

We came down on a bomb seamed airfield in Assam for a brief half hour and then took off on the last hop to Calcutta, reaching there about 6 pm. We were gladder to get out of the plane than we had been to get into it, 12 hours previously.

Not surprisingly, the rigors of travel had not improved Eric's back. Reluctantly admitting that he simply could not go on, he entered a Calcutta hospital for two weeks, but apart from the rest and food, the hospital stay was of no avail. When they heard of a ship leaving Bombay for the USA in early April, they determined to be on it, even though it was on the other side of the Indian subcontinent. In God's providence, the train from Calcutta to Bombay had only first class seats available, which meant the family had a private compartment, and Eric could lie down.

The ship was the SS *Mariposa*, a luxury liner chartered to the US government and converted into a transport. It sailed from Bombay on April 13, missing by one day a terrible accident in the Bombay harbor. The SS *Fort Stikine*, a freighter carrying explosives, caught fire and blew up in the harbor, sinking nearby ships, setting others on fire, and killing over 800 people.

By that time, in God's mercy, the Coxes were making their way out into the Arabian Sea, far away from guns and explosions. They were among 200 civilian passengers, mostly missionaries like themselves, and several hundred military personnel, all squeezed into cabins redesigned to hold as many as twelve bunks, rather than the normal two. "Our cabins were on the third deck down," Eric wrote, "and ports were left shut night and day. Men were on one side and women on the other." But there were no complaints. "Considering it was war time," he wrote, "we were very comfortable." The bounty and quality of food was something they had not seen in years, and they would they could share it with friends back in China, who had so little.

Because it was war time they traveled without news of any kind, even about their own ship. Reportedly, their escort ships sank a submarine on the first day out, but from then on they traveled without incident. Their route was kept secret, putting them blissfully out of touch with the world at war.

Not until they found themselves in port at Melbourne, Australia, did they realize that they had gone south through the Indian Ocean and around Australia. They were in port four days, though not permitted ashore. Eric took the occasion to write a brief card to his mother, which had to be cleared by Censor 336 before it could make its way to England. "Miriam has been ill with a form of measles but is better now," he told her. "Philip is very bonny. Everybody on board loves him and says what a good baby he is. Grace is well. I am about the same."

For Miriam, the highlight of being in port was the gift of a new stuffed toy, possibly her first. A seaman whom she called "Uncle Joe" had taken a fancy to her. Unlike passengers, seamen could go ashore, and when "Uncle Joe" returned with a stuffed wooly koala bear for Miriam, she was elated. She clutched *Mel* (for Melbourne), and with all the exuberance of a two-year old, hugged her "Uncle Joe" as he picked her up in his arms.

After Melbourne they were "lost in the vastnesses of the South Pacific Ocean," as Eric put it, heading up towards the Panama Canal. "[One day], when we were thoroughly accustomed to our loneliness, a big flying boat roared down on us, giving all of us who hailed from China quite a scare," he wrote. But its markings were USA, not Japanese, and they took heart: a land-based plane with USA markings could only mean they were nearing their destination.

Two more days brought them through the Panama Canal, and another week brought them safely to Boston, Massachusetts. The voyage from Bombay had taken a full six weeks.

Chapter 32

Home and Hospital

After a day in Boston and travel by train to CIM headquarters in Philadelphia, where they remained for a week, the Coxes boarded a long-distance train to Red Oak, Iowa. Unlike Naomi in the Book of Ruth, who had gone away full and come back empty, Grace had gone away empty and was coming back full, with a husband and two children to introduce to the family waiting on the platform.

The train stopped, and Grace was soon in their arms—nine years and eight months since she had said good-bye to them at that same station. People whom Eric had known only through letters and conversation with Grace were now flesh and blood, and as for them, they finally met, and grew to love, the man who had won her heart. "He sure is a wonderful boy," Grace's mother wrote to Eric's mother, "& I love him like my own."

It was his first visit to the United States, apart from the West Coast ports he had visited as a sailor some twenty years earlier. Certainly he had never been in the heartland, and now as he saw it in the first days of June his admiration was palpable. He wrote to their prayer partners:

> As this good land of America unfolded before us its early summer beauty, the wideness and busy order of its great cities, and the rich prosperity of its people, how could we fail to be moved. It is the very opposite of all we have left, of the daily scenes of our life these last 6

to 9 ½ years, respectively, and perhaps we had forgotten that a land could be so beautiful, and cities so splendid and people so wealthy in those things which make life rich and full. … Truly we stepped into a new world when we landed in Boston. How truthfully Americans can say, and should say, "The lines are fallen unto me in pleasant places, yea, I have a goodly heritage."

Home was to be a two-story house in Emerson, Iowa, provided and furnished by Grace's sister Flora and her husband, Sherman Allen. Like many others of that era, it would be considered rustic by today's standards. They pumped their water by hand, dried their clothes on a clothesline, and heated the house with coal, which Eric discovered was cheap by comparison with England. When winter came, he marveled at the "grand stove that warms the whole house," concluding in a letter to his parents, "…our methods of heating in England are utterly antiquated." Central heating would not become a standard feature of English houses for another three decades.

To Grace's delight, the property included an apple tree and space to plant a garden, which she did. "We have quite a large garden," Eric wrote a year later, "and it is now looking very flourishing with all manner of vegetables peeping above the ground. Grace does most of the gardening, and makes a very good job of it." Her cabbages did well enough that she took some to Sherman and Flora's farm to make sauerkraut, with the help of her ten-year-old nephew, Merrill. "We sat outside in the shade to shred it," he recalled.

Emerson was a small town of about 500 people, located seven miles north of the Allens' farm. At that time it had no street signs and no home mail delivery, so residents went to the post office for their mail, and the Coxes' address was simply Box 266. They were within easy walking distance of the post office and almost anywhere else they needed to go—the high school, where Eric spoke once a month; the Baptist Church, where he frequently attended the evening service; the Methodist Church; the grocery store, which was on the same street as a café named Shoops; and the corner where the Burlington Bus stopped, taking people to points east or west.

Since neither Eric nor Grace could drive, a neighbor picked them up on Sundays for the five mile drive to Champion Hill, the rural church where Grace's extended family attended. If they needed a doctor or a department store, they could usually catch a ride with someone from the family who was going "to town," meaning Red Oak (eleven miles west), or Shenandoah (eighteen miles south).

Likewise, when any of the family came into Emerson for groceries, or to visit the bank or post office, it was not unusual for them to stop at the Coxes'. If it was Grace's sister Flora, she might take Miriam back to the farm to play with Loretha, or Miriam might go home from church with her and stay the night. For her part, Grace kept Wanda's little girl, Clyda, after school until her parents could come from their farm to get her. Often she had a chocolate custard ready. "I loved it!" Clyda recalled years later.

Grace was still the winsome, warm-hearted young woman to whom the family had said good-bye nine and one-half years earlier. Back in the bosom of her family, she again enjoyed tête-à-têtes with her sister Flora, and her dear Aunt Flora, though her conversation now reflected some of Eric's culture (afternoon tea) and terminology ("nappies" for diapers; "porridge" for cereal). Yet she had changed. She was more cosmopolitan, and also more serious. Joe Allen, who had married her cousin Jean, remembered how easily Grace used to josh or tell a joke, but now seemed more subdued. "She wasn't as much fun," he said matter-of-factly. Still, for all of the sobering things she had endured, her sense of humor and irony was intact. She kept a little notebook for jotting down some of the children's antics and amusing expressions, and mischief.

For Eric, rural Iowa was a world totally new. His life experience had been solely among English people: at home, at school, in the British Merchant Navy, and then in the predominantly British China Inland Mission. He had an English accent and was by nature shy, but he soon warmed to Grace's family and grew particularly close to her Aunt Flora. "She has been just a mother to me," he would later write to his own mother.

Eric and Grace Cox with Miriam and Philip – June 1944

One of their early trips to Red Oak was to see Dr. Gladys Cooper, the Liddell/Allen family doctor, who readily realized Eric needed more help than she could give, and wrote him a referral to the Mayo Clinic. He left on a summer day in mid-July, 1944, traveling by bus and then by train overnight to Rochester, Minnesota, while Grace and the two children moved out to her Aunt Flora's farm, midway between Emerson and her sister Flora's farm, to await his return.

Grace and Eric had no idea what his expenses might be, or what kind of debt he might incur at Mayo Clinic. They only trusted that the God who had richly spread the table for them after their losses on the Burma Road would continue to provide for them. When they left China, the exchange rate was such that the bit of money they possessed had multiplied considerably; they were to find that in this way, their heavenly Father would enable them to pay not only for this visit to Mayo Clinic, but for others to come, about which they yet knew nothing. Though they were presented with doctor bills, hospital bills, transportation costs, and living expenses during two extended stays in Rochester, each time they had enough. The Widow at Zarephath, in the days of the prophet Elijah, would not have been surprised (1 Kings 17:7-15).

As in past separations, they wrote to each other daily, sometimes twice a day, letters replete with tender longings. "It was harder to say goodbye to you today than any time since Paoshan," Eric wrote the day he left. For her part, Grace confessed, "It has been a lovely Sunday, but oh! How I've missed you—all the time—everywhere."

Eric's address was a boarding house near Mayo Clinic, where rates were one and a half dollars per day. A nearby restaurant offered a chicken pot pie dinner for fifty cents, and at a café he could get a pancake breakfast with grapefruit and coffee for thirty-five cents.

After nearly a week of tests and x-rays at the clinic, the doctors diagnosed a slipped disc, which they proposed to remove, and a congenital weakness at the base of the spine, which they proposed to strengthen by means of a bone graft, splicing a piece of Eric's shin bone with the spine. They would perform this surgery at St. Mary's Hospital, where a single room was six dollars per day, a double was five dollars, and a five-bed ward was four dollars and twenty-five cents. As for the clinic, he still had not paid anything. He wrote to Grace,

> I don't know yet what their charges are. So far I haven't paid a cent & there has been no mention whatever about fees. But one sees quite a few apparently poor people in the clinic, so they must make their terms reasonable for those who are not rich.

He had come to admire the efficiency of the clinic, and the care and expertise of the doctors. "I am so glad I came," he wrote. "I feel that if [my back] can be fixed, under God, they will do it. I am sure He led me here."

But now that an operation was imminent, a disquieting possibility came to mind. Not wanting to distress Grace with it, he confided in Sherman and Flora. "I am confident that the Lord will bring me thro this operation," he wrote, "but it's only human to consider all the possibilities. I know that if I were called Home He would fully care for dear Grace & the little ones [and] my hope would be that God would keep them in the States...."

Little did he suspect that he, not Grace, would be the one left to decide the children's future.

The surgery was scheduled for Saturday, July 29, nine days after his initial visit at Mayo Clinic, and Grace determined to be with him. Eric found her a boarding house, she arranged for Miriam to stay with Flora and Sherman, and she and her Aunt Flora set out for Rochester with baby Philip, arriving the day before Eric's operation. He was a patient at St. Mary's for three and one-half weeks, and stayed with Grace at the boarding house for one more week before attempting the trip home.

That week gave Grace the opportunity to visit the Mayo Clinic herself. Though she seemed well, she couldn't seem to regain her energy, in spite of easier living conditions and good food. She also had a history of rather severe hemorrhoids, which the years of hard walking and horseback riding had not improved. But after a thorough physical exam, complete with x-rays and the most advanced tests of that day, the doctors found nothing untoward and dismissed her with a clean bill of health.

The week also gave Aunt Flora the opportunity she had been looking for—to take Grace shopping. Before they left Suyung, Eric had said that one of the things they looked forward to at home was getting Grace some "nice clothes." Having lost everything on the Burma Road, her wardrobe now consisted of hand-me-downs: though truly appreciated, they were still of a make-do nature, and her Aunt Flora was just the person to help her find replacements.

They went to a department store in downtown Rochester, where Grace spotted a suit she admired. However, one look at the price tag told her it was out of her reach, and she put it back.

"Why don't you try it on?" her Aunt Flora asked. "You could at least have the pleasure of wearing it for a few minutes."

So Grace tried it on, and it fit perfectly. But the price tag had not changed, and again she put the suit back, not noticing the wink Aunt Flora had given the clerk to save it.

After the week was up and Eric was dismissed to go home, they went to Aunt Flora's home while he continued to recuperate. When a package arrived from the store in Rochester, addressed to Grace, she assumed it was the sheets she had purchased and didn't bother opening it until Aunt Flora suggested she should.

"It was worth the price of the suit to watch her as she realized what it was," Aunt Flora recalled with a smile.

Chapter 34

An Ominous Shadow

In the fall of 1944, Eric was approved to be acting pastor of Champion Hill Church. It had been founded in July 1880 as a member of the Cumberland Presbyterian Church (CPC), so-called because of its beginnings in the Cumberland Valley of Tennessee as a protest against actions by the Presbyterian Church in the United States of America (PCUSA). However, in 1906 the CPC rejoined the PCUSA, and in 1907 Champion Hill became a member of the larger denomination. Being a small, rural church, it was a challenge for the congregation to support an ordained minister, and in 1944 it was once again without a pastor.

Eric was available and eager to help, and the church invited him to come, but the arrangement needed first to be approved by the presbytery, whose moderator at that time was the Rev. Charles Speagh, pastor of First Presbyterian Church in Red Oak. Although Eric had no theological education and was not ordained, the presbytery saw in him a widely-read and careful student of the Bible, if not a theologian, and recognizing his years of experience as a missionary, they approved him to serve as acting pastor at Champion Hill while he was on furlough. Because Eric and Grace were receiving a monthly remittance from the CIM, salary was not an issue, so the church agreed to send a monthly contribution to the Mission in appreciation for Eric's services.

This arrangement put Grace in the role of pastor's wife, and as such she sometimes spoke at women's meetings. On one occasion she was surprised with a household shower. At another she spoke from Luke 10, the account of Jesus visiting in the home of Mary and Martha, admitting wryly that she had more sympathy with Martha now that she had two little children to care for. For a time she also had her mother to care for. A widow since 1930, Lucy was no longer able to live independently, and Grace took turns with her nearby siblings, Flora and Virgil, at welcoming her into their home.

The months were busy, but without the strain of her life in China, she began to feel more rested. She could enjoy reading again. It was no longer a chore to concentrate. And she had a new baby coming at the end of July or early August. Eric had written confidentially to his mother that "God willing, you will have 3 little grandchildren to meet when we come to England, and not just two."

February 1945 brought to reality Grace's long-cherished dream of attending the annual Founder's Week conference at Moody Bible Institute. Leaving Philip with Grace's cousin, Jean Allen, Grace and Eric took Miriam and traveled by train to Chicago, accompanied by Sherman and Flora and their two children. They heard well-known speakers: Dr. Harry Ironside, Dr. Harry Rimmer, and "a young man named Irwin Moon," who would become well-known for his Sermons from Science movies. They took the children to the Field Museum of Natural History, the Shedd Aquarium, and the Adler Planetarium, and they had a meal in Chinatown. But Grace was disappointed in the thing she had most anticipated. Although she enjoyed meeting again many friends and former fellow-students, when she introduced herself to her favorite professors, they could not recall her. Ten years had been a long time.

Back at home, an ominous shadow began to form over their blessedly normal life. For two months, since the beginning of the year, Grace had been troubled with what they thought was a recurrence of dysentery. In March she sought the advice of a specialist in Omaha, Nebraska. Diagnostic tests at Methodist Hospital did seem to indicate dysentery, and she returned two and one-half weeks later for the treatment.

While she was in the hospital receiving the treatment, a second doctor, Dr. Simmons, took a look at her x-ray and spotted something else: a polyp in the rectum. He advised her to stay and have it examined, but it was Friday, and the earliest they could do it would be Monday. Rates were not exorbitant at four dollars and twenty-five cents per day, but she was loathe to remain over the week-end, especially since Monday was April 9, Eric's birthday. She returned home. They talked of going to Mayo Clinic instead, "but were advised against it because Grace was pregnant."

A month later she saw Dr. Simmons again, presumably for the rectal exam. If she had the exam, there is no record of what it showed, or what Dr. Simmons may have recommended. Three weeks later, by now in the seventh month of her pregnancy, she again saw Dr. Simmons, but that visit also seems to have been inconsequential. She returned home the same day, and life went on as usual.

Their furlough had officially ended at the end of April, by which time they had expected to be packed and on their way to China via England. However, the epic naval "battle of the Atlantic," as Churchill called it, was still raging, and German submarines were making trans-Atlantic travel too dangerous for civilians. Eric's contract with Champion Hill Church had also expired at the end of April, but at a meeting on April 20, moderated by Mr. Speagh, the church asked him to continue, in exchange for one hundred ten dollars a month. Since the CIM would not be sending the Coxes a monthly remittance until they resumed their work in China, it was a timely provision, and Eric welcomed the opportunity. He wrote to their praying friends:

> I have done more Bible study these months [at Champion Hill] than in any similar period since I was at Newington Green [in London], and since I lost all my notes with the rest of our things when we escaped from Lungling, I am going to find these very useful when we get back to China.

While they waited for a sail date, Eric was asked to take speaking assignments on behalf of the Mission. The first came at the end of April, when he was to speak at a five-day conference at Moody Church in Chicago. He was torn. Miriam had just sickened with measles, and no doubt Philip would be next. He wrote to Grace, even before boarding the train at Red Oak. "I sure hate to leave you dear, when I know you are not well, & Miriam is so sick, & Philip perhaps sickening, but I don't feel I could do otherwise. And I don't believe you would want me to, would you?"

Grace reassured him in a hurried P.S. "Eric, darling, … Of course I am glad you went & of course I wouldn't have it otherwise. God bless you & infill you. Your own love, Grace."

In June, Eric was asked to speak at a series of meetings in Waterloo, Iowa, and Grace and the children went to the farm to stay with Flora and Sherman. Of necessity, she had put herself on a liquid diet: eggnog, and chicken broth, which Flora made from one of their own fresh chickens. "I don't seem so well again," she wrote to Eric. "The symptoms seem more in evidence & the feeling of congestion in the colon persists. I don't know why it is."

On the day she expected Eric home, Grace asked Sherman to drop her off in Emerson on his way to Red Oak, thinking she could meet Eric's bus, and Sherman could take them back to the farm together.

What she didn't know was that Aunt Flora and her daughter, Jean, had gone fifty miles to Council Bluffs to surprise Eric by intercepting him and bringing him directly to Aunt Flora's for the night.

When he didn't get off the bus in Emerson, Grace assumed he would be coming on a later bus and left a note for him.

> First, Welcome Home, to our Daddy dear. ….
> I have picked <u>dozens</u> of radishes & want to pick some lettuce & a bouquet for the church.
> There is some bacon & two eggs in the refrigerator. I brought [from the farm] some of [this] morning's milk & hope it keeps sweet for [tomorrow] morning.
> My! It is so good to be in my own little home, & will be ever so much better when we all are here as a family.
> The children are both bonny as ever & Miriam will be <u>so</u> excited to see you, to say nothing of her mother!!

Chapter 34

A Namesake at the War's End

As August approached, an unexpected package arrived in the mail—a gift of baby clothes from Miss Grace Hoover. Her strange behavior towards Grace at Chengkiang remained a mystery, and this unexpected kindness was a mystery. Was it a tacit apology? It was at least a kindness, which Grace accepted at face value, asking no questions. For one thing, there wasn't time.

On Wednesday evening, August 8, Eric was leading prayer meeting at Champion Hill when a neighbor came to say that Grace needed him. Private phone lines were yet unknown in Emerson, Iowa, but Grace had called the central operator, and "Central" contacted the neighbor, who drove to the church and took Eric home, where he found Grace in labor. Another neighbor kindly drove them the eleven miles to the hospital in Red Oak, where little John David was born in the wee hours of August 9, 1945.

He was named for his Uncle John, Eric's nineteen-year-old brother, an air gunner with the RAF, who had perished over Yugoslavia three months earlier, just days before Germany surrendered. Ironically, the little namesake himself almost perished at birth. "It was touch and go," the doctor told Grace the next day. "I was afraid he was dead." He had been in a breech position, and after a very difficult delivery, the doctor had worked on him for fifteen minutes before he finally gave the welcome cry of life. Grace and the baby remained in the hospital for nine days, giving Eric the occasion to paint the kitchen, as well as keep pace with the garden and the church.

On the second day after John's birth came the startling news that the Japanese had offered to surrender. However, because of poor radio connections, Eric could get no confirmation of it until five days later, on August 14, as he returned from his daily bus trip to visit Grace. The driver announced to his passengers that the Japanese had surrendered, and World War II was over! As they approached Emerson, they could hear the siren blaring in raucous celebration, followed by the "fire truck, loaded with kids, careening around the city." That night Eric was asked to speak at a victory service at the Methodist Church, where he used Deuteronomy 4:1-8 as his text, and the next day the town took a day off: the bank and businesses all closed in celebration.

In a few more days there was celebration at the little home in Emerson. Grace and baby John were home, and on the following day, Miriam and Philip returned from the farm to make the family complete.

The Cox Family – September 1945

But all was not well. Grace seemed to grow more weak and wan by the day. Again they considered going to Mayo Clinic, but were advised to wait another five or six weeks. It was September 24 when they finally made the trip.

Chapter 35

Into the Darkest Valley

At the clinic there was no waiting. Grace was admitted as an emergency case, and their worst fears were confirmed: there was a tumor in the rectum, which subsequent tests proved to be malignant. The ominous shadow was the shadow of death, though an operation might prolong her life "a few years," the doctors said.

It was a stunning blow, and Eric reeled under it. "The Lord gave me composure, outwardly and inwardly, until we were alone together in our room [at the boarding house]," he wrote, "and then it seemed as tho my heart would break." Normally he would be reassuring and encouraging Grace, but not this time. It was Grace who comforted and counseled him. He could only marvel as he saw the reality of the peace of God steadying and keeping her, to the point that all the while they were in the Valley, "she was a tower of strength to me."

The doctors advised an immediate operation at St. Mary's Hospital, and Grace and baby John were admitted that same day: Grace to a room on the second floor, and John to the nursery on the sixth floor, so he could be weaned. On the way, they stopped at a photographer's, mindful that there might not be another opportunity, and regretful that Miriam and Philip would be missing. "I think Grace's face reveals the wonderful peace with which the Lord had filled her heart," Eric wrote.

Eric and Grace Cox with John, aged seven weeks

While she waited, Grace wrote letters to those she loved best, expressing no bitterness or regret, but no denial or facile optimism, either. She was not one for pretense and euphemisms. She knew the situation was dire, and the outcome dubious, but she also knew her heavenly Father. She wrote tenderly to her mother:

> Isn't it wonderful at <u>all</u> times to know Him, to trust in Him, to hide in Him, to love Him with all our hearts! How sweet too, to be given the grace at <u>all</u> times to say, "Thy will be done." Just as dear little Miriam & Philip look up into our faces and smile, so do we look into His dear face and smiling, say, "Thy will be done." His sustaining grace, His peace are most precious.
>
> If He should take me now or soon or years later, I know He will care for our precious babies. We gave them all to Him before they were born, and they are

His. He will guard them and keep them as the apple of His eye. And He will stand beside my beloved Eric, and sustain & comfort Him.

And I know, too, that His peace will garrison your heart, Mama dear, & that His comfort will flood your soul. ...

Our greatest, most blessed joy when we leave this world will be to see His dear face. "His servants shall serve Him & they shall see His face." Then there are all of the loved ones gone on before. How wonderful!

If He takes me before He does you, Mama dear, don't think of the grave. I shall not be there. That is just the house I lived in. But think of glory where I shall be with Him. Grace will not be in the grave, she will not be there, but "over there" with the Lover of our souls. ...

She wrote to each of the children, and she wrote to her faithful sister Flora, who was caring for them.

... Eric and I have perfect peace of mind when the children are with you, and neither of us can think of anyone with whom we'd rather leave them.

You and dear Sherman have been so kind to us and to our babies. We can never thank you enough. ...

God bless you, dear Flora. You are so dear because your love for Him is so deep & true. My pen cannot express the feelings of my heart.

She wrote to her mother-in-law, "My beloved Eric's beloved Mother."

Thank you, mother dear, for sending me that poem which reminds you of Eric.

From Saturday noon when they told us my trouble, until Tuesday when your dear letters came, I think I hadn't shed one tear. But I couldn't help it then. I have looked forward so much to seeing you because Eric has told me so much about you & loves you so much. But if we do not have the joy of meeting in this world, we shall have the blessed joy of meeting in Heaven.

The operation was scheduled for Thursday, October 4—their fifth wedding anniversary. The preparation was grueling, but on the day before the operation she received a wonderful boon in the person of her Aunt Flora, who had traveled by bus and train to be with her. "Grace was overjoyed to see her," Eric wrote, "and in talking to her was more animated & like herself than I have seen her for a long time."

That evening she wrote to Eric.

> Tomorrow is our wedding anniversary, the fifth, and what wonderful years they have been with you by my side.
>
> Your love for our blessed Saviour, your constancy in prayer and Bible study, your eagerness to speak to souls about their salvation, your courage to decry evil and to exalt Him, your husbandly solicitude—you were my slave beyond your power—your fatherly tenderness and care of our three darling babes; these and much else has been at once to me a rebuke, a challenge & a benediction. ...
>
> How I praise Him for the deep, strong abiding love which he gave us for each other, and for the multiple triumphs of this love....
>
> And tomorrow the operation! We don't know what our loving Father has in store for us, but we do know it is good and best. ...
>
> Oh! how wonderful, how wonderful it would be if He should spare me to you & our darlings, and how our hearts would bow before Him in humblest gratitude. Oh! how I love you, Eric darling, how I love you.
>
> How sweet to know that if He chooses otherwise, His is the balm of Gilead, His is the sustaining grace. Discipline your thoughts heavenward. That is where

your Grace will be, enraptured to behold His face, and overjoyed to meet loved ones gone on before.

My hope for you is, my beloved Eric, that you will accept His proffered grace, roll every burden & every day onto Him, commit to Him the Key to all unknown, & looking away unto Jesus go right on in your God-given, God blessed ministry for Him. …

I have no fear, my beloved, no fear at all of tomorrow. You will be by my side, & though unseen He will be there too, & is there now.

"Thanks be to God, which giveth us the victory through our Lord Jesus Christ."

She had been running a fever, and when "tomorrow" arrived, it was no better. Furthermore, a chest x-ray showed four shadows on her lungs, and there was a spot on her liver. The operation was postponed, and then postponed again, and finally the doctor advised that she not go through with it at all. "If you were a member of my own family I would say the same thing," he assured her. As an alternative, he recommended radium treatments to try to reduce the tumor.

A letter came from Jennie Fitzwilliam, who understood their travail all too well. Did Grace remember that the verse Jennie quoted was the same one given to her in Shanghai, when she was a new worker, fresh off the boat? It was Isaiah 26:3, but in a rendering suggested by C. H. Spurgeon: "Thou wilt keep him in perfect peace whose MIND STOPS AT GOD."

"That is just what we have found is so necessary," Eric wrote to Flora and Sherman, "not to think of 'might have beens' or 'might be's' but to think of God, our Father, Who has led us, & Who will lead us."

It was October 9, a classic fall day, when they transferred Grace to Worrall Hospital, where the radium treatments would be given. "The bright sun shining on the yellow leaves of the trees made it seem as tho we were driving thro a golden archway," Eric wrote. Situated just two blocks from their boarding house, the hospital would be convenient for visiting, and for bringing baby John to his mother's arms.

But the treatments were brutal, and after a week they were suspended. The cancer was everywhere, and the doctors told them frankly they did not expect Grace to live for more than five or six months.

This news was not wholly unexpected. From the beginning they had sensed the disease was terminal, and they had accepted it, bowing to the good and perfect will of their heavenly Father, however inscrutable it might be. But a sermon on healing made Eric begin to hope, and when other circumstances seemed to confirm it (a second sermon, a reading from *Daily Light*, and a prayer handkerchief they were given as "a tiny link of faith in the mighty Name & power of Jesus"), his hope became conviction.

Together they discussed James 5:14-15: "Is any one of you sick? He should call the elders of the church to pray over him and anoint him with oil in the name of the Lord. And the prayer offered in faith will make the sick person well; the Lord will raise him up." Together they agreed to do that. Eric had visited Rochester churches enough to know several Christian men who were willing to come. They anointed Grace with oil in the Lord's Name, and prayed in faith that God would raise her up.

Eric would later see his conviction for what it was: a desperate attempt to prove they had been mistaken in thinking this was a sickness unto death. Yet it gave him the heart to go on. "I could hardly bear to write this to you," he told his parents when writing of the doctor's prognosis, "except that I know God is going to heal her."

Chapter 36

With Jesus, Which
Is Far Better

Eric took Grace home to Emerson by ambulance on October 19, another glorious fall day. "The beautiful hues of the trees gave her such delight," he told his parents. For five days she was able to walk and seemed to feel "pretty good," but then came debilitating pain, which not even morphine could mask. It left her bedfast, and often unable to eat.

Sherman and Flora continued to keep Miriam and Philip at their farm, though they brought the children in as often as possible to be with Grace. She was confined to bed, but with supervision they could lie quietly beside her and chatter in their baby ways.

Meanwhile, Eric found himself "more busy than I ever want to be again" with the care of Grace, baby John, the home, and what attention he could give to the church. Aunt Flora began to come two days a week to help, and in the middle of December a fellow CIM missionary arrived, a nurse to care for Grace. She was Grace Emblen, who had been captured with Alfred Bosshardt and Arnolis Hayman in 1934. For Eric she was a veritable lifeline.

As in every year of her life, the month of December began with Grace's birthday and ended with Christmas, but neither one could be celebrated with the light hearts of the previous year. On December 1, Grace quietly turned 39, and for Christmas there was a little tabletop tree for the family to enjoy. Grace had devised a two-part gift for Eric:

first, a sweater, given "with all my love, which is much, much warmer," and the second, the promise of a typewriter to replace the one they had lost on the Burma Road. But when the opportunity came to make the promise a reality, he was obliged to do it alone, for in less than a month Grace was gone.

Her younger sister Merlie came at the end to help nurse her, and a letter from her older sister, Lucy, cheered her. The night before she died her beloved older brother, Samy, drove over three hundred miles on icy roads to see her. "She knew him, & kissed him, & put her arm round him." But it was Eric who watched by her side and took note of every change. "Dear, dear Eric," she would say, as with unsteady hands she tried to stroke his face and hair. "Eric is the one I love."

On January 15 she seemed very near the end, but while her sister Flora and Aunt Flora were visiting, she seemed to rally. As they and Eric sang together the "Doxology with Hallelujahs," they could hear her alto voice, sporadically but unmistakably, joining theirs.

The next day she was again only semi-rational. She still knew people, especially Eric. But her thoughts were more of the One who had taken the sting out of death for her. "Dear Jesus, Dear Jesus," she repeated in her semi-coma. A radio sat on the table in her room, tuned to the *Back to the Bible* broadcast. When the choir sang "Ready to go, ready to stay, ready to do Thy will," she slowly nodded her head in agreement.

The following day she murmured several times, "Tomorrow with Jesus." But it was three days later, on Sunday, January 20, that her breathing became imperceptibly light, and she was gone.

"It was the first time I had seen death come," Eric reflected, "and tho Aunt Flora, who had seen it many times, said it was a very peaceful death, it just wrung my heart, & wrings it yet. Thank God that Jesus…said [His own] should only 'taste of death.' That was all dear Gracie did, I am sure, & then she was with Him, where there is fullness of joy for ever more."

Dazed, but focused, he gathered Merlie, Grace Emblen, and Aunt Flora around her bed and gave thanks "for the beautiful life, lived to His Glory, and that she was now with Him."

His next sad task was to go to the farm and break the news to the children and the family there: Sherman and Flora, Merrill and Loretha, and Grace's mother, Lucy. Tenderly he explained to Miriam that Mama was now with Jesus. Two-year-old Philip was too young to comprehend, and at first Miriam seemed not to mind: Flora's motherly heart and welcoming lap were a providential cushion against that reality. But at night she was restless and wanted to be with Flora. Later, on a return visit to the house in Emerson, when little Philip ran to Grace's sick room and asked in surprise, "Daddy, where is Mama?" it was hard to explain.

The Comer Funeral Home had taken charge of her body, but on Monday and again on Tuesday a desolate Eric went to see once more "the earthly house of my dear one."

The funeral was on Wednesday, January 23, in Champion Hill Church. Since no one from the CIM could be present, Eric turned to the Rev. Charles Speagh to take the service. It was important to Eric that, notwithstanding the great sorrow, there be a note of joy and triumph, and he prayed that he be able to take part with composure. He read the Scripture, John 11:17-44, and after Rev. Speagh spoke on verses 25-26, he did indeed "[give] testimony, and a word of exhortation to the unsaved ones present." All her adult life Grace had been burdened for her siblings who showed no interest in the Savior she loved and served—writing to them, loving them, praying for them. She even went so far as to say that if it was through her death they came to him, it would be well worthwhile. So Eric spoke to them again on her behalf.

After the funeral a "big company" drove more than 30 miles over country roads in stormy weather to be at the graveside in Fairview Pioneer Cemetery, Oakland. The wind sweeping over the prairie was merciless, and mourners who had braved the weather pulled their coats tight as they witnessed Grace's interment next to her father, beside the church where he and her mother had met some fifty years earlier.

In writing of it to his parents, Eric concluded,

> So the "earthly house of her tabernacle" rests there beside her dear father's, until that glad day when the Lord Jesus shall come, with the voice of the archangel, and the trump of God, and the dead in Christ rise, and then we which are alive and remain are caught up together with them in the clouds, to be forever with the Lord. What a glad day that will be.

A simple upright granite stone marks her grave. The inscription Eric chose concludes with the promise Grace herself held most dear—Revelation 22:2-3 (ASV)—the promise which was now fulfilled for her:

His servants shall serve him, and they shall see his face.

She had needed no introduction. The passage of time had not dimmed her Savior's memory, the fog of war had not reduced her to an anonymous someone. Her name had been written on his hands since before the beginning of time, and she heard his glad welcome, "Well done, good and faithful servant."

AFTERWORD

At the end of 1946, my father returned to China, leaving us three children on the farm in Iowa with our Aunt Flora and Uncle Sherman and our cousins, Merrill and Loretha. It was a seamless transition. We had been with them since our mother's illness, and they loved us like their own.

Back in Yunnan, my father was designated to Longchiu, the Lisu village where my mother had lived. He labored there for three and one-half years before returning to Iowa in 1950, to an uncertain future. The Communists were taking over China and missionaries were being evacuated, not designated.

In 1951, Dad married another Yunnan missionary, Helen Madeira, who had recently been evacuated and had returned to her home in Elizabethtown, PA. Their marriage eventually gave me the baby sister I had hoped for, and two more brothers.

Since China was closed, the CIM branched into Southeast Asia, changing its name to the Overseas Missionary Fellowship (OMF). But the United States seemed closed too, as far my father was concerned. There was little call among churches for someone whose only credentials were a master's ticket from the British Merchant Navy, and thirteen years of missionary service in China.

When the OMF appealed for help in reaching the tribes of North Thailand, Eric and Helen answered, sailing in September 1952. They learned to speak Thai, reduced to writing the language of the Yao/Mien tribe, and translated the New Testament into that language before retiring in 1974.

John was young enough to go to Thailand with them for the first term, attending an elementary Chefoo School in Malaysia before joining

Philip and me in the United States, where we lived in homes staffed by OMF missionaries, and attended public schools. Each of us went on to college and graduated. We married, have children and grandchildren, and are active in our respective churches.

Although our childhood was irregular, even for missionary kids, I testify that our mother's confidence was well placed when she wrote from her hospital bed, "…I know He will care for our precious babies. We gave them all to Him before they were born, and they are His. He will guard them and keep them as the apple of His eye."

WORKS CITED

Bosshardt, R. A. *The Restraining Hand*. London: Hodder & Stoughton, 1936.

ccmhk.org.hk. June 30, 2011.

CNAC Home Page. cnac.org. June 24, 2014.

Crossman, Eileen. *Mountain Rain*. Singapore: Overseas Missionary Fellowship, 1982.

DeYoung, Kevin. "Andy Neselli on Why 'Let Go and Let God' Is a Bad Idea." thegospelcoalition.org. June 3, 2010.

"Fairview Pioneer Memorial Church." genealogytrails.com. September 22, 2014.

"History of Chinese Currency." Wikipedia. October 1, 2014.

Kuhn, Isobel. *In the Arena*. Chicago, IL: Moody Press, 1958.

Montsma, Lieuwe. "About Yunnan." tinyadventurestours.org. June 23, 2014.
---. "Bridges in Yunnan." tinyadventurestours.org. June 23, 2014.
---. "Burma Road." tinyadventurestours.org. June 23, 2014.
---. "Southern Silk Road." tinyadventurestours.org. June 23, 2014.

Packer, J. I. *Keep in Step With the Spirit*. Old Tappan, NJ: Revell, 1984.

Sawyer, M. James. "Wesleyan and Keswick Models of Sanctification." bible.org. February 26, 2000.

Tow, Don M. "The Doolittle Raid." dontow.com. October 6, 2014.
---. "Heroic and Critical Battles in Yunnan During WWII." October 6, 2014.

Wings Over Asia, Vol. 1, c. 1971 by the China National Aviation Association Foundation. Cited at CNAC.org. June 24, 2014.